THE HYSTERICAL MALE

new feminist theory

CultureTexts

Arthur and Marilouise Kroker   *General Editors*

Culture texts is a series of creative explorations in theory, politics and culture at the *fin-de-millenium*. Thematically focussed around key theoretical debates in the postmodern condition, the *CultureTexts* series challenges received discourses in art, social and political theory, feminism, psychoanalysis, value inquiry, science and technology, the body, and critical aesthetics. Taken individually, contributions to *CultureTexts* represent the forward breaking-edge of postmodern theory and practice.

Titles

The Hysterical Male: new feminist theory
edited and introduced by Arthur and Marilouise Kroker

Seduction
Jean Baudrillard

Panic Encyclopedia
Arthur Kroker, Marilouise Kroker and David Cook

Life After Postmodernism: Essays on Value and Culture
edited and introduced by John Fekete

Body Invaders
edited and introduced by Arthur and Marilouise Kroker

The Postmodern Scene: Excremental Culture and Hyper-Aesthetics
Arthur Kroker/David Cook

THE HYSTERICAL MALE
new feminist theory

edited and introduced by
Arthur and Marilouise Kroker

New World Perspectives
CultureTexts Series
Montréal

*New World Perspectives
3652 avenue Laval,
Montréal, Québec
H2X 3C9*

ISBN 0-920393-69-1
Published simultaneously in the U.S.A. by St. Martin's Press and in Britain by Macmillan

Canadian Cataloguing in Publication Data

The Hysterical Male: new feminist theory

(CultureTexts series)
ISBN 0-920393-69-1

1. Feminism. 2. Sex (Psychology)–Social
aspects. 3. Postmodernism. I. Kroker, Arthur.
1945- II. Kroker, Marilouise. 1945-
III. Series.

HQ1206.H98 1991   305.3   C90-090392-9

Printed and bound in Canada

On December 6, 1989, fourteen women were murdered at the Université de Montréal. "I want the women." "You're all feminists." That is what the twenty-five year old male dressed in hunting gear with a semiautomatic rifle in one hand and a hunting knife in the other shouted when he ordered the men to leave and the women to stay.

We dedicate this book to these fourteen women, murdered because they were thought to be feminists.

Attila Richard Lukacs, *True North* (detail)

CONTENTS

Phallus of Malice

Daddy's No

THE HYSTERICAL MALE
one libido?

Arthur and Marilouise Kroker

The hysterical male, then, as a prelude to the seduction of one libido.

If the image of the hysterical male can be so popular in cinema today (*Sex, Lies & Videotape, Dead Ringers, Total Recall, Robocop*), maybe that is because there is no longer a relationship between sex and power.

Power, fleeing its basis in sexuality generally and male subjectivity specifically, becomes now a *viral* power, a power which speaks only in the previously transgressive feminist language of absence, rupture, plurality, and the trace. A post-male power which leaves behind male subjectivity as a hysterical photographic negative of itself, and which disappropriates women of the privileged ontology of the Other.

Or is it just the reverse? Not the decoupling of sex and power, but a hyper-infusion of power by a male sex which, speaking now only in the fantasy language of one libido, seeks to hide the privileging of the phallocentric gaze by theorizing the disappearance of power into seduction.

The psychoanalytics of one libido, therefore, as one last playing-out of old male polyester sex theory, a big zero.

Or maybe it's neither. Not one libido theory nor its denial, but the production of neon libidos in the age of sacrificial sex, when sexuality too is both produced by power as a *trompe l'oeil* and then cancelled out. Sacrificial sex, therefore, as a time of the monstrous double, when all the sex differences are simulated and exterminated in a spiralling combinatorial of cynical signs.

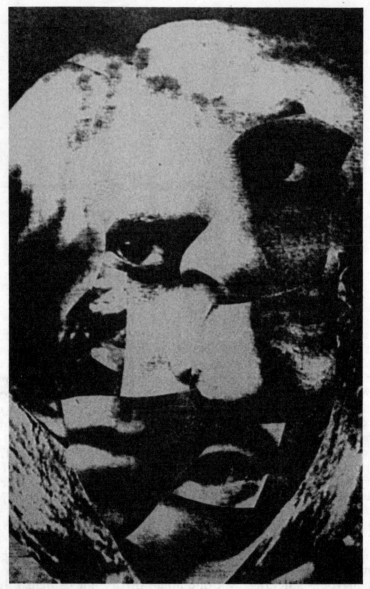

Marc de Guerre

The Penis as a Mutant Clitoris

The key to decoding the psychoanalytics of the hysterical male at the end of the twentieth century is to read Freud's theory of seduction, his theory of the hysterical female written at the end of the nineteenth century, in reverse image.

Here, there is only one sex: the female sex. Freud got it all wrong. He insisted that female hysteria had its sexual origins in the teenage repression of the clitoris as an erotegenetic zone and the forced shifting of the sexual register from the clitoris (Freud's "masculine sexuality") to the vagina. Freud's victory sign was the repression of the eroticism of the clitoris, and the celebration of vaginal sex as the triumphant sign of the double exclusion of women from their own sex. The lost clitoris, then, as an eternally recurring sign of penis envy for the female hysteric living within the horizon of the Victorian sexual prohibition, and for the political fate of women of having to learn their own sex through that ideological interpellation of male power—the Freudian vagina.

But why not the opposite? Why not the penis now as a sign of the mutant clitoris, as a postmodern clitoris under the sign of abuse value? No longer the clitoris as a minimalist penis, but the postmodern penis as a runaway outlaw clit—like Pinnochio's nose?

Or is it both? The nineteenth century clitoris as a failed Freudian penis (with the vagina as a sign of repressed absence), and the twentieth century penis as a hyper-inflated clitoris (with Freud's one male sex as itself as fatal theory of sexual flatlining). Freud's penile theory made this big mistake. It never gave credence to the sexual fact that women can ejaculate, and that, consequently, the dialectic of the clitoris and the vagina was that of one sex, a female sex, moving through a pleasurable libidinal sexual economy of discharge and bodily memory.

The female hysteric, then, as a *quintessential* sign of the repression of masculine denial. Not so much the hysterical female, but the first of all the existentialists—Freud's Dora—who can report her condition as "nausea and disgust" because she is surrounded by all the repressed signs of denial of the hysterical male: the male hysteric who desperately needs discharge, but who can't discharge directly, and does so through the conversion of sexual lack into emotionally cathected ideas.

Or maybe it is something more. Not just male hysteria in relation to sexual lack, but as the emblematic sign of a more primordial lack in postmodern society. Maybe male hysteria—the hysteria of the mutant sex—expresses a more fundamental inversion: the inversion of space over memory, of the ideological order of the phallus over embodied history. Male sex, then, as the sovereignty of desire as lack over libidinal history, which is to say of spatialization over the body. An endless revenge-taking by the mutant sex against the body, against the pleasures of the clitoris. Indeed, if Virilio can write so eloquently now about the

Photo: Marc de Guerre

postmodern body as a "war machine", about, that is, the indefinite combination of speed and politics into a new form of "dromocracy", maybe that's because as a privileged participant in the mutant sex he can understand so well the dialectic of lack and deterrence. Male sexual discharge as also a kind of deferral of knowledge of absence which, first having its basis in the penis as a mutant clitoris, expands rapidly into a universal political logic of revenge-taking.

The New Sacred Object

Why is the image of the erect penis now privileged as a cathected object for political prohibition?

A new drive towards male puritanism in which the Madonna image does a gender flip? No longer woman as 'sacred vessel', but the erect penis as a probibited object of the gaze. A sacramentalized penis which can fall under a great visual prohibition because it is now *the* sacred object. Perhaps a last domain of innocence for anxious men, desperate about all of the gains made by movements for sexual liberation. And so, the erect penis is encoded with all the liturgical trappings of a sacred vessel: the ideological probibition of the gaze, an unseen object of veneration, an erectile domain of semiotic innocence. The erect penis, therefore, as a key agent in a new discourse of semio-sex which can be so fundamentalist in its cultural prohibitions because it screens out the reality of a culture which is all about a ruthless patriarchal politics of back to the penis. Political injunctions against images of the erect penis, therefore, as also about the repression of denial.

But, of course, the question remains: You can cover it up, but will it go away? If the erect penis can be so semiotically innocent, that is because a great political reversal is now taking place. The erect penis can acquire a cultural discourse of innocence in direct and intense relation to the new material reality of a penile power which, under the impact of a decaying neo-conservativism moving from the political to the cultural sphere, is all about predatory power against women and children. Is the new penis censorship just a camouflage, then, for a new fundamentalist cultural politics based on a new order of phallocentric domination: violence against women, the sexual abuse of children, a whole sexual politics based on the libidinal economy of abuse value? The new sexual censorship, therefore, recapitulates the historical traditions of puritanical movements: the cultural reality of a sacred object as a displaced sign for a material reality based on sexual abuse. Consequently, the discourse of the erect penis as a sacred object is central to the newly resurgent ideology of the hysterical male.

Crash Subjectivity

The theorisations in this book are written under the sign of the failing penis as the emblematic mark of postmodern subjectivity. They originate in that shadowland where the real material penis disappears into the ideology of the phallus, and where the privileged figure of the masculine throws off its Freudian burden of repression, becoming what it always secretly coveted—fully hystericized subjectivity. That fateful point where the specular coherence of unitary male subjectivity shatters, and what remains is but the violent residues of the death of the old male cock. Crash male subjectivity, and crash male bodies too, as the hysterical sign of the fatal breakdown of the symbolic order of the unitary male subject.

The Hysterical Male: new feminist theory is a thematically focussed exploration of feminism in the 1990s. Initiated as a companion text to *Body Invaders, The Hysterical Male* traces out the logic of imminent reversibility in received patriarchal discourses in psychoanalysis, art, theory and culture. Here, under the sign of male hystericization, critical feminist theorists track the next stage of gender politics. From the theoretical fallout from *Daddy's No* (refusing the psychoanalytics of the Lacanian symbolic) and *Phallus of Malice* (where the image of the ejaculating woman substitutes for the disappearing penis) to the *Mirror of Seduction* (where women, too, are doubled in an endless regression of mirrored identities) and *Sacrificial Sex* (where feminism is encoded in a labyrinth of seductive images), *The Hysterical Male* nominates new feminist theory in light of the inverted world of the male hysteric. What results is an intense, provocative and creative theorisation of feminism under the failing sign of male hystericization—the death of the privileged ideology of the unitary male subject.

I

SACRIFICIAL SEX

1

THE THREE SISTERS OF TANYA MARS

Elke Town

Photography by David Hlynsky

Pure Virtue, *Pure Sin*, and *Pure Nonsense* compose a trilogy of performance works by Toronto artist Tanya Mars. They are the tales of two women and a girl, each in active pursuit of her desire. Elizabeth l in *Pure Virtue*, Mae West in *Pure Sin* and Alice (of Wonderland) in *Pure Nonsense*—a monarch, a sex queen and a character of the imagination—navigate the perils of politics, sex and psychoanalysis by seizing power, staying single and having an adventure.

In Mars's performances, Elizabeth I attempts the impossible—lying down and doing sit-ups—in a dress built for show and immobility. Alice's Wonderland is not a Victorian rabbit hole but a '60s psychedelic paradise in which the masters of psychoanalysis, Freud and Jung, stage their quarrels with Alice and each other to the musical strains of Jefferson Airplane and the visual backdrop of a light show. Likewise, Mae West steps off the 1930s movie screen and tries on a few other goddesses for size. She slips back in time to the beginnings of creation, there to confront the holy and unholy clamorings of priests, philosophers and historians who, by asserting that women are the source of original sin, construct mythologies that conveniently disguise their own guilt and sexual desires.

The three performance works are a hybrid form, amalgams of bur-lesque, carnival-like spectacle and cathartic theatre. Like other performance pieces by artists, Mars's work takes its structural cues from theatre, visual art and literature, but its ideological cues, true to Mars's own investigation of women's power, have their roots in feminism. Becoming progressively more complex in staging and casting from work to work, each work unfolds through a series of interconnected tableaux that incorporate projected textual quotes and images, props, costumes, music and a cast of broadly drawn characters representing everything from Zeus, atomic subparticles and the Tree of Knowledge in *Pure Sin* to Freud and Jung and the Mad Hatter and the White Rabbit in *Pure Nonsense*.

Mars's scripts abound in borrowed quotes and references from souces as disparate as Greek mythology, the Bible, Sophocles, Shakespeare, Freud, Elizabeth I's own poetry, Mae West's unbeatable one-liners and mountains of '60s psychobabble. This liberal borrowing amplifies the characters and provides a cultural subtext, a subversive, humourous climate in which nothing is sacred and no myth or text is so irrefutable that it cannot be scrutinized, toyed with and overturned. In *Pure Nonsense*, for example, after Freud and Jung have performed hypnotic hocus-pocus on Alice and put her into a trance, a projected text reads: "Woman has done for psychoanalysis what the frog has done for biology."

Performance art demands the presence of the artist as performer and indeed Mars is the central character in each work: she plays the lead role and dresses for the part (in costumes designed and made by Elinor Rose Galbraith). But Mars's performances are more than dressing up and her dresses are more than costumes. Mars is both a visual object and a performer. As an object, she is Elizabeth, Mae or Alice, a spectacularized representation that symbolizes who and what women are and how they got that way. As a performer, Mars identifies with and merges with each of her representations. In doing so, she combines her personal concerns as an artist with the politics of representation.

Each of Mars's performances is an inhabitation, a critical and comic feminist narrative about women's power, whether it exists in a kingdom, on a movie set or in Wonderland. By taking a character from history, film and fiction, Mars explores personal and social relations both as products of the social and political imagination and as producers and reflections of it. Mars fits herself into the dresses of women who, in the case of Elizabeth I and Mae West, created themselves and their circumstances, and in the case of Alice, challenged the existing order. For each, there was a price for power: Elizabeth, the Virgin Queen, was denied more earthly pleasures; Mae West was replaced by more malleable cinematic icons who held their tongues; and Alice Liddell was, after all, only the subject of Carroll's imagination and the object of his desire.

In rewriting the histories of her three characters and placing them at the centre of debate, Mars has constructed a trilogy that reads like the origins of the female species.

Photo: David Hlynsky

Pure Virtue

I am and not, I freeze and yet am burned, since from myself, my other self, I turn.

Elizabeth 1

Elizabeth 1, the "Virgin Queen", splendid in dress and mind, contemplates virginity, power, sex and death. She recommends means whereby chastity may be maintained and, if necessary, the loss of it disguised; she entertains the lords of war, religion and commerce for a picnic lunch à la Manet's *Dejeuner sur l'herbe*; she complains of men's desire for power in the state and in her bedroom; and finally, in the metaphorical shadow of the names of other women from history, fairy tales, fiction and film, Anne Boleyn, Sleeping Beauty, Marilyn Monroe—Mars/Elizabeth symbolically sacrifices herself and calls out for her mother.

Photo: David Hlynsky

Pure Sin

It isn't what I do, but how I do it. It isn't what I say, but how I say it, and how I look when I do it and say it.

Mae West.

Mae West, as herself and as a variety of mythological heroines—Lilith, Pandora, Hecate—confronts the longstanding myths of women as the source of original sin in history, religion, and philosophy. As she swaggers shamelessly into the re-creation void and the Garden of Eden, Mae shakes off this blame and repossesses her body and sexuality, redirecting the blame to the men who were its source. With her one-liners she acknowledges and condones men's lust and gives them a glimpse of what life could be like without their shame or their will to gain power and possession.

Photo: David Hlynsky

Pure Nonsense

*Why I hardly know, sir. In fact, I hardly
remember anything at all. Indeed I don't
even know where I left my penis.*
                        Alice to Jung

Alice investigates the social and psychic construction of sexual difference and challenges the essen-
tialist myth that anatomy is destiny. When Alice
discovers that she doesn't have a penis, Freud tells
her that she has "lost" it. Alice searches for the
privileged signifier in a world where the confusion
and riddles of Carroll's Wonderland merge with the
psychoanalytic theories of Freud and Jung. True to all
fairy tales, Pure Nonsense has a happy ending: what's
lost is found. When the musical game "You put your
left foot (arm, head, psyche, etc.) in" gets to "penis,"
Alice lifts her dress to discover that she indeed does
have a penis—in the form of a giant, permanently
erect, strap-on dildo.

Photo: David Hlynsky

Installation: Art in Ruins
Hannah Vowles/Glyn Banks

2

BIG JUGS[1]

Jennifer Bloomer

*I have given this paper two parts, which we might call
theoretical and practical (a construction), for the benefit
of those who think that architects are incapable of
thinking about what they do and even less capable of
talking about it; and for those who believe that nobody
needs to talk about architecture, one should just DO it. If
you fall into one of these categories, you may choose to
read only the appropriate part. Good luck in deciding
which one is which.*

Part One

Western architecture is, by its very nature, a phallocentric discourse:
containing, ordering, and representing through firmness, commodity,
and beauty; consisting of orders, entablature, and architrave; base, shaft,
and capital; nave, choir, and apse; father, son, and spirit, world without
end. Amen.[2]

In the Garden of Eden there was no architecture. The necessity for
architecture arose with the ordination of sin and shame, with dirty
bodies. The fig leaf was a natural first impulse toward architecture,
accustomed as it was to shading its vulvate fruit, its trunk and roots a
complex woven construction of undulating forms. Was it the fig tree that

was hacked up to build the primitive hut (that precursor of classical architecture)?

The primitive hut and all its begettings constitute a house of many mansions, a firm, commodious, and beautiful erection. The primitive hut is the house of my fathers. But there is the beginning of an intrusive presence in this house:

> She transforms, she acts: the old culture will soon be the new. She is mixed up in dirty things; she has no cleanliness phobia—the proper housecleaning attacks that hysterics sometimes suffer. She handles filth, manipulates wastes, buries placentas, and burns the cauls of new born babies for luck. She makes partial objects useful, puts them back in circulation—properly. *En voila du propre!* What a fine mess![3]

Julia Kristeva has written:

> As capitalist society is being economically and politically choked to death, discourse is wearing thin and heading for collapse at a more rapid rate than ever before. Philosophical finds, various modes of 'teaching', scientific or aesthetic formalisms follow one upon another, compete, and disappear without leaving either a convinced audience or noteworthy disciples. Didacticism, rhetoric, dogmatism of any kind, in any 'field' whatsoever, no longer command attention. They have survived, and perhaps will continue to survive, in modified form, throughout Academia. Only one language grows more and more contemporary: the equivalent, beyond a span of thirty years, of the language of *Finnegans Wake*.[4]

Broadcast throughout the text of *Finnegans Wake* are thousands of seedy little t's, those bits of letter written, devoured, excreted, and pecked by the hen. They are little micturition sounds, tiny trabeation signs. To make those posts on beams properly classical, let us add the prescibed third part: the T becomes an I. The I, the ego, the I beam, the gaze, the image fixer, the instrument of fetish. When I was a child in church, I was told that the great golden "I" embroidered on the altar cloth stood for "INRI". I wondered why the church didn't spell its Henry with an H. Hen ri—the hen laughs. Ha ha ha ha—the sound of H is pure expiration: laughter, sighing, and the way we breathe when we are giving birth to our children. BODY LANGUAGE. The sound of H is more than mere pronunciation of three marks on a page—two parallels, one bridge. It is a mark itself of invisible flows.

Much as David Byrne perhaps "eggoarchicistically" burns down the house, James Joyce has enjoisted an other construction:

> The boxes, if I may break the subject gently, are worth about fourpence pourbox but I am inventing a more patent process, foolproof and pryperfect (I should like to ask that Shedlock Homes person who is out for removing the roofs of our criminal classics by what *deductio ad domunum* he hopes *de tacto* to detect anything unless he happens of himself, *movibile tectu*, to have a slade off) after which they can be reduced to a fragment of their true crust by even the youngest of Margees if she will take plase to be seated and smile if I please.[5]

Here is the hatchery. Let Us Deconstruct: Margee is the marginal one, taking her place, seated and smiling, faking, being woman as constituted by the symbolic order. *Movibile tectu*: homophonous to *horribile dictu* (horrible to tell, unspeakable). This is a passage from Virgil—repeated throughout the *Aeneid* much as the hen's letter is scattered throughout the text of *Finnegans Wake*. And *movibile tectu* is also moving touch: the moving finger writes, and, having writ, moves on. Architectural references abound: boxes, Shed, Lock (as in locked out of the house), Homes, roofs, classics, domunum, slade.

The hatchery is an apparatus of overlay of architecture, writing, and the body. The hatchery is a kind of architectural anti-type, i.e., it refers to a kind of built structure (the chicken house), but the structure to which it refers does not belong to the domain of the architect. It is a house, but not architecture, and its relationship to the primitive hut is mediated to the point of extreme tentativeness, primarily because the form of the hatchery is irrelevant. The hatchery is not bound or bounded by theory, but is a para-theoretical device. The hatchery is that which is not represented when the architecture-making is done. The hatchery is Work in Progress, a critical instrument, intrusive and elucidating. It refers to the place of the hatching of chickens from eggs, the place of the life flow, a dirty (soiled) cacaphonous place full of litter, the residue of life (eggshells, excrement, cast-off feathers, uneaten food). In this sense, it is a kind of alchemical vessel, a container of ingredients for the Philosopher's Stone (*un vaisseau de pierre*). Its floor is inscribed with the imprints of chicken feet (hatchings and cross-hatchings).

The hatchery is a writing machine. The biddies, the *chicks*, scratch marks in the dirt. These hieroglyphs constitute an historical document, a mapping and a marking of movement. This act of hatching resembles and belongs to the acts of etching, drawing, and writing. It is the act of the hatching of lines and the hatching of plots.

The body is, in a sense, a multiply-constituted hatchery, a messy assemblage of flows—blood, organic matter, libidinal, synaptic, psychic. The metaphor for the throat—the primary entrance portal—is the hatch,

as in "down the hatch." This hatch is a door or passage. We describe our bodies and our constructions in terms of each other, with words as passages between one and the other. Writes of passage, hatcheries all.
   Alice Jardine:

> [W]hat fiction has always done—the incorporation and rejection of that space [the space of schizophrenia, the libidinal economy, that which has begun to threaten authorship, that which is connoted as feminine—see Jardine, p. 88] as grounds for figurability—new theoretical discourses, with rapidly increasing frequency, have also been doing. Seeing themselves as no longer isolated in a system of loans and debts to former master truths, these new discourses in formation have foregrounded a *physis*, a space no longer passive but both active and passive, undulating, folded over upon itself, permeable: the self-contained space of eroticism.[6]

The hatchery is a bridge between the sacred and the voluptuous, between *physis* and *techne*.
   In Frank Baum's *The Wizard of Oz*, Dorothy's house becomes disconnected at the point of the hatch (trap-door to the cellar underneath) and floats and rises gently in the center of the cyclone. When the house falls, it kills the wicked witch and Dorothy is construed as a sorceress in a country that is not civilized, and therefore retains a population of sorceresses, witches, and wizards.
   Dorothy falls and Alice falls, but into other worlds—worlds of magic and strangeness. Adam, Lucifer, Humpty Dumpty, and Icarus fell to less desirable ends. The boys attempt to rise to power and fail, lose, fall from grace. The girls drop out, fall down the hatch, use the exits, find the dreamworld of condensation and displacement, of strangeness, of *délire*.[7] The position to take is perched at the rim of the hole, at the moment of the closing of the trap door, ready to fall, not to fall from, but INTO. The "fall from" is hierarchical and you can hurt yourself. The "fall into" is labyrinthine, dreamy, a dancing fall, a delirious fall.
   "Her rising: is not erection. But diffusion. Not the shaft. The Vessel."[8] The Hatchery is both vessel and erection (the topology of erection is vesicular flow, after all), but it is neither of these things in the formal sense. The form must remain undefined to escape co-optation. (The aestheticization of the political is a patriarchal sleight of hand power play against which Walter Benjamin warned us long ago.) We can, however, emblematize it with its initial letter. The H is an I in which the shaft has been allowed to rest horizontal for a moment, forming a vessel, a container, a bridge, a conduit.
   The Hatchery might be, but cannot be, classified into categories. Political, unauthorized, and unauthored, it is about acts, not images; transitory, it is movement, but is not *a* movement. Hacking at the edges

of the architecture/state apparatus, it is all these categories. It is political and collective and moving.

Barnacles, engulfings, underminings, intrusions: Minor Architecture.[9] Collective, anonymous, authorless, scratched on the city and the landscape, they are hatched not birthed. (They are illegitimate—without father.) Bastard Constructions. In matriarchal societies, there is no concept of legitimacy. One is legitimate by virtue of existence. No-one knows a single father; all males are the nurturing fathers of all children. Children are born of the mother; they are legitimate by virtue of having made the passage from inside to out.

"Wee peeps"[10] appear locally upon the landscape of The Gaze. Wee peeps: we peeks, small chickens (chicks), brief glances, a hint of impropriety—micturition in public. Tattoos upon the symbolic order. They are the "lens" that "we need the loan of ... to see as much as the hen saw."[11] Like minor literature, or the little girls on Tintorelli's stair in *The Trial*, or the twenty-eight little girl shadows of Isabelle, or the rainbow girls in *Finnegans Wake*. Tattoos. T-t-t's.

"This battering babel allower the door and sideposts":[12] the hatchery, the place of babes and babble, both allows and lowers the supporting structure of the entrance to the House.

A biddy architecture (a surd and absurd[13] architecture): Around midnight, Atlanta, Georgia. Moving along Techwood Drive, the access road running parallel to Interstate 75-85, and accessing the House of Ted Turner. On the right: plantation image, tasteful, white sign with Chippendale frame—"The Turner Broadcasting System." On the left: parallax view of trees silhouetted against the glow of the here submerged interstate highway and, beyond, the city lights. Glimpsed among the trees: small constructions of sticks and draped membranes through which the lights osmose—so strange that you might be hallucinating. Against the membranes, blocking the glow with jarringly recognizable blackness: human figures here and there, existing for the moment between the lines.

Part Two: Jugs

In Florida, as perhaps in other places, we are situated upon a most peculiar landscape. We stand upon a ground not of rock resting upon rock, but of the merest slice of solidity barely breaking the surface of the surrounding sea. Furthermore, the ground beneath our feet is not reliable, not the solid architecture of stone piled upon stone, carrying its loading in the proper compressive fashion, that we like our ground to be. It is in fact an architecture of holes and crypts, filling and emptying with fluids, an architecture delineated by suction and secretion, of solids, fluids, and gases, in such a complex and everchanging configuration that to pin it down with a word seems illogical. But it *is* named by a word:

Alachua,[14] a word the previous residents of this place chose. Alachua: a vessel or jug. Alachua, a land of filling and emptying, of holes and crypts, a place where the superimposition of "order" is ridiculous. A place where entire buildings are swallowed up, disappear into the surface of the ground, leaving behind only pock marks, that will eventually fill with fluid. The consideration of such an architecture is not about imbuing a mundane thing with pumped-up significance, nor about projecting an image of the place. It is about how it works. Not about what it means or what it looks like, but what it does. The following construction is a mapping of this territory. It is the landscape of Edgar Poe, a territory of significant voids.[15]

This construction consists of a collision of three texts: an essay by Martin Heidegger titled "The Thing"; a character from Angela Carter's *Nights at the Circus*, Fanny Four-Eyes, who sports eyes on her breasts where nipples properly should be; and a third, the text of architecture, which in its over-Booked and boxed-in state, is pocked with more booby traps than those of us who practice it would like to think. It is possible that there is a fourth text, an oscillating text, quite "rudely forc'd."[16]

In a happenstance that gives me more pleasure than I can say, this text intersects with the conclusion of Catherine Ingraham's review, called "Milking Deconstruction, or Cow Was the Show?"[17], of the 1988 Deconstructivism Show at the Museum of Modern Art. Here, Ingraham constructs a situation in which the contemporary architectural phenomenon of "Deconstructivism" is allegorized in the contemporary corporate agricultural phenomenon of the "necessity" to re-engineer the structure of the new hormone-injected, super milk-giving cows in order to support their mammoth udders.

> The idea of the cow as a thing—like the cow-thing [a jug] we fill with milk and set on our dinner table—is what makes the crude tampering with its bone structure possible... Equally, the idea of deconstruction as a thing that can be built results in the crude surgeries of deconstructivism. It will ultimately be the shift in the idea of architectural structure—its dematerialization—that will interfere most substantially with the material surfaces of architecture, not so many jugs and pitchers cast in the shape of something called deconstructivism.[18]

Jugs and things are the objects of Heidegger's essay. If you will allow, I will recast this large and intricate vessel into a state that will accommodate an apprehension of a certain subtext. Despite the closure of space and time in the modern world, there is no nearness. We perceive that things are near to us, "[b]ut what is a thing?"[19] "A jug is a thing. What is the jug? We say: a vessel, something of the kind that holds something else within it."[20] "As a vessel the jug stands on its own as self-supporting."[21]

When we put it into our field of perception either through immediacy or representation, it becomes an object, yet it remains a vessel. The jug as a thing holds something. It is a container that must be made. When we understand it as a constructed vessel, we apprehend it as a thing, not as an object. We can never learn how the jug is by looking at its outward appearance; "[t]he vessel's thingness does not lie at all in the material of which it consists, but in the void that holds."[22] "Only a vessel ... can empty itself."[23] "How does the jug's void hold? It holds by taking what is poured in. It holds by keeping and retaining what it took in. The void holds in a twofold manner: taking and keeping. The word 'hold' is therefore ambiguous."[24] "To pour from the jug is to give."[25] "But the gift of the outpouring is what makes a jug a jug."[26] Even the empty jug suggests the gift by a "nonadmission" of which "a scythe ... or a hammer is incapable."[27] The thing is "nestling, malleable, pliant, compliant ..."[28] The thing is "modestly compliant."[29] "Inconspicuously compliant is the thing."[30] "Nestling" is the thing.

The logo of the Nestle Corporation—known for its milk-like products—depicts a perfectly round nest—a domestic vessel—resting on a branch from which three leaves grow in trinitary symmetry. Nestled in the nest are two small birds with straining bodies and eager beaks. Perched on the rim is a large mother bird in the position of offering something to her young. But, look closely at this picture: the mother holds nothing in her beak. The logo is a hieroglyph that gives up a secret. The logo is a figuration of the corporation's activities in third world countries, where a small supply of infant formula, which carries with it the image of first world magic, is given "free" to women who have just given birth. Inconspicuously—not readily noticeable, especially by "eyes which do not see"[31]—the Nestle Corporation makes empty vessels. The dry, petrified udder sells more man-made milk. This gift, mixed with promise and tainted water, is an outpouring of forced consumption, sickness, and death. The women are perhaps comforted by the "gift" of breasts imbued with first-world aura: breasts which have not been sucked are privileged as objects. They are firm and erect; they stick out.

Two Ways of Looking at a Jug

Aesthetic: "Stick 'em out just a little more. Yeah, now pull your tummy in all the way and let it out just a tad." Lifted and separated from the wall, the things appear twice their actual size and full and round as if to bursting. "Yeah. Now really push 'em up, hold your breath, keep your chin down and give me the look. Give it to me, baby, give it to me, yeah, yeah. Terrific!" Click!

Scientific: "Now, you've got to get the whole thing up on the plate. It'll feel a little cold, but it'll be over in a minute." The glass plate descends, pressing down, pressing, pressing the thing out to a horrifying, unrecognizable state: thin and flat, a broad, hideous slice of solidity criss-crossed with shocking blue lines. "Yes, that's it. Now hold your breath. Good!" Click!

"'Well now that's done: and I'm glad it's over.'"[32]

What is the secret that the firm, erect, sticking out thing holds? Unused, it is a frontier, where no man has gone before. What is the secret that lies beneath the power of this image, this object? What most desired and most feared thing is masked behind the desire to be the first, or the biggest? What does (M)other lack?

What is the secret that "oozes from the box?" Deleuze and Guattari:

> The secret must sneak, insert, or introduce itself into the arena of public forms; it must pressure them and prod known subjects into action ... [S]omething must ooze from the box, something will be perceived through the box or in the half-opened box.[33]

Corporate architecture is a certain return of the repressed.

In Thomas Pynchon's novel *V.*, a novel whose entire four hundred and sixty-three pages are devoted to a search for a figure which seems to be a woman, perhaps the mother of the protagonist, who exists only in traces and hints. V herself is masked by a seemingly infinite constellation of guises, forming the fetish construction that is the novel itself. Through the text there walks a figure known as the Bad Priest. Walks until, at a certain point of intersection, he falls down and falls apart, revealing himself to be a beautiful young woman who is in turn revealed, by the children and the imagination of the narrator who dismantle her body, as a machinic assemblage of objects: glittering stones and precious metals, clocks, balloons, and lovely silks. The Bad Priest is a fetish construction mirroring the novel. As Alice Jardine has pointed out, it is "an assemblage of the dead objects that have helped hold together the narrative thus far."[34] The Bad Priest and V are reconstituted objects of desire, constructions of what is most desired and most feared. They are a rewriting of the urge to the aesthetic. (You will recall that Aesthetics begins with the assemblage of the most beautiful, most perfect (and malleable, modestly compliant) woman by cutting the most desirable parts off many women and gathering them to make one woman-thing.) Like Pandora, whose box was not a box, but a jar, or jug. When the Bad Priest falls, the children cry, "It's a lady," and then: "She comes apart."[35] Into "[a] heap of broken images."[36]

"It's a Lady." Consider the Statue of Liberty, a fetish construction: she is a thing placed on a pedestal—to "lift and separate," to put on display. She is a spectacle. She is the hyper-reification of Luce Irigaray's gold-plated (in this case, copper-clad) woman: woman's body covered with commodities (make-up, fashion, capital, gold).

> The cosmetics, the disguises of all kinds that women cover themselves with are intended to deceive, to promise more value than can be delivered. ... Her body transformed into gold to satisfy his autoerotic, scopophiliac, and possessive instincts.[37]

This image of "Liberty for All" contains a secret, a purloined letter ingeniously hidden because it is there, in plain sight, a secret that calls into question the concepts of "Liberty" and "All." Beneath the surface of this woman's skin, beneath the implants which pump up the image, lies a "creeping disaster," [Irigaray] a crabby invasion, a crabgrass, a rhizome.

The Statue of Liberty is an allegory of desire and fear. It is a container, "a place where something is about to happen."[38] It is structure and envelope, image and machine. A gift. A Lady. And she comes apart.

In the summer of 1987, a consortium of French institutions (including *L'Institut Francais d'Architecture*) co-sponsored an international competition for the design of cultural artifacts commemorating the bicentenary of the French Revolution. The multidisciplinary and international intentions behind the competition were reinforced by the diversity of the jury, which ranged from the philosopher Jean Baudrillard to the structural engineer Peter Rice, and included writers, musicians, visual artists, and business people. The instructions for the production of the commemorative artifacts were vague, leaving site, event commemorated, media, and dimensions at the discretion of the authors. Attracted by the indeterminacy, two friends—Durham Crout, a former student presently teaching architecture at Clemson University and pursuing a Ph.D. at the University of Pennsylvania, and Robert Segrest—and I decided to participate.

Our project began as a project of exchange. As citizens of the United States constructing a monument to the French Revolution, we began with the simple idea of returning the gesture of the gift given by the French to commemorate the American Revolution. This gift, the Statue of Liberty, immediately generated a series of correspondences to other concepts delineated by the idea of gift: woman as presentation (both in the sense of the allegorical figure of Liberty and in the sense of woman as spectacle, as object of the gaze), woman as currency (both in the sense of the medium of exchange and in the sense of a flow that must be controlled, woman as fetish construction to be bestowed upon the imagination. We were struck by the way in which several constructs of power coincided in this woman-thing: war, aesthetics, the monumental, the reification of the female, history, the symbolic. We chose to commemorate an event of the French Revolution that bore potential correspondences to this construction of constructs, an event described by Marilyn French in *Beyond Power*:

When, on October 5 [1789], the market women discovered there was no bread in Paris, six thousand of them marched the twelve miles to Versailles to protest to the king personally. He promised to help them, and they marched triumphantly back to Paris with the royal family in tow.[39]

The itinerary that led to this choice is germane to an understanding of the project. Continuing along our line of the gift as generator, we selected nine sites on the body of woman/Liberty that are conventionally construed as (partial) objects of desire: eyes, lips, breasts, vulva, etc. These nine sites were made to correspond to nine sites of revolutionary points of intensity around the city of Paris through an operation involving sight lines, focal points, and the lens (a glassy instrument and the "mechanical" apparatus of the objectifying gaze). We then made nine incisions upon the body of the Statue of Liberty, slicing through each of the nine sites to produce a generating section. The irony of the similarity of our operation to those of slasher films and pornography was not lost upon us. The commentary of our work upon the recent work of contemporary architects whose work is tethered to the "aura" of mutilated and murdered women, we hope is not lost upon you. The nine sections were then to produce nine objects, to form a constellation of partial objects which, in their assemblage, would form a certain "gift" to the French. As is the way with well-laid plans, for a host of reasons including both fatigue and the powerful correspondence of the section through the eye and the site at the Palace at Versailles upon which it fell, we diverged from our original intentions and chose to operate only upon the eye and the march of the six thousand market women upon Versailles. The eye of the woman bears with it, after all, the potential to return the gaze; to return not merely in a sense of the conventional female aquiescence in sexual discourse, but also to re-turn, to deflect the power of the male gaze through a re-turn of the repressed, through the exorbitance of the female gaze. There is then in the project something of a reversal of the mechanics of the fascinus, a phallus-shaped amulet for warding off the "evil eye" of the fascinating woman. The evil eye, and to whom it belongs, is called into question.

It is the *unseen* in the body which is critical here. The sectioning of the statue is an act of incision and release. The incision marks the temporal and geographical point at which the image of the body gives way to the possibilities of the body. It becomes a gift of another kind, an insidious gift, with unseen agents hiding within, like the Trojan Horse. This hollow vessel, this monument, this gift to the state, holds within it the potential of undermining the state. In the Trojan Horse, the body masks the body politic. The Trojan Horse is a viral architecture: a sleek protein coat with invasive content.

The incision marking the initiation of generation is repeated as an incising inscription. A slash three hundred meters long and a meter square in section is made on the Palace grounds. This repetition is simultaneously a reflection (an other kind of repetition) of an already-there gash in the earth: the Grand Canal, a commanding axis of inscription terminating in a statue. Thus, that which marks the termination of the grand axis is the same (vessel, statue) as that which marks the initiation of our project. And again, this identity is marked in reverse, setting the project into interminable reflexivity: the western end of the trench stops abruptly at the base of an other statue: that of Louis Quattorze atop a, perhaps now suspicious, horse. The new incision is a reflection of the old; the radical project is a mimicry of the State project. Furthermore, it is a rational response to the existing topography: our trench is a physically inscribed reflection of that which is marked by the relationship of the incision of the Grand Canal and the vertical slicing plane of the west (mirrored) wall of the Hall of Mirrors. In other words, we have taken the image of what one would see if one could see through the mirror and projected it back into the world before the mirror, reversing the customary relationship of "reality" and "image" in the mirror. In this geography of the imagination,[40] the idea that the mirror is utterly contained within its grandiose vessel—the Palace—is simultaneously negligible and crucial.

The reflection works at another level as well. If one renders malleable the word for our gift, *un cadeau*, into a Franco-Italian hybrid of *ca d'eau*, there is here a house of water (a body), which parodies the wateriness, the flow, of the Grand Canal. A *ca d'eau* is a house of currency. The trench functions as a monumental pissoir, open to the public in a public place. But being pissed off, here, is a redundant gesture. Nestled (modestly and compliantly) in the floor of the trench are six thousand vessels, with pear-like shapes and copper skins. Each is lined with mirror tain and glass and each is full to bursting with body fluids. Their bodily secrets allow them to laugh away or write off the oppression of being pissed on. These reproducing cells (vessels, fluid-filled uteri) mirror a something disastrous going on beneath the surface of the court of history, of power. It is the injection into a Revolution of "Feed Our Children." An injection of what is more "powerful than" (beyond) power. A giving suck, an other, although not *the* other, side of a suck taken. A gift.

Its borders incised with alchemical glyphs signifying moons and months and body fluids, and marked by criss-crossing sutures of iron rods, this slice of void barely breaking the surface tension of the surrounding sea gives up its secret, a secret marked, as things which must remain properly hidden often are, with an X. The X is an emblem of Heidegger's fourfold, in which "each of the four mirrors in its own way the presence of the others."[41] X is a generic substitute for a thing. The thing is "nestling, malleable, pliant, compliant, nimble." Heidegger suggests circularity (O), but there is an X hidden here, an unknown, a secret. Heidegger's thing folds the fourfold along a hinge, which he suggests is a mirroring. An X hinged is two Vs folded at the point of intersection, the place where the secret is both enfolded and released. X is the doubled perspective on two canals intersecting in a mirror. It is a vanishing point. To X is "to delete, cancel, or obliterate with a series of x's."[42] X marks the (blind) spot(s) of history. "Cross your heart"—and hope to die and stick your finger in your eye. X is a cartoon convention marking "lidless eyes"[43] blinded by a surprise or blow to the head. As Catherine Ingraham has pointed out, the criss-cross of heavy mascara marks "eyes which do not see"—eyes which do not look beyond the look. X is a mark of non-identity, a non-identifying signature, like that of a person who is identified by the name of her father which, in a mirroring, is replaced by the name of her husband. Yet X is a chiasmus, signifying the alchemical androgyne—"blind, throbbing between two lives..."[44] X is the mark of Xantippe, who dumped a pot of piss on the head of her husband, Socrates. X is a kiss, both a "patronising"[45] and a nurturing gesture. A puckering, a sucking, an undulating architecture of solids, liquids, and gases.

A reverse *fascinus*, warding off the evil eye represented by the eye of the "one-eyed trouser snake" of Joyce, the Cyclopean eye of power invested in the Palace—the project is a defetishizing move, inviting the (male) body, refusing the power structure of the phallus that represses and corrupts the male body, and displaying the profound return of the repressed of the female body through an obscuring, a darkening, of the image, and a display of the generative—the jug is not a thing, but a magical machine—an interwoven system of apparatuses, a text.

> And Schreck would say: "Look at him, Fanny." So Fanny would take off her blindfold and give him a beaming smile.
>
> Then Madame Schreck would say: "I said, *look* at him, Fanny." At which she'd pull up her shift.
>
> For, where she should have had nipples, she had eyes.
>
> Then Madame Schreck would say: "Look at him properly, Fanny." Then those two other eyes of hers would open.
>
> They were a shepherd's blue, same as the eyes in her head; not big, but very bright.
>
> I asked her once, what did she see with those mammillary eyes, and she says: "Why, same as with the top ones but lower down.[46]

Notes

1. This is the expanded (or augmented) text of a lecture called "Jugs" that I gave for the "Body/Space/Machine" Symposium held at the University of Florida in March 1989. The expanded version, called "Big Jugs," was delivered as a lecture at Princeton University in October 1989. A substantial portion of the implant comes from a paper, "Architecture, Writing, The Body," delivered in the session, "Forecasting the Direction of Architectural Theory," at the Annual Meeting of the Association of Collegiate Schools of Architecture in Miami 1987.

2. In the pages of an alumni newsletter from the University of Virginia's School of Architecture, there appeared recently a stinging critique of the current state of the grove of academe: that the students are engaged in producing "flaccid classicism." *Webster's Third* tells us that "flaccid" suggests a lack of firmness and stiffness or vigor and force. So, we might deduce that the architectural projects being produced at Virginia are, to the alumnus' eye, ones in which the first Vitruvian requisite is missing. An architecture, then, of *commoditas* and *venustas*, but no *firmitas*. But is there any other reading of this clearly pejorative phrase?

3. *Hélène Cixous and Catherine Clément, The Newly Born Woman*, trans. Betsy Wing, (Manchester: Manchester University Press, 1986 [1975]), p. 167. The translator points out that the phrase "*En voila du propre!*" (the English equivalent of which is "What a fine mess!") is used in the text in places where that which is considered "appropriate" is called into question.

4. Julia Kristeva, *Desire in Language: A Semiotic Approach to Art and Literature*, ed. Leon Roudiez, (New York: Columbia University Press, 1980), p. 92.

5. James Joyce, *Finnegans Wake*, (New York: Viking Press, 1965 [1939]), 165.30-166.02.

6. Alice Jardine, *Gynesis: Configurations of Woman and Modernity*, (Ithaca: Cornell University Press, 1985), p. 100.

7. See Jean-Jacques Lecercle, *Philosophy Through the Looking Glass: Language, Nonsense, Desire* (London: Hutchinson and Co., 1985). Lecercle locates *délire*: "*Délire*, then, is at the frontier between two languages, the embodiment of the contradiction between them. Abstract language is systematic; it transcends the individual speaker, separated from any physical or material origin, it is an instrument of control, mastered by a regulating subject. Material language, on the other hand, is unsystematic, a series of noises, private to individual speakers, not meant to promote communication, and therefore self-contradictory, 'impossible' like all 'private languages.' ... Language which has reverted to its origin in the human body, where the primary order reigns." (pp. 44-45).

8. Cixous and Clément, p. 88.

9. The term "minor architecture" is both properly deduced from architectural historians' conventional use of the term "major architecture" to refer to canonical buildings in the history of architecture, and is illegitimately appropriated from Gilles Deleuze's and Felix Guattari's concept of minor literature. See Deleuze and Guattari, *Kafka: Toward a Minor Literature*, trans. Dana Polan, Minneapolis: University of Minnesota Press, 1986 [1975]).

   Minor literature is writing that takes on the conventions of a major language and subverts it from the inside. Deleuze's and Guattari's subject is the work of Franz Kafka, a Jew writing in German in Prague in the early part of this century. Minor literature possesses three dominant characteristics: 1. It is that which a minority constructs within a major language, involving a deterritorialization of that language. Deleuze and Guattari compare Prague German to American Black English. 2. Minor literatures are intensely political: "[I]ts cramped space forces each individual intrigue to connect immediately to politics. The individual concern thus becomes all the more necessary, indispensable, magnified because a whole other story is vibrating within it" (p. 17). 3. Minor literatures are collective assemblages; everything in them takes on a collective value.

Deleuze and Guattari describe two paths of deterritorialization. One is to "artificially enrich [the language], to swell it up through all the resources of symbolism, of oneirism, of esoteric sense, of a hidden signifier" (p. 19). This is a Joycean approach. The other is to take on the poverty of a language and take it further, "to the point of sobriety" (p. 19). This is Kafka's approach. Deleuze and Guattari then reject the Joycean as a kind of closet reterritorialization which breaks from the people, and go all the way with Kafka.

In transferring such a concept to architecture, already much more intensely materially simple and with more complex relationships to "the people" and to pragmatics, I believe it necessary to hang onto both possibilities, shuttling between them. This may begin to delineate a kind of line of scrimmage between making architectural objects and writing architectonic texts. What a minor architecture would be is a collection of practices that follow these conditions.

10. Joyce, .006.31-32.

11. Ibid., 112.01-2.

12. Ibid., 064.09.

13. That is, a voiceless, irrational construction characterized by a lack of agreement with accepted ideas (among other things). the relationships between the surd/absurd and architecture have been theorized by Jeffrey Kipnis. This represents the palest of allusions to his work.

14. My house is located a stone's throw from one of the numerous sinkholes in Alachua County, Florida. The architecture building at the University of Florida, where I work, is located at the edge of another. "Alachua" is a Seminole word meaning "jug."

15. See Edgar Allan Poe's *The Narrative of Arthur Gordon Pym*, for example.

16. T. S. Eliot, "The Waste Land," *The Waste Land and Other Poems*, (New York: Harcourt, Brace and World, 1962 [1922]), p. 37.

17. Catherine Ingraham, "Milking Deconstruction, or Cow Was the Show?," *Inland Architect*, September/October, 1988.

18. Ibid., p. 65.

19. Martin Heidegger, "The Thing," *Poetry, Language, Thought*, trans. Albert Hofstadter, (New York: Harper and Row, 1971), p. 166.

20. Ibid.

21. Ibid., p. 167.

22. Ibid., p. 169.

23. Ibid.

24. Ibid., p. 171.

25. Ibid., p. 172.

26. Ibid.

27. Ibid.

28. Ibid., p. 180.

29. Ibid., p. 182.

30. Ibid.

31. This phrase refers to the well-known chapter from Le Corbusier's *Vers une architecture* and to Catherine Ingraham's critique of it in "The Burdens of Linearity," a paper presented at the Chicago Institute for Architecture and Urbanism (Skidmore, Owings and Merrill Foundation) Working Session on Contemporary Architectural Theory, September 1988, as well as to its more transparent referent, the eye of power which sees only that which it chooses to see.

32. Eliot, p. 39.

33. Deleuze and Guattari, *A Thousand Plateaus (Capitalism and Schizophrenia)*,trans. Brian Massumi, (Minneapolis: University of Minnesota Press, 1987 [1980]), p. 287.

34. Jardine, p. 251.

35. Thomas Pynchon, *V.* (1963), (New York: Bantam Books, 1981), pp. 320-321.

36. Eliot, p. 30.

37. Luce Irigaray, *Speculum of the Other Woman*, trans. Gillian C. Gill, (Ithaca: Cornell University Press, 1985 [1974]), p. 114.

38. These are the words of Aldo Rossi, whose obsession with the idea of architecture as vessel is well-known and well-documented. See *A Scientific Autobiography*, trans. Lawrence Venuti, (Cambridge, Mass.: M.I.T. Press, 1981).

39. Marilyn French, *Beyond Power: On Women, Men, and Morals*, (New York: Ballantine Books, 1985), p. 191.

40. Many readers will recognize this allusion to the writing of Guy Davenport (*The Geography of the Imagination*, San Francisco: North Point Press, 1981), who has been an influential teacher to me.

41. Heidegger, p. 179.

42. From the *American Heritage Dictionary*.

43. Eliot, p. 34.

44. Eliot, p. 38. The androgyne here is Tiresias, blinded because his androgynous experience led him to speak the unspeakable (that the female's pleasure—*jouissance*—is greater than that of the male). The complete phrase from Eliot is: "At the violet hour, when the eyes and back/ Turn upward from the desk, when the human engine waits/ Like a taxi throbbing waiting/ I Tiresias, though blind, throbbing between two lives,/ Old man with wrinkled female breasts, can see/ At the violet hour, the evening hour that strives/ Homeward, and brings the sailor home from sea."

45. Eliot, p. 39.

46. Angela Carter, *Nights at the Circus*, (New York: Penguin Books, 1984), p. 69.

3

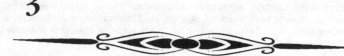

A GHOST STORY

Avery Gordon

[T]he importance of psychoanalysis is precisely the way
that it throws into crisis the dichotomy on which the
appeal to the reality of the event clearly rests. Perhaps for
women it is of particular importance that we find a
language which allows us to recognise our part in intolerable structures—but in a way which renders us neither the
pure victims nor the sole agents of our distress.[1]

Americans believe in facts, but not in facticity. They do not know that facts are factitious.... It is in this belief in facts, in the total credibility of what is done or seen, in this pragmatic evidence of things and an accompanying contempt for what may be called appearances or the play of appearances...that the Americans are a true utopian society.... You have to be utopian to think that in a human order, of whatever nature, things can be as plain and straightforward as all that.[2]

Look, you're tired and I'm going to tell you everything as if it were a story. It will do you good, it will change your ideas, and I'll tell it to you in the simplest way even though you won't believe me.[3]

Get Them at the Start[4]

I was on my way to a conference with an abstract and a promise. The path seemed straight-forward: a promise to speak professionally about a method of studying culture within the present historical landscape of what might be named postmodern America, a present that challenges the traditional distinctions between fact and fiction, between truthfulness and lying, between reality and fantasy, upon which sociological research methods are based. If increasingly the images of reality were becoming more real than the real itself then the methods and the desires to capture that reality and de-scribe it truthfully might need to be made problematic.[5] I was on my way to a conference with an abstract and a promise, but then I got distracted by a photograph and had to take a detour, a psychoanalytic detour which led me to follow the traces of a woman ghost.

There is photographic evidence of her absence.[6] I would not have noticed the fact that she wasn't there if I hadn't stumbled upon her existence by accident. I found her in a book entitled, *A Secret Symmetry*, a story of her as a link, a point of exchange between two great men.[7] I recognized her story as it called out my desire to know more and so I began to re-search the traces of a woman ghost, a woman who, the book cover proclaims, "changed the early history of psychoanalysis"; changed that history by virtue of being between Carl Jung and Sigmund Freud, and by virtue of not being in the photograph.

There is photographic evidence of her absence. The Third Psychoanalytic Congress took place at Weimar on 21-22 September 1911. The photograph displays 40 bodies, mostly male, and Sabina Spielrein is not there. Evidence also exists that in the past she had refused to pose for the eye of the camera because there is another photograph of her surrounded by her father and brothers shielding her face from the camera. It's possible she just didn't want her picture taken. After all, she was supposed to be there: in a letter to Freud at the end of August 1911, Jung had listed her name "Frl. Dr. Spielrein (!)" as part of the "feminine element" representing Zurich.[8] In a diary entry written almost a year before the conference, Spielrein wrote: "In my imagination I already saw my friend [Jung] in love with her, I saw her sitting next to me at psychiatric congresses, she—proud and contented as wife and mother, I a poor psychopath who has a host of desires and can realize none of them; renouncing love, my soul rent with pain."[9]

A woman was supposed to be someplace, but she never arrived. "The Weimar Congress, organized by Jung and opening on 11 [sic] September 1911 was supposed to include Sabina Spielrein among its participants, as Jung himself informed Freud, but we know from a calm and lengthy letter written by Jung to Sabina that she had found a psychosomatic pretext for not going to Weimar."[10] A woman was supposed to be someplace, but only a pretext was woven and delivered.

Here is her narrative, seductively displayed on the outer body of the book, an advertisement for a fascinating story, a story of fascinations: *Here is the fascinating story of Sabina Spielrein, a young Russian woman brought to Jung's psychiatric clinic in Zurich to be cured of a serious nervous disorder. Once cured of her illness, Spielrein falls deeply in love with her analyst. Despite his attraction to her, Jung chooses to break off the relationship when it threatens to cause a scandal. Spielrein then confides in Freud, Jung's mentor and father figure, and he becomes confessor to them both. Through Spielrein's diary and letters, published in paperback for the first time, the reader is presented with a rare glimpse into the essence of psychoanalytic work and into the lives of its key figures.*[11] The advertisement does not mention that Spielrein wrote about the death drive ten years before Freud published his seminal work on the death instinct, *Beyond The Pleasure Principle*,[12] nor does it mention the fact that Sabina Spielrein is not in the photograph of the participants at the Weimar Congress taken in the year she finished her dissertation.

Make Your Points by Ordering Events

I was on my way to a sociology conference with an abstract and a promise, a woman also hoping to remember later that she, too, was in the year she finished her dissertation. I was thinking about the powerful appeal of Régine Robin's statement that "something crosses over the disciplinary boundaries which only fiction can apprehend, like a trace of unassumed contradictions, as the only way to designate the locus of its own production."[13] Her statement, however, also harbors the danger implicit in forgetting the necessarily institutional construction of the boundary between a professional interest in facts and a professional interest in fictions. I was thinking about how even a professional interest in fiction may subvert the hegemony of facticity that characterizes the discipline of sociology while at the same time trying to avoid a romantic attachment to either literary criticism, another profession, or to textuality, "the locus of [our] production[s]." I was wondering how to describe and inscribe simultaneously the stories I was telling, all of which kept returning to the question of the materiality of the production of knowledge by intellectuals within the confines of the university. And so an abstract was written and it read partially, though thoroughly professionally, as follows:

What mode of knowledge production is possible and adequate in the postmodern world? The ethnography is a principal research method of studies of culture, both of our own and of others, yet the status of the ethnography as a window on the real needs to be rendered problematic.[14] How do we, as sociologists, rethink the ethnography in a world where the real is no longer self-evident, where the social fact may be more properly understood as an artifact, and where the description of cultural life is made problematic by the ritual mode of textual production? This essay offers a meditation on the limits and possibilities of sociological method within our present, an historical conjuncture which, of necessity and political desire, must question the boundaries separating the truth from the lie, the fact from the artifact, the real from the copy, science from literature, experience from interpretation, and the mode of producing knowledge from the product that mode creates. Perhaps the key problem facing sociology and cultural studies, more specifically, is to take up the historical, theoretical, and methodological challenges of our own changing cultural landscape and the theoretical/political interventions of what might be called a feminist poststructuralism. This implies grappling with issues related to the narrative structuring, fictive composition, and historical provisionality of claims to knowledge.

There are good reasons to be cautious of this abstract: the authoritative tone of the words, the materiality of its signification; the misleading stagings of identifications—"we, as sociologists"; the focus on ethnographic writing practices by someone who is not sure she is really an ethnographer; or the imperial gestures of global academic relief—"the postmodern world, our present." I could fix these and fix nothing of what is intolerable in the perfectly respectable statement concerning textuality and artifactuality in the social sciences, a question which ought to have some urgency for sociologists, who, even if protected against the seductive appeal of continental theory, must acknowledge the televisual conditions of the production of social reality for most North Americans.

[Sociology] today falls somewhere between the human and the social sciences. Its "hard" scientific aspect—the

collecting of data and empirical evidence, statistical research, linguistic analyses, for example—is nearly always
carried out to the accompaniment of its traditional human-
ism. The scientific [sociologist] works day to day in a
disciplinary field which is beset by questions of epistemology and interpretation and by concomitant philosophical
questions about the relation between observer and observed, about the constitution of ideologies and method-
ologies, and so on.[15]

I am also working within a field beset with these questions and at least
three others which multiply the fields and borders which situate the
woman writing in and out of a sociology falling somewhere between the
human and the *scientific*. The first question is: What constitutes the
social field in which the sociologist negotiates (or does not) between
what's hard and what's human? The sociologist is not only beset by
questions of epistemology and interpretation, and by questions of
ideology and methodology, but is also beset by the founding desire of the
discipline—to describe and analyze social reality. The problematization
of this desire is not only a function of being upset over epistemological
questions, but must be, for the sociologist, connected to questions about
the nature of social reality itself. Here, the social field includes, but is not
limited to academic discourses. The second question asks: Who is in this
field? This question, as a shorthand, must stand for the complications of
difference and power relations which such an asking and answering
gives notice to, and is related to the third question. How, when we ask
who, when, and where, does the field change dramatically?

It began with a question: what method have you adopted for your
research? Or more precisely, why do you use literary fictions as the "data"
for your research and teaching and name this mode of knowledge
production sociology, rather than, say, literary criticism? It began with a
question demanding to know the implications of understanding the
ethnography within an epistemology of the truth as partial, as an artifact
of the ritual mode of producing an understanding, a truth, the real. They
wanted to know what it meant to understand the real as an effect (as
something produced) and as an *affective relation* (as not simply rational
and conscious). They wanted to know how the real could be a powerful
fiction which we do not experience as fictional, but as true. They were
concerned about the implications of understanding social relations as
artifactual because entrance into this epistemological place blurs the
institutional, disciplinary, and political boundaries that separate the real
from the fictive without in any way diminishing the powerful self-
evidency of real fictions.[16] How can we tell the difference, they asked,
between science and literature, between sociology and literary criticism,
between the symbolic, the imaginary, and the real?[17] How can we tell the
difference between one story and an(others), a fundamental question of

how the sexual, racial, and national differences effected by social
relations of power and knowledge are inscribed within the social text?
Perhaps my method was ruinous. Perhaps there was some other interest
than a strictly professional one in fictions. Since I wanted to know why
the desire to know this difference was so powerful, I was struck by the
following answer given by Luce Irigaray to this question asked by those
judging her doctoral thesis at its defense. The question was: what method
have you adopted for this research? Her answer: "A delicate question. For
isn't it the method, the path to knowledge, that has always also led us
away, led us astray, by fraud and artifice."[18]

A detour has already begun. The question seems less than delicate,
hard actually. This is a hard question to answer and to be continually
asked. A persistent question. One asked within a certain tone of voice—
an almost imperceptible sigh of relief that the one asking is not the one
answering; the sound also of a powerful demand to know, a distanced
usually firm utterance capturing in its delivery the authority of the
interrogator. THIS IS JUST A TEST IN CASE OF A REAL EMERGENCY... I
am cautious about my answer since I know that Irigaray was later fired
from her job for what appears to have been an improper defense of an
institutional territory. The real is a terrifying place, says Jacques Lacan.
Not at all like the security observable evidence promises the ethnogra-
pher or the sociologist. Something is missing its mark, a detour has
already begun.

What method have you adopted for this research? "For isn't it the
method, the path to knowledge, that has led us away...from woman's
path," Irigaray adds. The question of method may be a matter of fraud and
artifice and this is why the singularity of Irigaray's woman and her path
troubles me, for the moment, even though women's paths are the paths
I am trying to mark and despite (or because of) the appeal of the certainty
of knowing the path of the detour. But they wanted to know how to tell
the difference between one story and another and in order to try to
provide some clues it will be necessary to speak of gender markings and
territorial dislocations. It will be necessary to take a detour.

A sentence about the duplicity of method is pursuing a rigorous
abstract promising to demonstrate the textuality of powerful claims to
knowledge, promising to give *evidence* of the *fictive* nature of claims to
truthful knowledge. Irigaray continues, "it was...necessary to note the
way in which the method is never as simple as it purports to be."[19] A
displacement then, a detour from abstract questions of method, from the
easier (because legitimate) question of the relationship between the
fictive and the real, the fact and the artifact, toward the materiality of
institutional story-telling. What I try to write about is not only how the
method "is never as simple as it purports to be," but how the focus on the
question of method at the metadiscursive level allows us to quietly pass
over the places least methodical in our work as intellectuals, the places
where our discourse is unauthorized by virtue of its unruliness. These are

the operations of the material rituals of the production of knowledge, those vectors of power—institutional, social, personal, sexual—which call us out to a desire to know and which the method will later authorize, which the method will later cleanse of all traces of the chaotic overdetermined mode of its production.

> The fiction of mainstream [sociology]—so generally "masculinist" that the adjective begins to lose all meaning—is that rigorous readings come into being in a *scientific field*, or in the field of legalistic demonstration of validity. The other view, coming from a mind-set that has been systematically marginalized may just as well be called "feminist": that the production of public rigor bears the strategically repressed marks of the so-called private at all levels.[20]

The question is: in what fields does field work occur? "How precisely, is a garrulous, overdetermined...encounter shot through with power relations and personal cross-purposes circumscribed as an adequate version of a more or less discrete 'other world' composed by an individual author."[21] How, precisely, to evoke the path to knowledge within an institution like the academy that is "shot through with power relations and personal cross-purposes" and yet so effectively disavows those "strategically repressed" marks of which Gayatri Spivak reminds us. How to enact the circuitous paths and detours along which desires to know become methods of producing products we recognize as knowledge?

These questions have everything to do with the ways in which theories are inscribed socially and institutionally and should be of special significance to feminist theory which is minimally committed to breaking down the distinctions between public and private force fields. Within the university, this implies grappling with:

> ...the disjunctions between what can now become the relative straightforwardness of an intellectual commitment to feminism and the compromising politics of university life; the libidinally driven articulation of gender differences in...academic settings; the often deluded sense of the state of theory produced by the narrow framing of the social terrain in which we do our intellectual work; the uncanny ways in which traditionally male academic practices can return to haunt us even as we try to disavow them.

The moments that in destabilizing theory may open up the possibility of theorizing differently, that is materially, reflexively. Finally, this implies grappling with the risk of shattering the safety net of traditional academic writing. [22]

Along circuitous paths, we enter into and exit out of our accounts, which are also willy-nilly, shot through with power relations and personal cross-purposes. If "we do not inhabit a clearly defined critical space free of [the] traces of complicity,"[23] what would it mean to acknowledge ourselves as being in our accounts, to foreground those repressed marks, the contradictory, "autobiographical" moments which must be circumscribed in order to produce the adequate version? (I flaunt the impropriety of the gesture here in Spielrein's name, although her story is not simply an allegory of my own). Perhaps the key methodological question is not: what method have you adopted for this research?—but what paths have been disavowed, left behind, covered over and remain unseen. In what fields does field work occur?

To a Definite Climax

I was on my way to a conference with an abstract and a promise but then I got distracted by a photograph and had to take a detour, a psychoanalytic detour which led me to follow the traces of a woman ghost, a woman who never made it to the conference which she had planned to attend. Why the detour? Why, now within North America, am I interpellated into psychoanalysis and into a story of a dead woman?[24] Why do some words come to me in the name of psychoanalysis which I am now offering you as an alternative promise to the one I made abstractly?

I say in the name of psychoanalysis because, as a feminist writing within and without the patriarchal institutions of Sociology and Psychoanalysis, Psychoanalysis, as an institution, remains a less than adequate home. But there may be a place for me as a white intellectual woman in relation to a particular psychoanalysis—a psychoanalysis somewhat surrealist; a psychoanalysis forged in critical political opposition to American ego psychology—a place constructed by a post-1968 generation of feminist women. "About 'and/or of psychoanalysis'.... It seems to me that this elaboration is surely not possible so long as psychoanalysis remains within its own field."[25]

Sabina Spielrein transferred from one field, madness, into another, psychoanalysis, and the story of that field work traces the institutional markings of heterosexual desire within an intellectual enterprise, within the institution of psychoanalysis itself. However, the work of Luce Irigaray, Catherine Clément and others have opened up the possibility of a field work that "disturb[s] the peace [and] disrupt[s] the order of discourse."[26] "And if, as a woman who is also in public, you have the audacity to say something about *your* desire, the result is scandal and repression...And at that point there are no two ways about it, you're shut out of the university, in fact you're excluded from all institutions."[27] My field work is a risky business, as was Spielrein's. She never made it to the

Weimar Conference, and of her paper on the death drive written ten years before Freud's "seminal" study was published, Freud had this to say: "...her destructive drive is not much to my liking, because I believe it is personally conditioned. She seems abnormally ambivalent."[28] Jung, after having written to Spielrein to say that her study was "extraordinarily intelligent and contain[ed] excellent ideas," wrote to Freud: "One must say: *desinat in piscem mulier formosa superne* ['What at the top is a lovely woman ends below in a fish'...]...She has...fallen flat in this paper because it is not thorough enough...Besides that her paper is heavily over-weighted with her own complexes."[29] Unlike Sabina I made it to the conference, but barely—the detours almost led me too far astray.

Why the detour through this psychoanalysis, a feminist, albeit white and intellectual psychoanalysis, in which some things are trying to escape their institutional borders? A simple answer first. I am engaged in re-searching women within the academic institution, our place and displacements within these confines. The ethnographic scene of my re-search is the scene I am in, a scene in which I look not through a window, a sociological metaphor for the probability of adequate recognition, but into a mirror, a psychoanalytic metaphor for misrecognition as the possibility of any recognition at all.[30] As I try to write the contours of this landscape in North America at the present time, as I try to write from the impossible place of attempting to demonstrate the "elusive historico-politico-economico-sexual determinations"[31] of our readings and writings, it is precisely the difficulty of articulating what produces stories such as Spielrein's (a story overdetermined by being *in* psychoanalysis) which leads me to a scene where storytelling is problematized. In order to write within a question concerning exclusions and invisibilities—a dead woman was not at a conference at which she was supposed to be—requires a methodology that is attentive to what can not be seen, but is powerfully real; attentive to what appears dead, but is powerfully alive; attentive to what appears to be in the past, but is powerfully present; and also requires attending to just who the subject of analysis is. To the extent that a feminist psychoanalysis is concerned with exploring and transforming scenes in which these binary oppositions (visible/invisible, real/imaginary, dead/alive, past/present) are *experienced as both fluid and maddening*, it may have some lessons for those of us who are also undertaking analysis which we think is of a different kind.

A brief digression on two psychoanalytic words which render the real, as the empirically given, problematic, two words around which much more could and should be said, two words which should not be taken as necessarily the most important ones. The first is "the unconscious."

> In setting itself the task of making the discourse of the unconscious speak through consciousness, psychoanalysis is advancing in the direction of that fundamental region [or field] in which the relations of representation...come into play. Whereas all the human sciences advance to-

wards the unconscious only with their back to it, waiting
for it to unveil itself as fast as consciousness is analysed, as
it were backwards, psychoanalysis, on the other hand,
points directly towards it, with a deliberate purpose—not
towards that which must be rendered gradually more
explicit by the progressive illumination of the implicit, but
towards what is there and yet is hidden, towards what
exists with the mute solidity of a thing, of a text closed in
upon itself, or of a blank space in a visible
text...[P]sychoanalysis moves towards the moment—by
definition inaccessible to any theoretical knowledge of
man, to any continuous apprehension in terms of signification, conflict, or function—at which the contents of
consciousness articulate themselves, or rather stand gaping.[32]

The unconscious draws us, as analysts, into another *region* or field
where things are *there and yet hidden*, where things *stand gaping*,
where the question of how we present a world, our own or another's,
becomes a question of the limits of re-presentation. "[T]o a knowledge
situated within the representable, all that frames and defines...the very
possibility of representation can be nothing other than mythology."[33] For
Michel Foucault, the three figures of Death, Desire and the Law, haunt a
psychoanalytic mythology.

Is death not that upon the basis of which knowledge in
general is possible....Is desire not that which remains
always *unthought* at the heart of thought? And the law-
language (at once word and word-system) that psychoanalysis takes such pains to make speak, is it not that in
which all signification assumes an *origin* more distant
than itself, but also that whose return is promised in the
very act of analysis?[34]

We are already far away from the world of the social scientist, a world
where the promise of science is precisely to ward off the mythological,
the place where things stand gaping; a world where the unthought is
violently expelled; a world where meaning is transparent within the
words it speaks, and in which there is no promise of re-turning only the
promise of a linear progression to a perfect analysis. At the most simple
level, the unconscious points us towards that which can not be seen but
which effects powerfully, points us towards the markings of exclusions
which are inscribed on our bodies and through our language, points us
to the process by which a real story is effected and enacted.
Foucault's evocation of the unconscious figures in his analysis of the
"otherness" which must be expelled, fetishized, and mastered in order

for a concept of Man, as a sovereign subject, as a knowing being and a unity knowable, to be discursively and historically deployed. The challenge to empiricity that the concept of the unconscious issues defies the promise of a unified subjectivity, either Man or Woman, utopian or otherwise. To the extent that the unconscious points us to the rituals and marks of exclusion, it points to the "full complexity of the personal,"[35] to the gaps, fragments, errant trajectories, the points of desire that are endemic to the representational field itself. What is the real story? How does it get written?

Within the analytic scene stories are effected and enacted within a field of intersubjectivity psychoanalysis names the transference-countertransference, my second word. The transference-countertransference is a chaotic field of energy in which, by virtue of the savage force of that field, memories are remembered and forgotten, desires are forged and reforged, a story is really just the effect/affect of the dynamics of storytelling (speaking and listening) within a dyadic relation. "It's a question of transferring not only old desires but also, continuously, what comes up in the real, what the patient imagines has existed. This is not the precise meaning dictionaries of psychoanalysis give to the word transference which describes, rather, a 'process' of fixation on the person of the analyst. But the word draws its own myth in its wake, and carries psychoanalysis back to its anchorage, to the very place it refuses to take into consideration. Transference unto the psychoanalyst; the transfer(ence) of populations; the crossing of streams, adrift, at the mercy of the waves of the river."[36]

It is the recognition of the transference, a demand "that insists on being recognized as *real*"[37] which throws into crisis what had previously been taken to be the real crisis (i.e., the "original" reason for the analysis). As Freud notes, "there is a complete change of scene; it is as though some piece of make-believe had been stopped by the sudden irruption of reality."[38] *It's a question of transferring not only old desires but also, continuously, what comes up in the real, what the patient imagines has existed.* A young Russian woman is suffering from a schizophrenic disturbance or severe hysteria. She enters into analysis as an object of analysis, as a subject to be transformed. Something happens in that field which paperback books call a love affair between the doctor and the patient; a reality is imagined. She is cured of her "original" illness, but now suffers from unrequited love. She becomes an analyst too, keeps a diary and writes about death. He writes about Her as the devil within his soul, gives this a name (the anima) for science's sake and later forgets about her when he writes a very long essay on transference, but remembers that the transference has something to do with alchemy and transformations.[39]

An acknowledgement of the transferential relations in any analytic encounter suggests that our field is often not what we thought it was—that the real is subject to and is the subject of reversals, displacements, and overdeterminations, that the real is just (but not only) a powerful and fascinating story.

"Academically, the term 'field' refers simply to some relatively circumscribed and abstract area of study. However, that particular sense gives no indication of how scholars operationally relate to their field; that is, *how* they study it. When we add the term 'research,' [or work, as in field work],...this adds a locative property. [It tells us that a researcher is in a field or fields.].... The field researcher understands that his field—whatever its substance—is continuous with other fields and bound up with them in various ways."[40] If the fields that are bound up and continuous with, the fields that overdetermine, any analytic encounter are not just other academic fields, but the social, economic, historical, political, and sexual fields in which as researchers we field what often appear to be academic questions, then the "real story" is always a negotiated interruption. Traversing fields, the story must emerge out of the field of forces which really attract and distract the story-teller.

A woman was on her way to a conference with an abstract and a promise but then she got distracted by a photograph and had to take a detour which led her to follow the traces of a woman ghost. The woman had to traverse fields in order to speak. The speaking was essential to her well-being, but it became harder and harder to keep track of the story. But she kept trying to remember that it involved death (a dead woman), desire (a photograph), and the law (a language trying to speak).

To the extent that psychoanalysis is organized along a dyadic model—speaker/listener, patient/analyst, student/teacher, its heterosexual and patriarchal structure marks the limits of its field at this time.[41] "The most significant event in Spielrein's young life was that whatever happened during her treatment by Jung at the Burgholzli...call it treatment, seduction, transference, love, mutual daydreams, delusions or whatever...it cured her. True, Spielrein paid a very high price in unhappiness, confusion, and disillusion for the particular way in which she got cured, but then..."[42] A limit is marked also by a story which understands "transfer(ence), from one stage to the next, from one wish to the next," as a cure.[43]

Nevertheless, Bruno Bettelheim's comments, which attempt to complicate the process of locating the source of the violence in Sabina Spielrein's story solely in the empirically verifiable actions of a powerful man, are significant. They are important because they echo Jacqueline Rose's concern that "for women it is of particular importance that we find a language which allows us to recognise our part in intolerable structures—but in a way which renders us neither the pure victims nor the sole agents of our distress."[44] Feminism, particularly American feminism, has desired and needed an "unequivocal accusation of the real,"[45] an empirical safety net, access to "what really happened" in order to politically challenge the powerful mechanisms which structure our exclusions, pains, pleasures, and violences. Maybe this is because there was/is no room within the academic institution for staging the kinds of remember-ings the (pyscho)analytic situation allows, for analytically inhabiting a really shifting reality. But there too the hope was that in opening up those "strategically repressed" markings *again*, a transfer(ing), a transforma-tion would occur. And this repetition the (psycho)analysis accomplishes by situating a story of the present as a complex staging of a past remembered and forgotten, but only as a memory of the present. A memory is never simply repeated within analysis because there was never a memory as a "thing" to remember in the first place. The repetition is always a repetition-as-displacement.

But because psychoanalysis recognized, but could not inhabit the space of the transference-countertransference *institutionally*, women's stories remained the seductive object of a writing, an analysis of secret symmetries based on "a model privileging symmetry as the possible condition for mastery in the non-recognition of the other."[46] Despite the lack of or overabundance of woman models imagined in North America, psychoanalysis seems to open up the question of a "dimension of reality all the more important for the subject because it goes way beyond anything that can, or needs to be, attested as fact." When "reality [becomes] nothing more than what can be empirically established as the case,"[47] the case studies we can write become (the sometimes) brutal fictions of established empires.

The focus within psychoanalysis on questions of desire, power, fan-tasy, memory, helps me to understand why I am haunted by a woman ghost; why the memory of her absence in a photo (which is both a real memory and an analytic staging) makes me attentive to the systematic exclusions produced by the assumptions and practices of a normalized social science. These normal methods fundamentally foreclose issues of power and gender because they foreclose the recognition of the exclu-sions, the sacrifices, required to tell a story as the singularly real one. At least "Freud problematizes any statement of method that would begin, putatively, 'I choose because...'"[48]

Yet the social scientist assumes that the analyst(me)/ethnographer is in a different field than her subjects and that with good intentions and methods, an object of analysis can become a non-violated subject of analysis, can speak her truth outside of the framing and narrativization, outside of the transferential intersubjectivity of the re-search process, outside of writing, of ritually enacting a story. But what if the material conditions and limits of our reading and writing, the "elusive historico-politico-economico-sexual determinants," necessitate that the ethnogra-pher, the sociologist, the psychoanalyst, must write "the theoretically impossible historical biography of that very self that is no more than an effect of a structural resistance of irreducible heterogeneity."[49] This is a tortuous language for trying to ask the question: in what fields does the ethnographer/sociologist write, because a subjectivity "neither simply achieved, nor complete," a subjectivity "leaving something in excess," is a tortuous process, a truly painful and institutionally risky embodiment. And because this subject never is nor was complete, except in an image, in an imagined moment of refraction where a mirror produced a myth, it always seems to be operating at a loss. But, for me, this is a significant lesson and promise of psychoanalysis: "Without reifying the idea of a pure fragmentation which would be as futile as it would be psychically unmanageable for the subject—only the concept of a subjectivity at odds with itself gives back to women the right to an impasse at the point of sexual identity, with no nostalgia whatsoever for its possible or future integration into a norm."[50]

If the ethnography has given us "writing reduced to method: keeping good field notes, making accurate maps, 'writing up' results...an ideology claiming transparency of representation and immediacy of experience,"[51] it has done so on the basis of a systematic exclusion of a "subject at odds with itself" and a systematic construction of a sovereign subject who can stand outside the window and de(in)scribe what he sees as separate from the relations of power that positioned him outside looking in to begin with. For men, the increasing challenges to that sovereignty, to that intersection of knowledge and power and the resulting ambiguity of cultural meanings—whether from feminism or from the de-stabilization of the real as a thing to be counted on generated by the simulation of white masculinity—may seem less hopeful, more terrifying. This is a fear which is translated into material forms of terrorism against all those others who, in their difference, challenge the very enclosure which makes a sovereign subject possible, challenge the very process of fetishization which allows the real to appear to his eyes as a discrete thing. As a white woman, already historically terrorized by that sovereignty, even where I benefit from the privileges of it, the loss of such a subject is perhaps not such a loss at all.[52]

Round Out to a Completion

Dear Sabina:

I'm uneasy about using your story, or the story of the places you were between as a pretext for speaking to the men (or to the women, for that matter) about methodology; about needing or seeming to need a dead woman to enliven matters, to make them have some material force. *Subjects repose in the archives, always inconsolable, never having the right to speak. They are, of course, spoken about—rumours of this reach them, but the materiality of their contents is forgotten.*[53] Is this why you have come back to haunt me because rumors of your re-covery have reached you? I found you by accident in a book which positions your diary and letters as evidence of your "decisive influence" on [Jung] and on the development of his system; your contributions, "of greatest significance, [to] the Freudian system" and the "startling new light [your life throws] on important aspects of the Freud-Jung correspondence."[54]

An aside: Perhaps, as feminists, we should be grateful for such a story. A young Russian girl, *the first child of intelligent, well-educated, well-to-do Jewish parents; her grandfather and great-grandfather...highly respected rabbis* is suffering from a *schizophrenic disturbance or severe hysteria*. In 1904, her *deeply concerned parents* take her to Zurich *to be treated at the world-famous Burgholzli mental hospital*. A patient of Jung's, by 1905, she has enrolled at the University of Zurich to study medicine, receiving her *doctor's degree in 1911 on the basis of a dissertation entitled 'The Psychological Content of a Case of Schizo-phrenia'.... The former schizophrenic patient had by then become a student of schizophrenia, a doctor treating mental disturbances, an original thinker who developed ideas that later became of greatest significance in the Freudian system.*[55] A young woman patient falls in love with her doctor. A doctor falls in love with his young woman patient. The history of psychoanalysis *is changed*. Perhaps as feminists we should be grateful for such a story, a story at least acknowledging that in the re-telling of an untold story an institution is "changed" by a love affair involving a great man and a young woman.

But what if this is just a ghost story marking the itinerary of one woman's desire for a woman ghost, marking a desire to raise the dead. "I don't want to listen to any more of your stories; they have no logic. They scramble me up. You lie with stories. You won't tell me a story and then say, 'This is a true story,' or 'This is just a story.' I can't tell the difference.... I can't tell what's real and what you made up?"[56] It's what the story opens up that's important. When a woman ghost is haunting a story about intellectual story-telling, what's important is not to be afraid.

Dear Sabina:

I'm writing to you again now. It seemed appropriate to pause for a moment and indicate the framing of your resurrection. I'm sure you will be interested in that part too, especially if these rumors reach you, just as the rumors of Jung's betrayal reached out for you. Do you think that the recovery of you may be just another cover up, another refusal of an alternative to scientific containment? I'm still stuck in the problem of acknowledging a truth of psychoanalysis, your field: that a dead woman (you) is alive for me haunting a story I'm trying to tell about intellectual story-telling.

This is a methodological problem, a political problem involving the "ethics of navigating the stagings"[57] of women's stories, our pains, our desires. It seems that I'm faced with a terrible and sometimes terrifying choice. On the one hand, I can't pretend that Sabina Spielrein, a proper name signifying a story of exchanges, could come alive as a fully constituted subject capable of speaking a truth uncontaminated by the narratives of patriarchal desire. What is *not* recoverable is a woman *not* confined by an exchange narrative, a value harboring desires forbidden and foreboding, linking two men; a woman who really wasn't in the middle of a great drama. And, I'm cautious about being complicit in the construction of another white utopian feminist subject. At the same time, I don't want to make you "disappear twice." ("Certain analyses, which describe flatly the statements of 'their patient,' make them disappear twice: a first time because their speech is inscribed in another discourse and a second time because their words-cries, their words-sufferings have become subduable and subdued under the analyst's Valium-pen."[58]) But I must confess to you Sabina that it is precisely the love affair, the story of a woman whose body and body of work was inscribed by the bodies of men who wrote books inspired by fractured women, that haunts me. The heterosexual theater that staged your story repeats itself into my present and it is a hope that the repetition of this story, a repetition with a difference made possible by the work of many feminists, may make possible our "taking the necessary risk of 'demonstrating' [just how] theory is necessarily undermined—as it is operated—by practice."[59]

Which Leaves the Mind at Rest

> The story is me, neither me nor mine. It does not really belong to me, and while I feel greatly responsible for it, I also enjoy the irresponsibility of the pleasure obtained through the process of transferring. Pleasure in the copy, pleasure in the reproduction. No repetition can ever be identical, but my story carries with it their stories, their history, and our story repeats itself endlessly despite our persistence in denying it. I DON'T BELIEVE IT. THAT STORY COULD NOT HAPPEN TODAY.[60]

"'It isn't so funny...Take it back. Call that story back' said the audience by the end of the story, but the witch answered: 'It's already turned loose./It's already coming./It can't be called back.'"[61] I was on my way to a conference with an abstract and a promise but then I got distracted by a photograph and had to take a detour, a psychoanalytic detour which led me to follow the traces of a woman ghost. And now at the end of the story, all that remains is an abstract that could not be realized, and the markings of a detour. Why the detour? Because I was haunted by something not seen, a woman who was not in a photograph, and I was looking for a field which gives notice to structures of exclusion and which does not enclose the landscape in only what can be seen.

Notes

1.   Jacqueline Rose, *Sexuality in the Field of Vision,* (London: Verso, 1987), p. 14.

2.   Jean Baudrillard, *America,* trans. Chris Turner, (London: Verso, 1988), p. 85.

3.   Luisa Valenzuela, *He Who Searches,* (Illinois: Dalkey Archive Press, 1977), p. 116.

4.   These headings/subtitles form a narrative of their own and are borrowed from Trinh T. Minh-ha's essay, "Grandma's Story" in *Blasted Allegories,* ed. Brian Wallis, (New York and Cambridge: The New Museum of Contemporary Art and The MIT Press, 1987), p. 26. "Grandma's Story" can also be found in Minh-ha's new book, *Woman, Native, Other: Writing Postcoloniality and Feminism,* (Bloomington: Indiana University Press, 1989).

5.   See Jean Baudrillard, *Simulations,* (New York: Semiotext(e), 1983).

6.   The history of psychoanalysis and the history of women's relation to the institution of psychoanalysis is inextricably bound up with the development and use of photography and the so-called documentary image. Jean-Martin Charcot, whose pioneering work on hysteria at the Salpêtrière clinic in Paris, produced the three-volume *Iconographie photographique de la Salpêtrière,* a photographic-classificatory scheme of female hysteria. "But, as for the truth, I am absolutely only the photographer; I register what I see." Quoted in Elaine Showalter, *The Female Malady. Women, Madness and English Culture 1830-1980,* (New York: Pantheon Books, 1985), p. 151. Charcot's early studies and "public lectures" on female hysteria were, of course, elaborately staged and theatricalized, documenting more than the signs of hysteria. As Showalter points out, "Women were not simply photographed once, but again and again, so that they became used to the camera and to the special status they received as *photogenic subjects*" (p. 152, emphasis mine). Posed, stylized and seductive, the hysterical image could have severe consequences. "During the period when [Augustine, a young girl who entered the hospital in 1875] was being repeatedly photographed, she developed a curious hysterical symptom: she began to see everything in black and white" (p. 154). Freud studied with Charcot from October 1885 to February 1886, but the replacement of the visual spectacle with the talking cure marks the transition (through Josef Breuer and Anna O) to psychoanalysis proper. Both Catherine Clément in *The Weary Sons of Freud* and Jacqueline Rose analyze the contradictory implications of the shift from the centrality of the visual and the spectacular to the oral and the interior. Rose's argument is most apt here: "[Freud] questioned the visible evidence of the disease—the idea that you could know a hysteric by looking at her body.... [B]y penetrating behind the visible symptoms of disorder and asking what it was that the symptom was trying to *say*...Freud could uncover...unconscious desires and motives.... Freud's challenge to the visible, to the empirically self-evident, to the 'blindness of the seeing eye'...can give us the strongest sense of the force of the unconscious as a concept against a fully social classification relying on empirical evidence as its rationale." In Jacqueline Rose, "Femininity and its Discontents," *Feminist Review,* 14 (1983):16. Rose's important argument that psychoanalysis challenges "empiricist forms of reasoning" is key to understanding forms of subordination which are not and cannot be made fully visible, and for my particular problem: how to research from within a photograph where a woman is seemingly not-there.

7.   Aldo Carotenuto, *A Secret Symmetry: Sabina Spielrein Between Jung and Freud,* trans. Arno Pomerans, John Shepley, Krishna Winston, with a commentary by Bruno Bettelheim, (New York: Pantheon Books, 1984). The book contains Spielrein's diary from 1909-1912, her letters to Jung written between 1911-1918, and her letters to Freud and his to her. Almost all this material is fragmentary. Although Carotenuto makes reference in his extended analysis of these documents to Jung's letters to Spielrein, permission by Jung's family to publish them was not granted.

8. Ralph Manheim and R.F.C. Hall, trans., and William McGuire, ed., *The Freud/Jung Letters*, (Cambridge: Harvard University Press, 1988), p. 440.

9. Carotenuto, p. 29.

10. Ibid, p. 182.

11. Ibid, book jacket.

12. Sigmund Freud, *Beyond the Pleasure Principle* (1920), trans. and ed. James Strachey, (New York: W.W. Norton & Company, 1961).

13. Régine Robin, "Towards Fiction as Oblique Discourse," *Yale French Studies*, 59 (1980), p. 235.

14. See James Clifford and George Marcus, eds. *Writing Culture: The Politics and Poetics of Ethnography*, (Berkeley: University of California Press, 1986); James Clifford, *The Predicament of Culture: 20th Century Ethnography, Literature and Art.*, (Cambridge: Harvard University Press, 1988); George Marcus and Michael Fischer, *Anthropology as Cultural Critique: An Experimental Moment in the Human Sciences*, (Chicago: University of Chicago Press, 1986); Richard Harvey Brown, *Society as Text: Essays on Rhetoric, Reason and Reality*, (Chicago: University of Chicago Press, 1987). See also, Patricia Clough, "Understanding Subjugation: The Relation of Theory and Ethnography," *Studies in Symbolic Interaction*, 7, Part A (1986); and Michel de Certeau, *The Writing of History*, trans. Tom Conley, (New York: Columbia University Press, 1988).

15. Paul Smith, *Discerning the Subject*, (Minneapolis: University of Minnesota Press, 1988), p. 83.

16. The issue here is not whether "real" events or experiences exist and can be reported. "The fact that every object is constituted as an object of discourse has *nothing to do* with whether there is a world external to thought, or with the realism/idealism opposition. An earthquake or the falling of a brick is an event that certainly exists.... What is denied is not that such objects exist externally to thought, but the rather different assertion that they would constitute themselves as objects outside any discursive condition of emergence," Ernesto Laclau and Chantal Mouffe quoted in Gayatri Chakravorty Spivak, *In Other Worlds: Essays in Cultural Poetics*, (New York: Methuen, 1987), p. 242. As Spivak elaborates, "This understanding...does not entail ignoring what it is that sentences report or tell. It is the precondition for the analysis of how the what is made.... Not even the simplest reporting or telling can avoid these maneuvers. Foucault asks us to remember that what is reported or told is also reported or told and thus entails a positioning of the subject. Further, that anyone dealing with a report or a tale...can and must occupy a certain 'I-slot' in these dealings.... That history [or sociology] deals with real events [facts] and literature with imagined ones [fictions] may now be seen as a difference in degree rather than in kind.... What is called history [sociology] will always seem more real to us than what is called literature. Our very uses of the two separate words guarantees that. This difference cannot be exhaustively systematized" (p. 243). What interests me is the relationship between the "I-slot" and what Roland Barthes called "the effect of the real"; I am concerned with the implications of acknowledging that "history"/fact may not always seem "more real to us" and with the difficulty of demonstrating that *both* the investigating subject (or analyst) and her subject (of analysis) are involved in negotiating and producing a real story.

17. The play here is on the subversion of the common-sense connotations of these words at work in Lacanian psychoanalytic discourse. See Chapter 3 of Ellie Ragland-Sullivan, *Jacques Lacan and the Philosophy of Psychoanalysis*, (Urbana: University of Illinois Press, 1987), pp. 130-195 for a discussion of Lacan's three orders and how they displace our more common understanding of the Imaginary as the order of the imagination, the

Symbolic as the order of symbolism, and the Real as the order of reality, objectivity, or the empirical.

18. Luce Irigaray, *This Sex Which Is Not One*, trans. Catherine Porter with Carolyn Burke. (Ithaca: Cornell University Press, 1985), p. 150.

19. Ibid.

20. Spivak, p. 15.

21. Clifford, *The Predicament of Culture*, p. 25.

22. The quotation is from Cary Nelson, "Men, Feminism: The Materiality of Discourse," *Men in Feminism*, ed. Alice Jardine and Paul Smith, (New York: Methuen, 1987), p. 155. I discuss some aspects of these issues in my essay,"Masquerading in the Postmodern," *Cross Currents Recent Trends in Humanities Research*, ed. E. Ann Kaplan and Michael Sprinker, (London: Verso, 1990).

23. Gayatri Chakravorty Spivak, "'Draupadi' by Mahasveta Devi," in Elizabeth Abel, ed., *Writing and Sexual Difference*, (Chicago: University of Chicago Press, 1981), pp. 262-3. Spivak's preface and translation are also included in *In Other Worlds*, pp. 179-196.

24. The question of why the turn to psychoanalysis now has important strategic implications for feminist politics. According to Laura Kipnis, "This recourse to psychoanalysis (which provides no theory of social transformation and historically offers no evidence of political efficacy) in both Marxist and feminist theory seems to take place at a particular theoretical juncture: one marked primarily by the experience of political catastrophe and defeat. The political appropriation of psychoanalysis appears to signal, then, a lack—of a mass movement or of successful counterhegemonic strategies. The disastrous absorption of the European working-class movements into fascism, the decline of the political fortunes of feminism (outside the university) from those boisterous years when it seemed on the verge of becoming a mass movement, these are the events that have preceded the respective detours through the psychoanalytic.... The political use-value of psychoanalytic theory would...seem to be its updated account of the organization or etiology of *consent* to patriarchal or capitalist orders," "Feminism: The Political Conscience of Postmodernism?" in *Universal Abandon? The Politics of Postmodernism*, ed. Andrew Ross, (Minneapolis: University of Minnesota Press, 1988), pp. 150-1. This is not the place to respond to Kipnis's often insightful analysis, and her central concern—the implicit valorization of a modernist avant-garde aesthetic and the denigration of the popular cultural and 'real' world politics which she sees as issuing from the psychoanalytic turn and its focus on interiorization. (In the larger work of which this essay forms a part, I take up Kipnis argument about the "real" world and real world politics.) However, I would argue that the focus on consent is not only legitimate, but necessary, in the context of these defeats. Moreover, a feminist or Marxist politics which cannot address the very complicated ways in which people are *mobilized* or cathected to change both themselves and the social relations of power in which they are subjects and to which they are subjected will remain defeated. It has been in this context that certain features of psychoanalytic theory have been seen as providing insights into the possibility of a political practice beyond ideology-critique.

25. Irigaray, p. 125.

26. Irigaray, p. 145; Catherine Clément, *The Lives and Legends of Jacques Lacan*, trans. Arthur Goldhammer, (New York: Columbia University Press, 1983); Catherine Clément, *The Weary Sons of Freud*, trans. Nicole Ball, (London: Verso, 1987); Hélène Cixous and Catherine Clément, *The Newly Born Woman*, trans. Betsy Wing, (Minneapolis: University of Minnesota Press, 1986).

27. Irigaray, p. 145.

28. Carotenuto, p. 146.

29. Ibid, p. 183.

30. Jacques Lacan, "The Mirror Stage as Formative of the Function of the I," in *Écrits: A Selection*, trans. Alan Sheridan, (New York: W.W. Norton & Company, 1977).

31. Spivak, p. 15.

32. Michel Foucault, *The Order of Things*, (New York: Vintage Books, 1973), p. 374.

33. Ibid, p. 375.

34. Ibid.

35. Rose, "Femininity and its Discontents," p. 19.

36. Clément, *The Weary Sons of Freud*, p. 75.

37. Rose, *Sexuality in the Field of Vision*, p. 42.

38. Freud, quoted in Ibid, pp. 42-3.

39. Carl G. Jung, "Psychology of the Transference," in *The Practice of Psychotherapy. Collected Works*, Volume 16, trans. R.F.C. Hall, (New York: Pantheon Books, 1954), pp. 163-321.

40. Leonard Schatzman and Anselm Strauss, *Field Research.*, (Englewood Cliffs: Prentice-Hall, Inc., 1973), pp. 1-2.

41. The focus here on the heterosexual implications of the psychoanalytic "couple" should not detract from the equally problematic class and race-bound assumptions of psycho-analytic theory and practice. What I would consider a historically-informed social-psychoanalytic approach informs my reading of memory in Toni Morrison's novel *Beloved* in my dissertation, *Ghostly Memories: Feminist Rituals of Writing the Social Text*; Homi Bhabha's essay on mimicry also comes to mind here, "Of Mimicry and Man: The Ambivalence of Colonial Discourse," *October* 28, (Spring 1984):125-33.

42. Carotenuto, p. xxxviii.

43. Clément, *Weary Sons of Freud*, p. 74.

44. Rose, p. 14.

45. Ibid, p. 12.

46. Irigaray, p. 128.

47. Rose, p. 13.

48. Gayatri Chakavorty Spivak, "The Rani of Sirmur: An Essay in Reading the Archives," *History and Theory*, 24,3 (1984): 257.

49. Spivak, *In Other Worlds*, p. 16.

50. Rose, *Sexuality in the Field of Vision*, p. 15. See Spivak's very interesting and thoughtful critique of Rose's book, *Sexuality in the Field of Vision*, and this specific passage in "Feminism and deconstruction, again: negotiating with unacknowledged masculinism" in *Between Feminism and Psychoanalysis*, ed. Teresa Brennan, (New York: Routledge, 1989), p. 208. With respect to this particular passage, Spivak states: "This desire for an

impasse is not unlike the desire for the abyss or infinite regression for which deconstruction must perpetually account. I do, of course, declare myself bound by that desire. The difference between Rose and myself here is that what she feels is a right to be claimed, I am obliged to recognize as a bind to be watched." I suspect that Rose's (or my?) political and rhetorical purpose here is to push feminism to make the initial move Spivak's position already implies: that is, to claim a bind which can then be watched, not normalized.

51. Clifford and Marcus, *Writing Culture*, p. 2.

52. See Paul Smith's chapter on the human sciences, appropriately concerned with paranoia, in *Discerning the Subject*, pp. 83-99. Although feminism is the explicit subject of a later chapter of this important book on subjectivity, it clearly informs Smith's argument about the relationship between paranoia and the "controlling subject" of the sociological enterprise.

53. Robin, p. 234.

54. Carotenuto, p. xvi.

55. Ibid.

56. Maxine Hong Kingston, *The Woman Warrior: Memoirs of a Girlhood Among Ghosts*, quoted in Minh-ha, p. 3.

57. This phrase was shared with me by Jackie Orr who is also working with this question in her writing on the gendered history of panic.

58. Robin, p. 235.

59. Spivak, *Other Worlds*, p. 17.

60. Minh-ha, p. 7.

61. Leslie Marmon Silko, *Ceremony*, quoted in Minh-ha, p. 18.

4

BEHIND MASTER MIND UP ON TIME
MISPRISONERS ONCE ESCAPE LITERATURE*

Charles Noble

i asymmetrical signs
   a) Always lying to lower his head to get the good stuff into his brain,
      poeia-turned; politically horny, pretextually self-de-disabused,
      with "a bit of fun before ya get tucked under" spermatic Ezra Pound
      over perfectly spinny control, of his words, and, admittedly, after
      his prostatectomy: "they've made me into a cunt"
   b) The bellies have it! W.H. Auden, witness, at the police line-up. The
      missing crime? Sexual competition.
      #1: infant terribly erect,
           belied.
      #2: pregnant women
      #3: the beer belly
         (after the show #3 nurses his synecdoche, replays, etc.
         (will the real Mackenzie King Brothers
                         stand up, *sit calm*?
   c) Mailer, of the infamous PENis conference, has with *Tough Guys
      Don't Dance* (Nice Girls Don't ... *infinite equation*) finally re-
      norman-ized his Big Bang existentialism, married the self-parody
      he'd *roled over* anyway, a kind of James (Junk) Bond issue he'd
      floated, stealing back—the mis-taken identity—as limply totalitarian

---

* Hysterical title, positively, setting the two.one, quite a little number (not Job's daughter,
   Eye-shadow), a job that won't quit.

or simply "blasted"?—*onco* Sam taking another half-life—to weed(s)?
d) Fifty year reunion of the Normal School teacher training—my
mother cleaning out the closet of *Playboy* magazines up to the
early 70s (*mail*-er trouble?) for expected visitors. Heavy, glossy
mags burning poorly. Individual attention to the pages of naked
"tit" in the burn brabarrel. Closet gazes hang down—McLuhan's
clothes: ?barrel—of laughs or displaying the emperor's buy-us-as
                    or Noah's
                    arch rival
                          revival
                          reviral
            holy-grammared rib-
                              bed-rockship
                    proofoflacktic-ed off
      & regaled by the indented hull
      a new pair-o'-graFF(e) (s) (in fact floods)
                    typO
         All displays of virality, feminine
              hoho: & bottle it!
In the dregs of the closet mother finds stash of old letters from
aunts in Scotland, and one from her mother. Sits down, reads with
relish and emotion. Closet redressed! *Roxanne* come out in the
Milky Way. Light reading. Holy cow! Lifting off the parody-raised,
moebius, loop-sided roof projection.
Fractured, fractal allegory, signed disasymboled immanence mas-
cara-rading/mas*cow*ting out—putting out!—little Klee-shade fires
of creation. Rocky theatre in the asymmetrical shied-away nose *is
as big as your* ... pause, laughs from the set up chorus of ludic
matrons but no comeback comet Yeti in Nelson, A.D. flush with
the last scene where-ing the honestly untouching—
         down movie
         /
         the howlful "breasts like pillows"
from the mouth of the wolf1 naif other-wise
                    well
                    / -spoken
              Rousseau-piped-up
         Roxanne really nowhere too, dissolved
into the name-saken movie about projection thoughtfully "anti-
absorptively" screening the audience out—onto the street again
following the nose extended to the play in plain as your background noise held-over nightly till the *longueur* dawng Brecht
face
              /
         key-oaty

So left with: Jerk. Around
       re-mark-able nose account
        numb-ering(21) into a/cute
         sense of small
           onederloss
Mr. Universe, old midwife, climbs into his farty old coverall
combine harvester. From deep without orders a "wrench"
                    with an 'r'
                    = "jerk around"
                    getting a handle on
  wife *after* wife
no baby talk intended, goes from grease nipple to zerk, takes
another look at the monkey spiral
             top up: the phoney angel
        bottom down: the hilarious
               bawdy under class
of nuts & dolts
           gluons, fig Newtons
         & naturally—selected combine parts!
—not the intervening para-shooting prairie pheasant
           colored clay pigeon
hole   home on the bracketed de-coy
            flushed, pretty boy flesh
       no hoser-ann-*ah* either
    unless we're talkin' viral spiral
       which we are.
1 Not Whorf, B.L., *amateur* linguist and fire prevention engineer.

ii a suite of single symmetries

  a) He Laughed In His Face

    The first man to see the first man
    came on a plush leather horse
    that breathed fire into the snow.

    The first man was fed up in the snow
    right to the eyes so the lids wouldn't close.
    His arms had folded long ago
    unto themselves.

    The first man struck the first man
    as funny.

    The horse galloped around and around
    the stake in the snow.

The first man grabbed the tail
and the circus dragged on
into the night of its death.

The first man on the one horse open
was splitting
and didn't want to have to slay
the first man over the snow
and be laughing all the way.

b) Leviathanless Canadarm A Plug For Escaping Canadians
   Limp On The Ground. Curved Stick In The Memory

A huge Yellow Turtle
huddled across the western sky.
The Grey Cup skipped
over the chocolate snow dunes,
the prairie hooted at the hedge.
A Canada goose
hung outside the picture window
his head tied in the all year round
Christmas lights wire.
The boy said, "look at the part
of a 'V'".
The farmer blurted out,
"what would you like
for Christmas son?"
"A boomerang that
can do my homework,"
the boy replied.

c) Having A Premature Retro Fit

Christmas for baby brother
was like baptism in the already rain.

A dry, one-way culture would soon
drive him.   To.

He would smash a golf ball
into a tree; it would fire back
in December just when he had forgotten
get him in the Christmas spirit.

Yet we are born outside the family tree
so why not cut it off
a fixed date
from the rotor roots
let our backward selfish gifts be
a spark in heaven
over our heads a guided mistletoe,
the impossible w*eigh*t of our
reflexive, imm*a*nent birth.

d) Phantom Of The Operation

Down the dark basement of the shop
was a little lamp on a workbench.
A watch back was open with a succession
of larger and larger wrenches
coming from a tiny gear.
On the big steel handle of the last wrench
a man pulled just hard enough
for his teeth to show but he seemed
not to move he went so slow.

Outside a man sprinted across the yard
reached out a long wooden wrench
and batted into a feedlot five bales
that had begun dropping off the stack.
He pivoted, pounded towards the chicken coop
where a weather vane turned and nudged a hen
who took three careful hop-steps
and gracefully booted an egg off the roof peak.
As the man came near he adjusted the wrench
and then took the plummeting orb
on the run into the gentle jaws.

When a stranger asked him,
"Who's the boss around here?"

He answered, "Well there's just me
and m'brother. Pop teetered into the *well*
when we was just tots."

e) Space Burgher. Reproducing The Way To His Heart.
Empty Blindness. Wurst a la Kant.

Wearing a new shirt into
a plush men's wear shop
cool walnut panelling
back from the clean cement
the soft leather shiny shoes
pivot on. Addressing the thin
men hung on the racks. Like
a field marshal. Finding
a fortune cookie in the dark
platonic pocket.

Outsided a sports stadium
high white wall
lots of lawn in the afternoon
sun, lazy and hurting with some
energy. Play with the buffalo
for a while.

Going with your belly
ballooned out of your navel
in the back of the half-ton
bouncing to dinner
with the spare tire
over the fields eating dust.

II

MIRROR OF SEDUCTION

Photo: Critical Art Ensemble

5

THE CONFESSION MIRROR:
PLASTIC IMAGES FOR SURGERY

Carole Spitzack

Introduction

The lucrative business of cosmetic or "plastic" surgery presents an intriguing site for the deployment of contemporary power relations.[1] The highly *material* "illness" of physical/aesthetic imperfection is "cured" through complex and overlapping mechanisms of confession and surveillance. A patient confesses inadequacy to a physician-confessor who sees and evaluates; in the confessional process, the patient is supplanted with the eye/I of the physician who functions together with the discourses of desire and consumerism.

As Michel Foucault tells us in "The Eye of Power," the evaluative gaze within institutional practices achieves its effects not because it emanates from an all-powerful individual, but because the gaze is housed in an apparatus of hierarchical power relations.[2] In this "complex play of supports," Foucault writes, the "summit and the lower elements of the hierarchy stand in a relationship of mutual support and conditioning, a mutual 'hold' (power as a mutual and indefinite 'blackmail')."[3] As in the case of Bentham's panopticon, power functions optimally when those who are imprisoned come to guard their own actions, to embrace the logic of surveillance in which they are caught and by which they are defined. Prison officials and convicts are equally "trapped" within the institutional gaze.

Cosmetic surgery as a cultural phenomenon, characterized by confession and surveillance, acquires particular significance for an analysis of contemporary power tactics with the realization that women, more often than men, are the consumers of beauty enhancements and products.[4] Foucault suggests that, during Eighteenth Century practices, the bodies of women were thoroughly saturated with sexuality.[5] When integrated into social/clinical discourse, then, the bodies of women were viewed as inherently pathalogical or diseased because they were, in effect, "reduced" to sexual functions that were seen to account for a host of neuroses and maladjustments. At the same time, the reduction to sexual functions highlighted the danger posed by feminine sexuality. The female body, perhaps epitomized in the mythology of Adam and Eve, was capable of destroying its (male) victims. In the linkage between illness and danger, the bodies of women were deemed unhealthy and deviant, in need of ongoing scrutiny and surveillance. A diseased sexual identity placed the female body in a polarity of health and disease, legitimizing a host of efforts to monitor and correct the bodies of women, to make them whole while highlighting their fragmentation.

In her analysis of the female "look," Rosalind Coward notes that in contemporary culture, female body appearance is linked to sexuality, health, and personal power.[6] The cultural obsession with the female body "makes women the bearers of a whole series of preoccupations about sex and health. For the exhortations to good health are exhortations to take control of your life, and are in no way separate from ideologies of working at becoming sexually attractive."[7] Similarly, Mary Daly's analysis of cross-cultural gynocological practices reveals a historical connection between feminine sexuality, clinical discourse, and a fixation on the appearance/exterior of female bodies.[8] Daly's investigation is important because it clarifies the operative ruse in feminine sexuality as defined androcentrically. Namely, in clinical efforts to correct and monitor the female body, the bodies of women in fact became "disabled." Corrective procedures *underscore* female disease and reposition women within the discourses of disease and sexuality. In the Chinese practice of footbinding, for example, a "medical procedure" transforms the feet into sexual signs or fetish objects; at the same time, the feet become unhealthy (completely non-functional for the body's inhabitant) in the process of transformation. A woman who hobbles on "lotus hooks" is both a sexual vision and a disabled person.

In the scenario of the cosmetic surgeon's office, the transformation from illness to health is inscribed on the body of the patient. The reformed nose or breasts, similar to the bound foot, increase sexual desirability and thus, through the discursive linkage between feminine sexuality and health, are seen to empower the patient. The female patient is promised beauty and re-form in exchange for confession, which is predicated on an admission of a diseased appearance that points to a diseased (powerless) character. A failure to confess, in the clinical setting, is equated with a refusal of health; a preference for disease. A healthy patient, then, demonstrates a capacity for free will (choosing health) through the admission that she is unhealthy/unattractive, i. e., in need of cure. Yet she is not capable of enacting her own state of health, as implied by her presence in the physician's office, much like the convict's presence in the penal system. The choice to alter oneself announces, simultaneously, health and disease because the cure signifies the hold of prescriptive beauty standards over the patient. A change in the body secures the patient's position within the discursive machinery that has deemed her unhealthy and dangerous.

Practices such as cosmetic surgery are difficult to critique precisely because they are seen to be elective and empowering. In his later work, Foucault demonstrates that contemporary power strategies function not through bodily repression, but through stimulation or desire.[9] "Mastery and awareness of one's own body can be acquired only through the effect of an investment of power in the body: gymnastics, exercises, muscle-building, nudism, glorification of the body beautiful. All of this belongs to the pathway leading to the desire of one's own body . . . "[10] As Coward explains, the investment of power in the female body is cast in the language of deficiency and desire: "dissatisfaction [with the body] is constantly recast as desire, desire for something more, as the perfect reworking of what has already gone before—dissatisfaction displaced into desire for the ideal."[11]

Beautifying one's body is premised on the assumption of free choice, unlike chemotherapy, for example, where the "option" is death and thus the patient is seen to be powerless in making a choice. Concomitantly, the choice to repair an unsightly physical feature is met with the approval of society, particularly when the choice is made by a woman. The choice is connected to personal strength and self-love—seeing oneself as desirable. As Susan Brownmiller writes, a women who is judged to be unattractive within society is seen as a person who does not care about herself.[12] An illustration is provided by comments directed toward the woman whose appearance is not socially sanctioned: "she must not like herself." The irony in concepts of beauty and health that fundamentally efface and deny the bodies of women, recasting them in images of the ideal, remains veiled by the promises of power and self-love; the promise of uncovering the real.

In pondering my diagnostic tools for an analysis of cosmetic surgery as a confessional phenomenon, I initially consulted published texts. I wanted to find out what numerous experts had said about the practice of surgical body beautification. I also paid close attention to media advertisements for cosmetic surgery, most of which are given credibility through medical or "expert" ensorsement. Cosmetic procedures are regularly marketed for mass audiences, distinguishing them from many other medical procedures (e. g., gall bladder surgery). In fact, an important shift in the domain of cosmetic surgery is that cosmetic procedures are no longer restricted to the very wealthy or famous: carving the body for social sanction is now mundane and available to everyone.[13] In addition to explicit advertisement, news programs and talk shows regularly include segments on cosmetic surgery. Physicians typically appear with "before" and "after" success stories; the patient relays her positive experience with surgery and encourages others to follow in her footsteps. Finally, I considered more subtle forms of encouragement for increased attractiveness, such as the pervasiveness of anti-aging creams and the models used in advertising who represent physical "perfection": the ideal.

During the process of collecting data, I wrote to several cosmetic surgery clinics and requested further information, posing myself as a prospective patient. In response I not only received pamphlets which provided cursory overviews of specific procedures; also enclosed were invitations for free consultations. Initially I discounted the invitations, finding them useful only as a case of the urgency that accompanies modern consumerism. In several cases, I was even sent bank loan application forms, underscoring the easy availability of a physical trans-formation. Upon further reflection, however, I decided to go to a clinic for a consultation. In part, my decision was based in an academic desire for thoroughness in my investigation; but another part of me, in pouring over the information concerning cosmetic surgery, had become in-trigued by the prospect of a changed appearance. Although I trusted my critical faculties to prevent me from agreeing to surgery during my first visit, I was very interested in the clinical mechanisms that encourage the fabrication of a new identity.

I was fully prepared to let my own clinical experience serve a tangential function in my research on cosmetic surgery. Like most academics, I had been trained to view the personal as an intrusive and distorting presence in scholarship. During and after my visit to the clinic, however, I began to see that the workings of confession and surveillance are far more visible in the clinical setting than in disparate sources such as books, advertising, and cultural beauty standards. I was able to keep a distance from these sources and thus my own entrapment within cultural dis-course remained safely hidden from view. I trusted an actively critical 'self' to keep at bay any 'common' or politically incorrect desires. The clinical experience forged a coalescence among numerous support mechanisms which fuel confession and consumption, and prompted a realization of my own entrapment. What follows is an account of my experience, the subtle splitting and jarring that prompts intense self-scrutiny, leading to an externalization and internalization of disease.

A Visit to the Cosmetic Surgeon

With a newspaper coupon for my free consultation gripped firmly in hand, I step into the elevator. In the mirrored ceiling overhead, I inspect myself, liking my reflection but also knowing the perceptual limits of bending back and looking upward. I look like I look when lying down, impassive. The elevator door opens onto a floor, a faint perfume odor engulfing me as I walk to the correct(ive) office. Strange, I think, for a medical building. Ground floor offices smelled of antiseptics and rubbing alcohol, familiar signifiers. My sensibilities encompass beauty and medicine. The door leading into the fourth floor office presents a list of names—physicians, psychologists, and people whose names are not followed by degrees. Another medical aberration or supportive gazes?

Stepping into the office, I am transformed into another world, devoid of clinical overtones. Elegant Oriental sofas and chairs, vivid oranges and blues, a beautiful featureless woman positioned at a reception desk, sipping espresso from a delicate china cup. I notice that the deep amber birds on the cup match her nail and lip color. All around here are what appear to be prospective clients. I say "prospective" because I can't imagine why these women are here. Each woman is finely dressed, following closely the dictates of seasonal hemlines and shade combinations. Great care has been taken to replace the natural face with one streaked by manmade color and definition, without evidence of fabrication. They know the secrets, they have mastered the look. Susan Griffin writes that the 'objects' of male sexuality are "somehow magically . . . reduced to only matter."[14] I see these objects before me, seemingly pure surface, carefully orchestrated and magical.

I feel as though all eyes are on me as I approach the desk. Here disease is worn externally, detectable even to an untrained gaze. The receptionist surveys me, asking, "How may we help you?" I trade my coupon for a medical history chart and find a seat in the corner, near a television set.

I think initially that video equipment in a physician's office is out of place. I imagine a soap opera blaring, the woes and triumphs of fantasy life, ironically placed in the "serious" world of medicine. But I soon realize, this television has an instructive purpose, a medical function. Complete with Hollywood actresses, beauty consultants, and the team of physicians from this particular clinic, a videotape presents the miraculous transformations afforded by cosmetic surgery. Phyllis Diller, the comedic actress and recipient of some 50 surgeries, hosts the show. After a general presentation of before and after photographs of herself and others, Diller begins a series of engaging interviews.[15] Among her guests are several sets of identical twins, only one of whom has had cosmetic surgery. The unaltered twin is made to see her own possibilities by being presented with her beautified double, in what appears to be their first "post-surgery meeting." Several variations of the prearranged chance meeting are played out. In one instance, the unsightly twin bursts into tears, overwhelmed by her sister's beauty and lamenting her own comparative unacceptability. Another case shows the beautified twin crying, mourning the pitiful existence of her formerly unattractive self staring back at her. The ugly twin ("ugly" I imagine, is the term they would use to contrast beautification) exhibits embarassingly high levels of self-consciousness, to the point of speechlessness, while the corrected twin proceeds through the interview with ease and grace, an uninhibited outpouring of discourse. A lengthy moment of silence occurs as the ugly twin decides her fate, the camera scanning her closely. Her desired identity or twin appears in split screen so that viewers can intervene to judge, to divide themselves like a pair of twins, seeing for themselves the only reasonable option.

The ugly twin, we learn, has always been more cautious and skeptical. She has a tendency to avoid challenges and would rather have others make decisions for her; she lacks motivation and self-confidence. Her clothing is outdated just to the point of looking tragic. They say it's worse, I remember, to appear fashion conscious and fail than to seem oblivious. Moreover, she fears change, which manifests itself in rationalized excuses having to do with pain and financial cost. In the space of a few minutes, she is embued with powerlessness and an absence of will or strength, which surfaces in physical unattractiveness and social ineptitude.

Diller asks the beautiful twin, "Did any of your surgeries hurt?" "Not a bit, not even a tiny bit," is the response, underlined with a broad smile. The cost of specific operations is not discussed directly, but the interviews are laden with subtle references: "I can't put a price on the way this has made me feel"; "I was always using some excuse, money or time"; "For a long time I didn't even bother to find out that insurance can cover these costs." At the end of the inteview, the ugly twin is converted. The positive rewards stare her in the face, dressed and packaged to minimize resistance. Her double is everything she is not, everything she can become. With support from her sister, and the silent interviewer, she promises to schedule an appointment for consultation/catharsis.

After waiting just long enough to see the video from start to finish, I am led into a room to have my photograph taken. Enlarged covers from *Vogue* magazine grace the walls of the room. All around me, one who does not know, the eyes of judgment, from persons who know. The receptionist carefully places her mane of black curls behind her, so as to see clearly through the photographic lens. Everything about her now, engaged in a mundane task, seems non-functional. In motion she looks artificial, like a doll impersonating a woman. She is another cover from *Vogue*, except she cannot fully manage the image because she has to move while taking my picture; she is inhibited by the fact that she is human. I can see black marks on her cream-colored high-heeled shoes. One of her amber nails is crooked too. More signs of her 'failure.' She says, "We take pictures because the doctors remember faces in addition to written histories. Please smile for the first one and look serious for the second." I had known from feminist work that smiling is a particularly feminine activity, but had never had its contrast so vividly articulated for me. "Can I be both at once," I ask jokingly. She smiles and says nothing, answering my question. We remain in the small room until the Polaroid photos are developed. Upon seeing the results, she remarks, "Dark colors don't look very good in these pictures . . . they tend to drain you." "You" doesn't necessarily mean me, I think. Yet, as I look down at my gray sweater and black trousers, I recall that a sales clerk once said I should not wear dark colors because they are unfeminine, and it occurs to me that the receptionist's observation does refer to me.[16] Looking slightly annoyed with my questionable taste, a bit sympathetic actually, she ushers me to a third room.

The next room is an absolute study in contrasts, a symphony of imagery placed so carefully that it looks, and may be, haphazard. Signs of medical authority are plentiful. Enlarged, framed medical degrees cover one wall, along with awards for recognized excellence in the practice of cosmetic surgery and magazine reviews outlined in silver. A second wall consists of floor-to-ceiling bookshelves, making me slightly uneasy. Doctors are supposed to *know* these things, the technical secrets of their profession. They should not, in mid-surgery, have to consult the written word, the doctrine. But in an odd way, the secrets are demystified, no longer frightening, when placed so clearly in my visual field. Adding to the demystification is another video machine; this one showing actual surgical procedures. A staff of happy professionals surrounding a relaxed patient, the needles and knives almost beside the point, fading into the background, into the skin, the body. The patient appears happy about the prospect of her own effacement.

My eyes shift back to the bookcase, scanning a row of intimidating and impressive titles, mostly having to do with the reconstruction of body parts—eyes, nose, breasts, thighs, chin, stomach, neck, ears. Suddenly I see other kinds of expertise, *The Psychology of Body Image*, *Beauty Through The Ages*, telling me that my potential judge is schooled in the ways of mind and culture as well as physiology. To underscore cultural and political acuity, an eye for historical shifts, there before me are also the biographies of Henry Kissinger and Gerald Ford, among others. Covering a third wall and much of the table space are magazines of many varieties. *Playboy* and *Penthouse* to *Better Homes and Gardens*; mother and whore, wife and mistress in the same room, confronting one another. As Elizabeth Janeway observes, the images of virgin and whore, entrapped in each female body, serve to fragment a woman and perpetuate a seemingly self-imposed mistrust of her body: "Female a priori knowledge, then, cannot be taken as valid by the female self who is required by the laws of otherness to live as a displaced person not only in man's world but also within herself."[17] Here, in the physician's office, the mistrust works to encourage confession and consumption because the male physician, the "other," is both knowlegable and "centered," i. e., he, unlike the fragmented female patient, is in a position to render an a priori judgment.

The scope of reading materials in this room gives the impression of an omniscient inhabitant, both streetwise and well-schooled. There must be little he does not see, little he does not know.

On a table in the center of the room is an array of pastry and sugar-free beverages, displayed on fine china. The receptionist appears and offers me to partake. She watches as I select my refreshments, coffee and a packet of sugar, then leads me back to a different chair, next to a desk, placing the tray of sweets before me, asking, "Would you rather have Sweet-n-Low for your coffee?" Collecting my used packet of artificial sugar and positioning the tray of pastry within my grasp, she leaves the room, missing completely the irony of her actions.

At the very corner of the desk, only inches from me, is an intriguing mirror. Two panes of glass are bent inward, touching one another, to form a 90 degree angle, with two additional panes at the top and bottom. Any slight turn toward the desk, facing the doctor, requires a simultaneous look into the mirror. And the mirror's construction insures a reversal of the image, such that the reflection is my face as others see it. Looking into the mirror, everything seems wrong, distorted and somehow displaced. The face I had come to recognize in my own bathroom mirror now looks like the face of a familiar stranger, a double of sorts. The twins. The intrusive double invades my perception as I turn to face the doctor's chair. Now there are two judges in the room: the doctor's felt presence and my double. Thankfully, I realize, the lighting has been dimmed to provide some escape from myself, from his keen vision. I recall the comment regarding my color sensibilities, wondering if he will notice, wondering if she would notice.

In the midst of my scrutiny, a well-dressed man enters and introduces himself as my consulting physician. To my self-conscious displeasure, he asks me to follow him into a room with "more adequate lighting." This room has no books, no food or drink; only the business of serious body work represents itself here. Several enlarged photographs of "real" women (not fashion models) reflect his work in the form of before and after contrasts—mostly facelifts, fatty tissue removal, and breast augmentation. I am disappointed. The real women look ordinary, as though they clean and cook and care for children. In being more than 'only matter,' the real women become less attractive, flawed, imperfect.

On the split screen of an elaborate computer system are pre- and postoperative sketches of nose surgery. Instead of positioning himself in the chair behind his desk, the doctor sits directly across from me, no more than three feet away. He studies me for a seemingly endless moment, up and down, saying "hmm" and "ahhum," waiting for me to speak. Flashes of the Freudian blank screen run through me and I decide to remain stubbornly silent. He doesn't want to rule anything out. Yet I also fear that I might not identify my problem correctly, which would certainly not be missed by this man who sees and knows. Finally, with a sigh, he says, "So, what brings you to us today?" I reply, "I'm unhappy with my nose."

He briefs me on the psychology of self-esteem, emphasizing that most people are unaware of their own problems, then leads me to a blank wall. Did I make a mistake in problem identification? I studied his face when I said "nose" and he hadn't seemed surprised, but perhaps he sees additional imperfections. Almost miraculously, he pulls from the wall three full-length mirrors, framed in fluorescent lights. The two outermost mirrors are brought forward in order that we might see me from multiple angles. He places his hand on my back, holding me gently in place, only inches from the mirrors. He asks me to remove my jacket in order that we might see what he calls the total picture. Pictures are representations, not reality. My comfort in theoretical knowledge is diminished by seeing my own body, the 'reality' of me in the glass before my eyes. Now I am conscious of many *parts* of my body. I can no longer see a whole person in the mirror.

Each feature must be seen in relation to the others, he says, interrupting my thoughts. Musn't fragment the body. He says, "Yes I see what you mean . . . your nose is quite unfeminine . . . would you like to have a more feminine nose?" I stammer, "um . . . I don't know, more feminine? I never thought of my nose as being unfeminine, just asymmetrical." Yes, he intimates, "you probably inherited your father's nose." A masculine feature contained in a female body. With a single utterance my gender identity is called into question: my otherness is suspect. I recall Brownmiller's discussion of the feminine difference, "It must constantly reassure its audience by a willing demonstration of difference, even when one does not exist in nature."[18] He surveys my face with the same look the receptionist had when taking my photograph—judgmental and sympathetic. I say the lighting is severe; I don't really look like that. "You're not used to seeing yourself so *clearly* is all," he observes.

My nose can be dislocated or broken, he says blandly, then carved and reshaped with minimal difficulty. Having one's nose broken calls forth violent imagery; physician as bodily harm, as villain. By this point, I am feeling awkward, slightly fearful, and attempt to step back, away from the mirror. My fear is oddly directed at myself. The villain is my mirror image, which he is either forcing or enabling me to confront, piece by piece. His hand holds me in place as I try to back away from myself. I decide to ask him a question, figuring it may distract him from my now criminal reflection. "Oh, I also wanted to ask you about," I am interrupted and he finishes my sentence for me, "your skin" he offers.

A new insight. "What about my skin?", I ask cautiously, knowing it is too late. Skin is a big category, covering my whole body. Before giving him a chance to respond, I find myself confessing to a history of skin problems and attempted remedies. I want him to know that I am aware of my deficiencies, particularly after his lecture about the psychology of ignorance, blindness. More silence on his part, more speech on mine. I am careful not to spare any details. How can he render a diagnosis if I am not honest with myself? With him? With the creature in the mirror? At the end of my confession, he explains that he can see I am extraordinarly bothered by my skin. I say, "Well, actually, I usually don't think about it." But you just showed me that you do, is what he is thinking. She agrees.

Two operations, one on my nose and the other on my skin, are necessary if I am to demonstrate my self-knowledge: my free will, my otherness. The total cost is five thousand dollars and we can say the surgeries are necessary in order that insurance will pay the fees. We will be cohorts in deception, like lovers committing a crime. Deception is a small price to pay for wholeness, for the death of my flawed/fragmented reflection in the mirror, for his/our approval. His knives and business acuity will cure me/us at a minimal cost. I will be able to love myself, without self-deception.

I am mystified by the skin operation and ask, "But wouldn't my skin have two different shades if you take off the top layers in specific areas?" He explains that I'm a perfect candidate for the operation because "your skin is naturally very pale, very little color, and oily," shaking his head sadly. Encouragement through insult, I tell myself. We are back in our chairs and with his observation, he moves closer to me, leans forward, almost whispering, "You could do with a bit of make-up, it would make you look more naturally feminine . . . so the surgery won't produce shading problems." Make-up and natural femininity, he said, in the same sentence. I demand, "I want to know if there will be a difference in skin tone if I am *not* wearing make-up." Yes, he offers, there will be a difference, but not if you wear cosmetics which, in the long run, will enhance your femininity.

The problem of skin tones in his scheme, I realize, rests with me, with my insufficient femininity, not with his medical competence. Part of me resists his oppressive view of femininity, but another part of me is in doubt, ready to acquiesce. He is, after all, the expert. And he is simply reiterating the views within my culture: he makes sense. I have heard this before. I have felt this before. A staff of experts, he says, again invading my thoughts, can help me to learn about the secrets of cosmetics, under his supervision. "And perhaps some about fashion, too," he adds, scanning my choice of clothing. I lower my head and see a designer insignia on his brown stocking. Christian Dior, I think it is, the 'C' and 'D' locking in an embrace.

He switches into another reflective mood and says, "The nose would be done for yourself, the skin for other people." The "irregularities" of my nose are probably not extremely noticeable to others, but my skin, he explains, is blatantly problematical, "distracting" is the word he uses. I think momentarily about the word 'distracting'. Clearly his word choice is meant to criticize, but is not 'distracting' precisely what I want to be? Beautiful women are meant to distract, to draw attention, to preoccupy. He explains, "The skin you were meant to have is buried underneath the surface and unfortunately people cannot see the skin you were meant to have." My own body has betrayed me, as I feared when I saw my reflection. My body distracts me such that I cannot be distracting. Or am I confused? Momentarily, I imagine skin as volitional, even vindictive, making me look foolish by hiding itself from others. Or a battle of two skins; one visible and one suppressed. Both of my personages surface.

The procedure, this attempt to uncover my real skin, sounds horrid. Several layers of skin surface are sanded away, left bleeding, and eventually new layers replace them. One must avoid the sun for several weeks because ultraviolet rays cause post-operative disfigurement. "Some people are sun-worshipers and that causes problems," he says, again absolving himself of responsibility. I can have it done during spring break, during the rainy season, he suggests, because the healing process begins immediately and my students would hardly notice upon returning to class. Even if they do, they will find the scars less offensive than my current skin, than me. "They'll probably appreciate your efforts to better yourself." I say I have to think about it. "I wouldn't wait too long," he cautions, closing my file and cueing my departure.

I make a quick exit, head lowered, refusing to look at the fashion models hung on walls or the immaculate-while-motionless receptionist. My entire being seems deficient, in spite of myself, apart from my critical sensibilities. My body is cumbersome. It does not want to move. Each step pulls me in two different directions: toward me and away from me. Two women sit in the first waiting room, laughing. I am certain that I am the object of their laughter. I enter the perfumed corridor, step into the elevator and don't look up this time. Upon reaching the street I put on my sunglasses, though the sky is overcast. As perhaps a meager gesture of protest, I light a cigarette . . . throwing it into the street almost immediately: smoking causes the skin to age.

Notes

1. An article titled "Snip, Suction, Stretch, and Truss" in a recent issue of *Time Magazine* reported that in 1986, $250 million U.S. dollars was spent on cosmetic surgery in the U. S. A. September 14, 1987, p. 70.

2. Michel Foucault, "The Eye of Power" in *Power/Knowledge*, ed. by Colin Gordon, New York: Pantheon Books, 1980, pp. 146-165.

3. Ibid., p. 159.

4. Although men are also consumers of cosmetic surgery, albeit to a much lesser extent, the marketing strategies designed for male and female consumers vary tremendously. For women, strategies center on a correlation between surface beauty and self-knowledge; for men, surgeries function to provide competitive advantages, but are quite removed from the so-called pleasures of becoming a fantasy-ideal based on appearance alone.

5. Michel Foucault, *The History of Sexuality, Vol. I: An Introduction*, trans. by Robert Hurly, New York: Vintage Books, 1980, pp. 102-104.

6. Rosalind Coward, *Female Desires: How they are Sought, Bought, and Packaged*, New York: Grove Press, 1985, pp. 19-84.

7.   Ibid., p. 21.

8.   Mary Daly, *Gyn-Ecology: The Meta-Ethics of Radical Feminism*, Boston: Beacon Press, 1978.

9.   For an explanation of Foucault's shift from repression to stimulation see, Michel Foucault, "Body/Power" in *Power/Knowledge*, pp. 55-62.

10. Ibid., p. 56.

11. Coward, p. 13.

12. Susan Brownmiller, *Femininity*, New York: Fawcett Columbine Books, 1984, pp. 13-19.

13. Although it is arguable that cosmetic surgery is still restricted by economic circumstances, the shift in emphasis from elite to ordinary is significant as a power issue. The shift *implies* easy availability; hence the rationale of "I cannot afford it" is discounted as psychological blockage.

14. Susan Griffin, *Pornography and Silence: Culture's Revenge Against Nature*, New York: Harper Colophon Books, 1982, p. 37.

15. The before/after imagery is seductive because it contrasts the real and the ideal. For an extended discussion of this phenomenon see, Carole Spitzack, "Confession and Signification: The Systematic Inscription of Body Consciousness", *The Journal of Medicine and Philosophy*, 12 (1987), 357-369.

16. For a discussion of the internalization of "fashion sense", see Coward, pp. 27-36.

17. Elizabeth Janeway, "Who is Sylvia?: On the Loss of Sexual Paradigms" in *Women: Sex and Sexuality*, ed. by Catharine R. Stimpson and Ethel Spector Person, Chicago: University of Chicago Press, 1980, p. 6.

18. Brownmiller, p. 15.

6

BLONDES

Teresa Podlesney

Blonde in Black (The) 1903
Blonde Beast (The) 1923
Blonde Saint 1926
Blonde or Brunette 1927
Blonde For a Night (A) 1928
Blonde Crazy 1931
Blonde Venus 1932
Blonde Captive (The) 1932
Blonde Bombshell (The) 1933
Blonde Dynamite 1937
Blonde Trouble 1937
Blonde Cheat 1938
Blonde For A Day 194?
Blonde Inspiration 1941
Blonde From Singapore 1941
Blonde Comet (The) 1941
Blonde and Groom 1943
Blond Fever 1944
Blonde From Brooklyn 1945
Blonde Ransom 1945

Blonde Savage 1947
Blonde Ice 1948
Blonde Dynamite 1950
Blonde Bandit (The) 1950
Blonde Bait 1956
Blonde Blackmailer 1957
Blonde in Bondage 1957
Blonde Sinner 1957

"They are nearly always blonde; before the Fifties there was no Blonde Fever, the Love Goddesses had gone all across the spectrum from dark blondes like Dietrich to redheads like Hayworth to brunettes like Gardner. Blondes were so unheralded that both Harlow and Turner took advantage of black and white film to play explosive redheads; in the opening moments of the late Thirties' *Ninotchka*, the narrative talks of the good old days when 'sirens were brunettes, not things on police cars'. But for the crumbling man, blonde is essential—blonde, like a little girl! Shirley Temple with sex appendages!"[1]
Blonde Alibi 1946

"It's time ... that the blonde glamor girl dropped her modern offhand manner and assumed the seductive ways of the traditional charmer. Blondes today are sexy and exciting. But we should go further than that. We should be dangerous characters."[2]

JeanHarlow-MarilynMonroe-DorothyMalone-MamieVanDoren
VeronicaLake-GraceKelly-BrigitteBardot-JodieFoster-SandraDee
KimNovak-MaeWest-LanaTurner-CaroleLombard-BettyGrable-Di-
anaDors-ConnieStevens-AnitaEkberg-ElkeSommer-JayneMans-
field-JulieChristie-JeanSeberg-TuesdayWeld-TippiHedren-
ShelleyWinters-BarbaraPayton-IngerStevens-CaroleLandis-Car-
rollBaker-LeeRemick-FrancesFarmer-GoldieHawn-JeanneEagels
MarleneDietrich-JudyHolliday-AngieDickinson-EdieSedgwick
MarionDavies-ThelmaTodd-CarolLynley-VirnaLisi-GingerRogers
ZsaZsaGabor-JanetLeigh-SueLyon-IngridBergman-Constance-
Towers-DorisDay-PhyllisDiller-ShirleyTemple-EvaMarieSaint-
JoeyHeatherton-JeanWallace-KimBasinger-ShereeNorth-Ma-
donna

I don't know. I 'member one time I went to see Clark Gable and Jean Harlow. I fixed my hair up like I'd seen hers on a magazine. A part on the side, with one little curl on my forehead. It looked just like her. Well, almost just like. Anyway, I sat in that show with my hair done up that way and had a good time. I thought I'd see it through to the end again, and I got up to get me some candy. I was sitting back in my seat, and I taken a big bite of that candy, and it pulled a tooth right out of my mouth. I could of cried. I had good teeth, not a rotten one in my head. I don't believe I ever did get over that. There I was, five months pregnant, trying to look like Jean Harlow, and a front tooth gone. Everything went then. Look like I just didn't care no more after that.[3]

Once upon a time I thought that I can be engaged in theory by writing it upon my body. Once upon a body, my body, once upon my body once upon a time I bleach my hair blonde. I am, as they say, interpellated into the filmic discourse of womanly glamor. I take Edie Sedgwick one step further. I color my hair white, not only in a counter-cultural *homm(e)age* to the Hollywood studio stars, but also, glibly, as an anti-culture critique of the manipulation of women's images in the name of male desire. Gentlemen prefer blondes, but only if their roots don't show. I am determined to make mine visible.

* * *

There exists a signifying effect, "the blonde phenomenon", that is not peculiar to the fifties US but is, rather, one of the emblems of that place/time. Any woman who has chosen to bleach her hair blonde at any time, in any place, since then has willfully/willingly written herself into the image matrix created with and inscribed upon the memory of those blondes in their pre-corpse state (death comes so horribly, tragically, to the blonde, yet fulfills and continues the process of her signification),

Geoffrey Bendz

augmenting, with her look, an accretion of meaning that of necessity reflects/refers to the perfect post-WWII product, that ultimate sign of US global primacy, the bottle-blonde Hyperwoman. The blonde phenomenon is a problem body, currently involved in an analytic situation. What follows is a fragment of that analysis. The fragment is a story. Or at least a suggestion of one.

The analytic dissection of the blonde phenomenon has revealed four (apparently) conflicting genealogies. The first three genealogies read as histories, intimately connected to/constructed by the 50s US, indicating that "the blonde" is a product of/for this time. What becomes clear in the fourth mapping is that the blonde is a product of/for *all* time.[4]

1—the inscription of difference upon the body of "the blonde" which takes place within the film work[5] of each of the 50s blondes in question. Difference is also inscribed by fans and the clubs and shrines they devote to their favorite blonde. Any (mostly male) (mostly white) fan will tell you that *no* blonde can compete with *his* blonde. This fervor is apparent in gay fans as well as straight. I will tell you the same.

2—a will to simulation read through the films' "accessories"—Hollywood publicity such as promo material and trade film reviews. Also in the category of "accessories", but operating within a different order of simulacra, are the graphies, both bio- and autobio-. The graphies peel back the mask to reveal the "real" body behind the blonde; as we read about their "private" lives we read how fucked up, lonely and miserable *all* the blondes "really" were.

3—the Hollywood blonde body as the limit and promise constructed by discourses of white phallo-supremacy, discourses which include Part II numbers 5 and 6 of The Production Code of the Motion Picture Producers and Directors of America, Inc.: "White slavery shall not be treated. Miscegenation (sex relations between the white and black races) is forbidden."

4—the 90s blonde, hyped in all major US fashion glossies as this year's must, still has her roots in Hollywood: "Women across the country are lightening up, thanks to Hollywood stars and wizard hairstylists."[6] Subtle hints at re-instating a world-wide, post-WWII-US cultural hegemony— "Blond will always be America's hair color."[7] The re-articulation of the blonde body as limit and promise; some post-feminist re-adjective-ization of the "new" blonde as "smart" and "natural-looking" (i.e., well-educated and white), *choosing* to color her hair because it's easy and fun and hence not prey to the tragic aspect of the 50s (pre-feminist) bottle blonde. Despite all the proscriptions against the bottle blond look—various fashion "rules" repeated endlessly in endless fashion mags by endless experts—the blondes who are at the center of media attention are still the women who choose the bottle. The blondest of these blondes, and with forty years of the blonde phenomenon informing her every move—the perfect site for exploration—, the blondest blond ever, is Madonna.

As with any problem body at the beginning of the analytic encounter, the blonde phenomenon is best glimpsed through the symptoms it makes manifest:

> Malone, Dorothy. *Actress. Born Dorothy Eloise Maloney, on Jan. 30, 1925, in Chicago...It wasn't until the mid-50s, more than a decade after her film debut, that she began to emerge as a fine dramatic actress, projecting an erotic blend of strength and vulnerability.* [8]

> Mansfield, Jayne. *Actress. Born Vera Jayne Palmer, Apr. 19, 1933, Bryn Mawr, Pa. d. 1967. Bosomy sexpot of Hollywood films of the 50s and 60s...She...repeated the role [of] a breathless, dizzy blonde à la Marilyn Monroe...in most of her...films. But repetition didn't seem to induce improvement no matter how many times she played the same role...* [9]

> Monroe, Marilyn. *Actress. Born Norma Jean Mortenson, June 1, 1926, Los Angeles. d. 1962... [S]igned to a year's contract in August 1946,...[and] typically cast as a dumb platinum blonde,...[by] January of 1954,...[h]er wiggle, her pout, her husky voice, were becoming the object of women's imitation and men's dreams. She exuded breathless sensuality that was at once erotic and wholesome, invitingly real and appealingly funny.* [10]

> Novak, Kim. *Actress. Born Marilyn Pauline Novak, on Feb. 13, 1933, in Chicago. Blonde star of Hollywood films whose somewhat bland blend of standoffish coolness and earthy sensuality combined to mold her into a properly cryptic sex symbol of the 50s and early 60s.* [11]

> Winters, Shelley. *Actress. Born Shirley Schrift, on Aug. 18, 1922, in St. Louis; raised in Brooklyn, N.Y...Her film career amounted to little before 1948, when...[s]he quickly rose to lead roles in films that, typically, emphasized her earthy sensuality.* [12]

These five women, actresses, erupt from the blonde phenomenon as the most striking symptoms, examples. Hollywood products all, they emerge as a synonym when packaged and promoted by the publicists. In spite of their differences, in their lives off or on screen, these women were all a function of their hair color. These women were blondes. What more is there to say?

There is only one woman. She just has many faces. [13]
*[I]n three other cases, her character has no biography beyond being
"the blonde".*[14]

Why blondes? Why *blonde*? Is "the blonde" only a Hollywood construct, or is she created at the crossroads of other American discourses,
social, cultural, and political? How do the mainstream discourses of
beauty in the fifties advocate the malleability of the female form? How
does the appearance of the first issue of *Playboy* magazine (1953) affect
these discourses? Is it crucial that Marilyn Monroe graced the cover of the
first issue? Does the publication of Simone de Beauvoir's *The Second Sex*
affect the same reading public? What is the response to the Kinsey report
on female sexuality? How has "the blonde" come to signify a "certain kind
of woman"? Why is the blondest of the blondes, the bottle blonde, the
paradigm? Is the obvious and excessive fakeness of this image the key to
understanding the function of this image in the iconography of the fifties?
Does the excess signified by these women function in a similar way "today"
as it did in context? Is the somewhat overwhelming and vaguely frightening aspect of these excessively womanly women offset by the *mise-en-
scène* of the films they appear in? Or is it constructed as part of the *mise-
en-scène*, the blonde as one of the new cinema technologies?

*This is true of all platinum blondes or whatever you call the highly dyed
jobs we have out here...If their hair is not touched up and coiffured
exactly right, if they're not gowned perfectly and their make-up is not
one hundred per cent, they look gruesome. This is not peculiar to
Monroe: it's peculiar to every other synthetic blonde I've ever known in
the picture business. There are very few [natural] blondes in Hollywood and, so far as I know, there have been no natural platinum
blondes in mankind's history, except albinos. They are strictly a
product of the twentieth century. They're created blondes, and when
you create a blonde you have to complete your creation with make-up
and dramatic clothes, otherwise you've got only part of an assembly
job.*[15]
*She'll never be able to act, but that doesn't matter. She's got star
quality.*[16]

Film work and the inscription of difference:[17]

Dorothy:
    Written on the Wind (Douglas Sirk, 1956)
    The Tarnished Angels (Douglas Sirk, 1958)
Jayne:
    The Girl Can't Help It (Frank Tashlin, 1956)
    Will Success Spoil Rock Hunter? (Frank Tashlin, 1957)

Marilyn:
>   *The Seven Year Itch* (Billy Wilder, 1955)
>   *Some Like It Hot* (Billy Wilder, 1959)

Kim:
>   *Pal Joey* (George Sidney, 1957)
>   *Vertigo* (Alfred Hitchcock, 1958)

Shelley:
>   *The Big Knife* (Robert Aldrich, 1955)
>   *Odds Against Tomorrow* (Robert Wise, 1959)

How does the fifties blonde figure as an object of desire for women?

> The root of the matter is identification, specifically with
> what *I* construe as the Other:[18] the Perfect Woman, the
> Hyper Woman. Hating my body, hating my self, I see
> Dorothy Malone and I realize (she is realized by me)
> everything that I am not. My desire to darken and negate
> my own "femininity" sees its negative double in the
> blindingly white excess of womanly markers that consti-
> tute the screen image of Dorothy Malone.

*... outwardly she acknowledges and admires the virtues of "feminine"
women.* [19]
> *How much do we know about women?* [20]

1953
Dr. A.C Kinsey's report, *Sexual Behavior in the Human Female*
English translation of Simone de Beauvoir's *The Second Sex*
The first edition of *Playboy* magazine

> I was once told that there was a possibility of excess. Once
> upon a time, there was uncontainability. (Certain move-
> ments, certain images.) Certain promises could not be
> restricted by the filmic frame. (A look—no, a glance.)[21] Is
> the gaze male?[22] Once, there was meaning outside of
> language, there was the notion that certain images (you
> know I mean images of women) were able to signify much
> more than narrative convention would allow. (The camera
> moves.) The reason for this excess of/in signification?
> Perhaps the condition of unrepresentability of women's
> desire within the hegemonic and patriarchal structure of
> cinematic codes. More likely, this "excess" can be attrib-
> uted to "the mental habit of translating women into meta-
> phor".[23] (Someone lied.) I realize that "excess of meaning'
> really means "overdetermination". Every possibility of the
> image of a woman on film to signify something other than
> male desire (or male fear, same thing)[24] has always already

been accounted for. Playing the futures market in images. Certain promises can not be restricted by the filmic frame— that is, until the camera moves.

What has come to stand for the female body?

Dorothy Malone was one of the screens most beautiful blondes. Of course, she started out as a brunette but it is as a blonde that she is known. [25]

The job of taking a young girl and turning her into a glamorous movie star is quite a production out in Hollywood. They call it "processing"...Given a girl who seems to have a rather unusual personality, Hollywood will, by physical tortures only the experts can dream up, begin the business of making her as completely unlike herself, when she came to them, as possible. [26]

An hour and a half later,..."only the eyes are still recognizable. She seems to have grown with the makeup, the legs seem longer, the body more willowy, the face glows as if lit by candles..." [27]

Marilyn was quickly transformed by Columbia's elaborate manufacture-a-movie star-machine. Studio makeup experts went to work to create a "new" Novak, having a perfect foundation on which to build— an utterly blank surface; almost a faceless face. [28]

I hate glamor poses. The studio always makes you take them. It's part of the Hollywood routine—like heavy pancake make-up and false eyelashes and false romances and wearing adhesive tape on your forehead so you don't grow wrinkles. [29]

While the trades and beauty mags devote much attention to the practice of "processing" new talent, as soon as a starlet becomes a star, the notion that she has been "processed" all but disappears from the promo publicity surrounding her. The blonde's status as an obvious image construct is now rendered transparent, and the search begins for the "real" woman behind the mask. In a very complex process of assigning identity, the blonde is constructed so that she may be de(con)structed, all in the name of entertainment and spectacle.

Does the blonde, characterized as mere image, mere haircolor, make possible the emergence of the "real" man, the sensitive man of the 50s? Because one half of the screen is so obviously and transparently constructed, the other half, reflected, can be seen as "real", not constructed, "natural".[30] This project of "naturalizing" the male actor was undertaken largely at the hands of Elia Kazan and Lee Strasberg at the Actors Studio in New York.[31]

The Actors Studio had given actors a chance to explore their emotions in a new technique of preparing for a role. This technique, "the Method", called for greater concentration by an actor in order to enable him to draw on inner experiences, "private moments", to create a "natural" response to situations constructed within a script. If an actor could "feel" the role, acknowledge those traits in the scripted character that the actor shared, if he could "become" the character, his performance could be so much more believable because it would be so much more "real".[32] "The world began to take notice. Within a few years,...the terms *Actors Studio* and *the Method* would be bandied about as many came to consider the workshop and the acting technique to be *the* theatrical phenomenon of the fifties."[33] "In the public mind...Marlon Brando and James Dean...were the quintessential Method actors—intense, instinctive, rebellious."[34]

Masculinism started with the Method. The Method Actor looked at the Sex Doll and thought her empty and unworthy; he turned to the mirror and the other man. [35]

"Desirability" is the quality that women in the fifties were urged to attain in order to make men (and thereby themselves) happy...[W]hat constitutes desirability in women...is a set of implied character traits, but before it is that it is also a social position, for the desirable woman is a white woman. The typical playmate is white, and most often blonde... [36]

Why Blonde?
Several discourses that (en)gender the blonde phenomenon locate and play themselves out in the biography of Kim Novak. Kim is the last complete construction of the studio system (Jayne Mansfield being the last incomplete construction), the final image of Woman created by Harry Cohn before he died. Cohn actually advertised his stars as creations, proud of the fact that he manufactured Kim to replace Rita Hayworth and compete with Marilyn Monroe. Two of the films that Novak stars in are films precisely about the construction of a woman in another woman's image, inspired by the (necrophilic) desires of a man (*Vertigo,* dir. Alfred Hitchcock, 1958 and *The Legend of Lylah Clare,* dir. Robert Aldrich, 1968. In *Kiss Me Stupid,* dir. Billy Wilder, 1964, Kim plays a B-girl who imitates a man's wife, at his suggestion.). Kim states frequently that she never wanted to be an actress, a job that the other blondes in this essay fought actively for. Kim Novak's whole story is one of being "done-to", not against her will, but because she had none. Her story allows entrance into another story that would seem to be excluded from discussion by the very nature of the (blonde) body under analysis: Kim is the first big Hollywood blonde to become involved in an "interracial scandal"—a romance with Sammy Davis, Jr.—, a scandal that addresses directly Richard Dyer's notion of the blonde as, first and foremost, a *white* woman.

It was in someone's best interest to create the bottle blonde Hyperwoman as paradigmatic ideal. Who were the people she could never be?

Be all that you can be. Which means nothing. Cheated and mistreated. Big fucking deal. Aftershave on your collar told a tale on you. Social climbers. Eurotrash. Expensive leather shoes from London. And here I am, guilty of it all because I want to bleach my hair so he'll be interested in me again. It won't work. We both know it won't. Two weeks later I go through his stuff looking for clues. I find a copy of *Black Beaver* and *Lesbian Lust.*

The first time I bleach my hair it is spring. Two days later, it is Easter weekend. I am wearing an Easter bonnet. I step off the bus and into the crowd. Recognizing me through the process of elimination, mom smiles Catholically, revealing/reveling in years of suffering. "Why did you do that? When I was in high school, only a certain kind of girl bleached her hair."

The procession of blondes parading across the silver screen of fifties America is led, some would argue, by Marilyn Monroe:

In our book, Jayne [Mansfield] is just one more fake platinum blonde trying to pull herself up by Marilyn Monroe's bootstraps. There have been dozens before her, including Mamie Van Doren, Sheree North, Cleo Moore, and even England's Diana Dors, to name but a few. And frankly, we're getting mighty tired of the whole phony business. If we want to see Marilyn Monroe, we'll go see Marilyn Monroe. We won't go to see any ersatz bargain basement sample.[37]

Yet, to read the press surrounding Monroe's own beginnings, one sees that the procession is, in fact (!), led by the original (!) blonde bombshell, Jean Harlow:

Marilyn:

...she got sex on a piece of film like Jean Harlow (Leon Shamroy, cameraman). Not only was Jean Harlow one of Monroe's idols; Monroe had her hair peroxided by Harlow's beautician.[38]

Kim:

As with...Jean Harlow, something in Kim's nature caused her to embrace the film camera with a soulful abandon...[39]

Shelley:

Movie-goers with long memories have already begun to compare filmdom's newest rising star Shelley Winters with the great star of the

Thirties, Jean Harlow. The startling resemblance between those two is not merely physical... [40]

The gradual disappearance of the "original" is made apparent, as the procession of blondes turns into the precession of simulacra. "Who was first, and in what order did the others follow?" is a question whose answer is moot. The "first" blonde in the series is not any more "real" than her copies, and, *at this point and place in time (fin-de-millenium US),* the meaning engendered by her image is neither different nor prior to the meaning created through image multiplication.

[F]rom now on there is no longer any difference: the duplication is sufficient to render both artificial...The relation between them is no longer that of an original to its counterfeit—neither analogy nor reflection—but equivalence, indifference. In a series, objects become undefined simulacra one of the other...Only the obliteration of the original reference allows for the generalized law of equivalence, that is to say the very possibility of production. [41]

When it was fashionable to wear one's hair à la Bardot, *each girl in style was unique in her own eyes, since she never compared herself to the thousand other similar girls, but each to Bardot herself, the sublime archetype from whom originality flowed. To a certain extent, this is not stranger than having four or five Napoleons in the same asylum. Consciousness here is qualified, not in the Real relation, but in the Imaginary.* [42]

Do you know the easy way to discover the top actress in Hollywood? Just stand on a street corner anywhere and watch the girls go by. Right now you can count Kim Novaks by the dozen. [43]

"I'll know I've arrived," said Sally, "when I see a woman with the same hair color as mine." [44]

The will to simulation is strong, ultimately always already making a discussion of difference obsolete, but I am nostalgic. [45] Always ready to defend what I obstinately refer to as my own originality, I must also defend the originality of those objects of my desire. I love those blondes because they are blonde, sure, but I love them for different reasons. I want to tell you, differently, why I love them differently. I want to tell you why my love for them is different. I want to tell you of their differences, which cause me to love them. But before I tell you all this, I find that I have to relate why it makes no difference, their difference.

Within the value economy of capital, difference is annihilated in favor of a more manageable conception of the relation between two or more things. The new relation, that of exchange value, succeeds in describing things in terms of their possible equivalence, not in terms of what makes them, well, *different*. Any Hollywood actor, from chorus girl and boy to box-office star, is a replaceable commodity. Stars merely wear the hype of "the one and only" to market in order to mask the similarity of their functions. It comes as no surprise that fifties America, a time of the glorification of the mass produced object ("Keep up with the Jones's! You can have one *just like theirs!*"), a time of WonderBread and subliminal advertising,[46] should also be a time that revels in/reveals a preference for replaceable babes on screen.[47] But, why blonde?[48]

> We were smoking cigarettes and talking about blondes, "plaid perfume on my breath. I mean I've been drinking scotch."[49] True confessions. I am telling why I bleached my hair. "Why'd you bleach *yours?*"

Invoking the name and image of Marilyn Monroe, both Richard Dyer and Angela Carter attempt to theorize the blonde phenomenon.[50] Richard Dyer begins with the notion that the "ultimate embodiment of the desirable woman" is above all a white woman, "and not just white but blonde, the most unambiguously white you can get...Blondeness, especially platinum (peroxide) blondeness, is the ultimate sign of whiteness."[51] For Dyer, the blonde "works" because she is "racially unambiguous" (p. 44), able to signify in her petrified state "the most prized possession of white patriarchy." (p. 44) If the blonde is the most prized possession of white men, it follows that, in white patriarchal discourse, she would be "the envy of all other races." (p. 43)

[A]ll the world had agreed that a blue-eyed, yellow-haired, pink-skinned doll was what every girl child treasured. [52]

Dyer continues by moving into the binary universe of white/black, good/evil, sexual/chaste; a series of images engendered by ancient Christian and Victorian morality, yet maintaining their associations well into the godless world of fifties advertising US. "Thus in the elaboration of light and dark imagery, the blonde woman comes to represent not only the most desired of women but also the most womanly [read: chaste] of women." (p. 45) I read this, I agree; but there must be more.[53]

What does it say about racial purity that the best blondes have all been brunettes (Harlow, Monroe, Bardot)? I think it says that we are not as white as we think. I think it says that Pure is a Bore. [54]

Angela Carter picks up on the connection between chastity and blondeness in her analysis of the blonde phenomenon, yet her reading differs from Dyer's in that the race of the blonde is considered as a given, i.e., it is not considered at all. Rather, Carter reads the chaste blonde through Sade's story of Justine.[55] Carter argues that, because a woman's success in Hollywood is first and foremost about sex, but a woman's success in American society is first and foremost about virtue, a tension arises in the fifties. "The cultural product of this tension was the Good Bad Girl, the blonde, buxom and unfortunate sorority of Saint Justine, whose most notable martyr is Marilyn Monroe."[56] Carter's analogous analysis is severely limited, though poetic. She asserts that "[t]he identity of the blonde was the most commercially viable one available". But *why* blonde? Certainly this commercial viability is part of the blonde phenomenon, not the cause of it. The argument continues to wander afield as Carter maintains that, "if she voluntarily took up blondehood, she always voluntarily took upon herself the entire apparatus of the orphan" (p. 65). Again off the mark, Carter speaks of the blondes' "physical fragility"—"Her fragility is almost the conscious disguise of masochism..." (p. 65). While Justine is indeed a frail, masochistic orphan, I suggest that none of the blondes in this essay conform to this image, at least, not on film or in the Hollywood press. It is only as we read about their "private" lives that we read how fucked up, lonely, and miserable all the blondes "really" were. Each of the blondes in my story has her own, pathetic, lonely, "please-take-care-of-me" story.

When the roots start to show, you can easily see that she's no natural blonde. Mind you, not that she ever thought she was fooling anyone. "Just like the girl next door", she'd say. Just like.

Blond is hot—so say the hair-color hotshots east and west. Hotter than it's been since Monroe and Bardot. The reason? Hair color has followed fashion's lead into a more glamorous era, and blond has never been easier to attain or more natural-looking. It all sounds good, but some basic home truths have to be faced before the decision to change hair color is made...The good news is that there is a world of difference between the maintenance necessary yesterday and today. First, colorists had to learn that coloring hair all one color (giving birth to the term bottled blond *) resulted in only artificial looks and the perennial problem of dark-root grow-out. Eventually they learned to color hair strand by strand, often at oblique angles, intermingling new color with original, resulting in more natural-looking hair that could also grow out more naturally.*[57]

Blonde is hot. Hotter than it's been since Monroe and Bardot. The reason? Any woman who has chosen to bleach her hair blonde at any time, in any place, since the fifties has willfully/willingly written herself into the image matrix created with and inscribed upon the memory of those blondes in their pre-corpse state (death comes so horribly, tragically, to the blonde, yet fulfills and continues the process of her signification), augmenting, with her look, an accretion of meaning that of necessity reflects/refers to the perfect post-WWII product, that ultimate sign of US global primacy, the bottle-blonde Hyperwoman. Hair color has followed fashion's lead into a more glamorous era. Could this more glamorous era have anything to do with a widespread backlash against feminism, a "post-feminist" call for girls to be girls? (Remember post-WWII US and the propaganda drive to get women out of the factories and back into high heels.) Hair color has followed fashion's lead. Why is fashion's lead away from "exotic" parts of the world—recently-conquered in fashion's search for "global beauty", i.e., "ethnic types", i.e., dark haired, dark eyed and dark skinned models—and back to a celebration of the land of blonde, blue-eyed girls-next-door?[58]

One shouldn't look to the discourse of fashion to include women of colors other than white, unless it is a discourse that was created to specifically sell or sell to these women. The chemical technologies (and the language) that have made bleached blonde hair "more natural-looking" were obviously not developed for African- or Latin-American women, whose desire for blonde hair is many things, but rarely a search for natural color. Yet due to the improved bleaching systems, it is just these women who now have access to truly blonde hair—older systems were only capable of "lifting" their hair to a reddish-orange color.[59] "[B]lond has never been easier to attain", and it is for this reason that fashion proscribes strict rules against un-natural hair color while it continues to hype the blonde. Paradoxically then, the blondes who are the center of media attention are still the white women who choose bottle blonde. The blondest of these blondes—and with forty years of the blonde phenomenon informing her every move, the blondest blonde ever—is Madonna.

> I wanted to get my hair really white, as white as Edie, but I am poor and can't afford to have a pro dye it for me so I do it myself, so I leave the bleach on for six hours. I get into the shower to rinse the bleach out of my hair and the hair, short, is slimy, like seaweed. It is also falling out. A chill runs through my body as I, fascinated, keep lifting my hands to my head, running my hands through my hair, rinsing my hands under the water. The hair is clogging the drain. At last it or I stop, get out of the tub. I am missing a patch of hair in the front of my head, but the hair that's left is white.

If I have blond hair, I attract attention.[60]

In prose that harkens back to the best publicity of the fifties, the *Los Angeles Times* hyped Madonna as part of the promo surrounding her new tour and movie:

Madonna watchers, get ready for another eyeful. The woman who has influenced the fashion scene more than anyone else in the 80's is about to reveal three—that's right, three—new looks. They are all dramatically different, but all basically blond...The world's most famous chameleon is about to slip into three new looks for the '90s. Copycats take note.[61]

Not since you could "count Kim Novaks by the dozen" has there been such a spate of women unabashedly imitating the style of a star. I remember with some amusement the "wanna-be's" of the mid-eighties—adolescent girls slipping deliriously into bustiers, crop-tops, crucifixes and mousse, as oblivious to their status as simulacra as Baudrillard's Napoleons ("It's a nice style. It's different. Nobody else does it.").[62] Theoreticians of popular culture, fixating upon the droves of teens rushing to purchase a "look", needed to somehow figure how and what Madonna signified—"amoral vixen [or] post-feminist libertarian"?[63] The semiology of fashion had made style fodder for theoretical journals and TV's "culture experts" as well as the trades; forgetting what "Sally" had known about the signifiers of media success thirty years prior, academics acted like ad-women and -men, conspiring with Madonna's publicists to construct the enigma.[64] Fans, being fans, tend to ingest any and every bit of information they can about their idol, and the discourse of cultural studies blended with newspaper- and fanzine-speak into one big information pool. Having heard that they embrace Madonna's style because they "never had the nerve to rebel themselves",[65] or because she showed them that it is okay to flaunt femininity—contra the lesson that "feminists" had been teaching for the last two decades—, and suddenly being in the center of media (and family) curiosity and attention, asked, finally, why they like the things they like, the pre- and adolescent "wanna-be's" began to de/in-scribe their desire in the terms they had gleaned from the media. These articulations of desire, constructed from and for the media but rendered natural—the "real feelings" of this frequently-silenced but recently-recuperated group—served as a base for more investigation into Madonna-as-signifier-of-historical-importance, quotations used to legitimize the tautological methodology of this type of cultural studies. That annoying ode to naivete, "Out of the mouths of babes", becomes in this instance a relatively simple, safe and marketable way to answer the eternal question, "What do women want?".[66]

Or is it all about Madonna playing Monroe? She's been updating the role for five years, since she imitated the dress, the voice and the hair, and called it "Material Girl", her hit song of 1985.[67]

The culmination of the Boy Toy period is the video for "Material Girl". It is in the way she wears her hair. Her head was "always" (i.e., ever since the media can remember) a variation on blonde, sporting multiple and various streaks and highlights—a mocking play on the codes of true blondeness, a refusal to be read as seamless image. As she impersonates Marilyn Monroe, she becomes, finally, the Real Thing—a complete bottle blonde. What had begun as a play with signification now becomes serious business. She is no longer able to resist totalizing interpellation into the blonde phenomenon. The Marilyn Moment inaugurates Madonna's appetite for ever-changing looks, her plasticity as icon, in a desperate denial of this one fact: Madonna has become a function of her hair color. She both loses and lifts weight, copping a few Madonna-jog-ging-looks-like-Marilyn-jogging photo opportunities along the way. She tries to act in pictures. She bleaches her hair even blonder, cutting and styling at what feels like increasing speed. Then, suddenly, shockingly, Madonna is a brunette.

Dark hair is for those times when I want to be anonymous.[68]

The speed at which Madonna changes looks has become so fast that movement seems like stasis. The parade of new looks from "the perfect femme fatale for the *fin de siècle* "[69] appears to have become a theater of multiple and multiplying personalities. Madonna parodies/imperson-ates/is Greta Garbo, Marlene Dietrich, Jerry Hall, Marilyn Monroe and Madonna in her "Vogue" video, resemblances so uncanny as to serve as the perfect visual equivalent of this essay, an illustration of that accretion of meaning, the signifying effect which is the blond phenomenon. Appearances, however, want to deceive. Madonna is sometimes dark haired, sometimes fair, sometimes both at the same time.[70] The flirtations with dark hair would seem to disqualify Madonna as a blonde, the ultimate displacement of the signifying effects of the blonde phenome-non; to the contrary, her dark moments function to make her more blonde. Madonna's black(brown)(auburn) hair operates like the fetish, signifying the absence of that which makes it possible, doubly inscribing its importance.

Cynical Madonna—heralded for (mis)(re)appropriating the iconogra-phy of the blonde bombshell in a cynical defiance of the rules of sexuality codified by patriarchy. Madonna says, "I think the public is tired of trying to figure out whether I'm a feminist or not...I don't think of what I do as gender specific. I am what I am, and I do what I do."[71] "It has nothing to do with whether I am a man or a woman. I think I am a sexual threat..."[72] It is absurd to figure Madonna as androgyne, ridiculous her incredible assertion that her "sexual threat" and her million-dollar bank account have nothing to do with the fact that she's a woman. "Although she's made $90 million in the last four years and is the president of each of her companies, she doesn't like to talk about business, and it irks her even to be thought of in those terms. 'The public shouldn't think about this,'she flares..."[73] The public shouldn't think about Madonna as businesswoman, making money by selling herself as that which racist, sexist global capitalism would never tolerate in its marketplaces. The public shouldn't think that Madonna-as-androgyne, Madonna-as-original, is really some-thing else, someone more painfully familiar to all of us in this "post-feminist" US. Madonna-as-transgression is really Madonna-as-sacrifice, of-fering herself up in a multi-media staging of denial.

Madonna's current Blonde Ambition World Tour—a gut-wrenching spectacle of denial. Advance publicity for the tour, newspaper page-size spreads, featured photos of Madonna, blindingly white, in a Harlow pose, hair soft and tousled, bare back to the camera, clutching a sheet around her breasts. Since all tickets are sold in advance, purchasers purchased on the basis of this image, anticipating that the goods so exquisitely displayed for them in these photos and on MTV would be delivered at showtime. Madonna's image for the performances themselves, however, feature a phallus-ized body encased in Jean-Paul Gualtier's fetish wear, bound and wrapped, all feminine "excesses" tightly and firmly controlled. Her face is made up in an orientalist vision of an evil ice goddess, and, hair pulled tightly back from her face, she sports a white fright wig that cascades in a ponytail down her back. The movement on stage—dancing, if you will—consists of Madonna strutting about like a power-lifter, hands clenched and arms extended, a constant display of flexed musculature. Madonna's spectacle is a denial not just of her own position within the blonde phenomenon, but a denial of the construction of *all* women in relation to this phenomenon. Realizing the impossibility of ever "delivering the goods", Madonna-as-sacrifice for all of us women: the alcoholics, the junkies, the overweight, the anorexics, the bulimics, the women who love too much; those of us who have tried to make our bodies disappear because we couldn't be the blonde ideal, and those of us who have tried to make our bodies disappear because we could.

People are surprised by my new blonde look—lipstick, the whole bit. When they ask me why I bleached my hair, I smile and tell them that it's because Madonna's blonde again. They think I'm just being witty. I tell them I'm quite serious; they think I'm cynical.

Notes

1. Julie Burchill, *Girls on Film* (New York: Pantheon Books, 1986), p. 38.

2. Kim Novak, quoted by Stanley Handman for *WEEKEND* Magazine (vol. 7 no. 20, 1957), p. 18.

3. Toni Morrison, *The Bluest Eye* (New York: Washington Square Press, 1970), pp. 97-98. This text is part of a work in progress, known in certain circles as The Blondes Project. I would not have been able to offer up this fragment of analysis without the critical readerly support offered by Avery Gordon, Andrew Haase, Sandra Joshel and Art Simon.

4. Dissection because, of course, "we" have to get inside of a thing to fully and completely understand it. Although this (scientific) notion seems to conflict with the thesis acknowledged in note 19, a thesis that implies that, as a woman, my understanding, that is, the connection between perception of a thing and complete comprehension of its significance, is instantaneous and is in no way dependent on protracted contemplation. Unfortunately, the meaning that is immediately apparent to me, the meaning that I receive in the blink of an eye, cannot be disseminated as rapidly and thus requires that I enter into protracted contemplation (that is, engage in an epistemology that is alien to

my "nature"), if only to find the "right" words with which to share my knowledge.

5.   "Film work" also, but not only, considered in the manner of Christian Metz in *The Imaginary Signifier* (Bloomington: Indiana University Press, 1982) as analogous to Freud's conception of dream work.

6.   US *ELLE*, vol. V, no. 10 (June 1990), p. 4 ("Go Blond", by Mary Ellen Banashek).

7.   Ibid., p. 174.

8.   Ephraim Katz, *The Film Encyclopedia* (New York: Perigree Books, 1982), p. 768.

9.   Katz, p. 773.

10. Katz, pp. 819-820.

11. Katz, p. 866.

12. Katz, p. 1243.

13. Says an angel to Jesus in Martin Scorsese's *The Last Temptation of Christ*.

14. Richard Dyer, *Heavenly Bodies: Film Stars and Society* (New York: St. Martin's Press, 1986), p. 21.

15. Pete Martin, *Will Acting Spoil Marilyn Monroe?* (New York: Pocket Books, Inc., 1957), pp. 17-18.

16. Max Arnow to Harry Cohn on the occasion of Kim Novak's second screen test. Quoted by James Haspiel, "Kim Novak: Yesterday's Superstar". *Films in Review*, vol. 29 #2, Feb. 1978, p 76.

17. These films will have to "speak for themselves"; in this fragment there is no place for a discussion of them.

18. For me, of course, not allowed to be my mother, who, by the way, does not have blonde hair now, but did as a child, but, of course, always conscious of the working of the unconscious desire not to acknowledge her as Other, but as a "bad object" and therefore my self [see Melanie Klein, "A Contribution to the Psychogenesis of Manic-Depressive States", in *The Selected Melanie Klein*, edited by Juliet Mitchell (New York: The Free Press, 1986), pp. 116-145.] .

19. Joan Riviere, "Womanliness as a Masquerade", reprinted in *Formations of Fantasy*, Victor Burgin et al, eds., (New York: Methuen, 1986), p. 42.

20. Question posed on the cover of *LOOK* magazine as a caption to the cover photo of Kim Novak's face and bare shoulders as she apparently lies in bed looking out at the viewer (31 May 1955).

21. "A mere glance is enough for her to see the difference right away, 'and, it must be admitted, its significance too'. What is it, then, that she notices so quickly?" Sarah Kofman, *The Enigma of Woman: Woman in Freud's Writings,* translated by Catherine Porter (Ithaca: Cornell University Press, 1985), p. 171. The quote within the quote is from Sigmund Freud, "Femininity", 1932. Kofman's source is the German version of *Gesammelte Werke*, 18 volumes (Frankfurt and London, 1952-1968), which Kofman translates into French herself because "the existing French translation is quite dreadful" (p. 14). This reference is to the connection between perception and knowledge; in this (female) case, *immediate* knowledge, with respect to the controversy over Freud's theory of female castration.

22. "The gaze is not necessarily male (literally), but to win and activate the gaze, given our language and the structure of the unconscious, is to be in the masculine position." E. Ann Kaplan, "Is The Gaze Male?", in *Powers of Desire: The Politics of Sexuality,* Ann Snitow, Christine Stansell, and Sharon Thompson, eds. (New York: Monthly Review Press, 1983), p. 319.

23. Rosi Braidotti, as quoted by Teresa de Lauretis in *Technologies of Gender* (Bloomington: Indiana University Press, 1987), p. 24.

24. "[T]he horror inspired by Medusa's head is always accompanied by a sudden stiffening (Starrwerden), which signifies erection...Woman's genital organs arouse an inseparable blend of horror and pleasure; they at once awaken and appease castration anxiety." Kofman, p. 85.

25. *Hollywood Studio* Magazine, May, 1982.

26. Boyd Martin's Show Talk, a syndicated column printed in *The Courier-Journal* of Louisville, Kentucky, 1 March, 1959. This particular column is titled, "Now Take Jayne Mansfield: She's an outstanding example of 'processing', the Hollywood technique for developing stars."

27. Actress Hildegard Knef's reflections on Marilyn Monroe, quoted by Anthony Summers in *Goddess: the Secret Lives of Marilyn Monroe* (New York: Onyx, 1986), p. 57.

28. "Kim Novak: Yesterday's Superstar", p. 76.

29. Shelley Winters, quoted by Maurice Zolotow in his article, "A New Shelley Winters?", *The American Weekly,* 12 February, 1956, p. 6.

30. By referring to "the other half of the screen", I do not mean to imply the actual co-stars of any given film. This term was suggested to me by Sandra Joshel as a way to talk about the iconic construction of radical difference necessitated by the gendered image discourse of the fifties. Because I was seeing "the blonde" as the female component of this image discourse without asking the question "Who does this image necessarily reflect?", Sandra suggested that I look at the other half of the screen. Who were the most famous male actors of this period, and how were *they* constructed?

31. The Actors Studio served as training ground for many women as well, but Method actresses were the unglamorous antitheses of the blondes; these women worked at their acting, while the blondes just had to *be.* Shelley Winters and Marilyn Monroe both trained at the Studio, after they became invested in acting as a "craft" Winters actually dumped her blonde sexpot image after her time with Kazan and Strasberg, staying away from Hollywood for almost four years and doing "serious" work, to excellent reviews, on Broadway. Monroe, however, was unable to live outside of the blonde phenomenon, even as she struggled to be taken seriously. She exemplified the impossibility of a blonde being anything but a blonde, in spite of the spate of biographers who insisted that she possessed more intelligence than she was given credit for.

32. The use of "real" emotion to create a fictional character within the 2-D spectacle of the cinema is a paradox that ties in to the same problems of fixing identity referred to in the discussion of "processing" blondes. Thank you to Art Simon for emphasizing the importance of a fixable (in the sense of controllable, nameable) identity in US society of the fifties. Art has also contributed many other crucial comments to this fragment; among them, the importance of the blond as a function of *mise-en-scène,* and the "invisible question" referred to in note 48.

33. *The Actors Studio: A Player's Place,* by David Garfield (New York: Collier Books, 1984), p. 115. For the purposes of my essay, I refer to the Method with the generalizing tendencies of the 1950s media and popular opinion, because "the use of the term with

those overtones of cultic significance it developed during the early fifties originated outside the Studio" (Garfield, p.168). A discussion of Method acting is, of course, "not as simple as that", and for those readers concerned with a richer description of the Method and its history, Garfield's book will prove quite helpful.

34.   Garfield, p. 155. While these actors (and others) may have been hyped as "real" and "natural" by the (hetero) press, gay men constructed of these images an iconography of a different sort (see Kenneth Anger's *Scorpio Rising*[1964] for an illustration).

35.   Burchill, p. 175.

36.   Dyer, 1986, p. 42.

37.   Clipping dating from 56-57; no further source information available.

38.   Summers, pp. 31, 82, 210.

39   Peter Harry Brown, *Kim Novak: Reluctant Goddess* (New York: St. Martin's Press, 1986), p. 34.

40.   Anonymous clipping dated 1950.

41.   Jean Baudrillard, *Simulations* (New York: Semiotext(e), 1983), p. 18 and p. 97. Translated from the French by Paul Foss, Paul Patton and Philip Beitchman.

42.   Baudrillard, *Selected Writings*, Mark Poster, ed. (Stanford: Stanford University Press, 1988), p. 26, footnote #8.

43.   Joe Hyams, "Everybody's Copying Kim", *THIS WEEK* magazine, October 12, 1958, p. 22. In 1958, Kim Novak simulated herself simulating another woman who was simulating yet another woman, "the original", in Hitchcock's *Vertigo*.

44.   Ibid., p. 23.

45.   "When the real is no longer what it used to be, nostalgia assumes its full meaning." Baudrillard, *Simulations*, p. 12.

46.   In the already-cited article on Kim Novak by J. Haspiel ("Kim Novak: Yesterday's Superstar"), one can find (p. 77) a reproduction of four frames from Joshua Logan's *Picnic*; "Kim Novak frames used for subliminal advertising gimmick." Hungry? Eat Popcorn.

47.   "Finally this is very democratic. What more could the freeworld offer than the ability to become the ideal through buying a bottle. In this context, non-conformity is clearly willful. If I'm not blonde, then I'm clearly a communist." This comment, offered to me by David James, continues the observations on the hysterical theater of identity that was fifties US society. The absurdity of these positionings—bottle blonde as ideal woman, simulacra as ideal US citizens—is replaced by something more like terror when we realize with what force the validity of these positionings is still being manufactured.

48.   The notion of history seems to come too easy in this analysis. If "Why blonde?" is the question that most visibly motivates this analysis, the invisible question is "Why the fifties?". This fragment of an analysis cannot adequately tell the story of all areas from which the blonde phenomenon creates the possibility of signification. All it can do is suggest which stories there are to be told.

49.   Lyric from "Under the Big Black Sun", sung by Exene Cervenka, music by Cervenka and John Doe. From the album of the same name by the band X (©1982, Elektra/Asylum Records, Los Angeles, CA).

50. Dyer, Chapter One of *Heavenly Bodies;* Carter, *The Sadeian Woman and the Ideology of Pornography* (New York: Pantheon Books, 1978).

51. Dyer, *Heavenly Bodies*, pp. 42-43. All further page references to follow in the text.

52. Morrison, p. 20.

53. And indeed there is more. Richard Dyer writes an essay for *Screen* magazine: "The Last 'Special Issue' on Race?" (vol. 29 no. 4 Autumn 1988). Dyer's essay is entitled "White". Throughout the essay, Dyer has been accumulating evidence in favor of his thesis that, through the history of American film, black characters are put into the service of representing "life" (lust, sensuality, emotion, non-rational behavior) within the confines of a rigid, bourgeois, Reason-centered frame. "If blacks have more 'life' than whites, then it must follow that whites have more 'death' than blacks." (p. 59) At the end of the essay he returns to his thoughts on Marilyn Monroe. In my essay, this fragment of an analysis, there is no room to tell a story of how death could possibly fit into "the blonde phenomenon", but there is room to say that there is a story.

54. Burchill, p. 103.

55. Sade tells two stories of two sisters, Justine and Juliette, children of the bourgeoisie, who are left to fend for themselves at the beginning of their adolescence when their father dies and leaves them penniless. Juliette chooses to make her way in the world any way she can, and in a Sadeian world, this amounts to whoring, killing and stealing. Justine, by way of subtle contrast, clings to the lessons she learned as a good bourgeois girl. She refuses to cheat, steal, and lie, but above all else, she refuses to sacrifice her virginity. As a Sadeian woman, Justine's "purity" is viewed as the cause of her misfortunes, and she is punished for some 300 pages for her stubborn (and ridiculous) adherence to her Christian teachings.

56. Carter, p. 63. All further references to follow in the text.

57. William Geist, "blonds", US *Vogue*, Feb. 1990.

58. "Ben Wattenberg of the American Enterprise Institute sees [the US] as the 'unipower' that has vanquished all other contenders. Under a doctrine he calls 'neo-manifest destinarianism 'he would spread [the US's] unique 'culture' to benighted corners of the globe via the aggressive marketing of movies and the franchising of U.S. university centers abroad." "What, Us Worry?", editorial in *The Nation* , May 21, 1990, p. 692.

59. "Finally this is very democratic. What could more could the freeworld offer than the ability to become ideal through buying a bottle." See note 47.

60. Madonna, as quoted in the *Los Angeles Times* , 2 March 1990 ("Thoroughly Modern Madonna", by Barbara Foley, page E1).

61. "Thoroughly Modern Madonna", p. E1.

62. Jean Anne Difranko, the 1985 winner of Macy's (a New York department store that devoted a whole "boutique" to the Boy Toy style) Madonna Look-Alike Contest.

63. Ron Givens, "Madonnarama", *entertainment WEEKLY,* 11 May 1990, p.40.

64. Cited earlier in this text, Sally says, "I'll know I've arrived when I see a woman with the same hair color as mine" (note 44).

65. "Madonnarama", p. 40.

66. If it's taken ten years of theories of feminisms and representations plus the acquisition

of the discourse of post-structuralism to enable me to even begin to think about mumbling something about my desires as a woman, if I can't tell you why I want to be Madonna, why should a twelve-year-old be assumed to have the answer?

67. *L.A. Times*, p. E5.

68. Madonna, from the *L.A. Times* article, p. E1.

69. "White Heat", p. 147.

70. Witness the blond Madonna on the cover of April's *Vanity Fair*, and the simultaneously raven-tressed Madonna on the cover of *Cosmopolitan*.

71. "Madonnarama", pp.39-40.

72. Kevin Sessums, "White Heat", *Vanity Fair*, vol. 53 no. 4, April 1990, p. 148.

73. Ibid., p. 148.

Photo: Mark Lewis
He Licked His Lip Until It Bled

1306

2.50 11306
October

Harlequin Presents...

SALLY HEYWOOD

love's sweet harvest

7

CONFESSIONS OF A HARLEQUIN READER: ROMANCE AND THE MYTH OF MALE MOTHERS

Angela Miles

Like most women, I think, I have read one or two Harlequins over the years when nothing else was available. All I saw, at first, were sexist, predictable, often poorly written stories with boorish heros and embarrassingly childish heroines. They have a rigid formula which, unlike many other aspects, has remained unchanged over the years. In fact, the guide sheet for aspiring authors warns that the plot must not interfere with the romance and asks them to make their manuscript approximately (!) 188 pages in length. As one romance writer succinctly put it: "In the *Roman rose* the plot is always the same: attraction followed by repulsion; despair at the hero's indifference; jealousy; reconciliation on the last page."[1] That means the last page, literally. Never earlier.

Imagine my surprise when I first found myself actually enjoying a Harlequin. It was one summer when I stayed at a friend's cottage and it rained for days and days. I lay on a comfortable sofa, beside a warm wood stove and read what was available. The third Harlequin was a very different read from the first, and I found myself enjoying it. Once the pattern was familiar (it is so predictable that it's clear by the third book), it becomes interesting to see how each author works variations on a theme; however, there is much more involved.

Knowing the Harlequin formula made reading the books an emotional experience in a way that I didn't begin to understand until much later. In this paper I will argue that the enormous emotional power of Harlequin reading, and the romance fantasy in general, can be explained by the fact that the hero is in fact a mother figure for the reader/woman. When a reader knows the Harlequin formula she can identify the hero figure immediately, anticipate the pattern of events, and is involuntarily caught up in an extremely active and demanding psychological interaction with the text, one that has been called, without irony or exaggeration, "the Harlequin experience." Readers who don't know the formula do not and cannot participate in the same emotional and psychological way and have a very different reading experience that is much more dependent on the quality of the plot and the writing.

After I returned to the city and the pressures of thesis writing, I continued to read the occasional Harlequin; but I sometimes *chose* to read them when other books were available. At the time, I explained my pleasure in them by the fact that I was very, very busy and tired and needed a break. I didn't bake, garden, exercise, or do crossword puzzles or any other things that would make a welcome change from intellectual work. No wonder, I thought, that I like to sink into a mindless, predictable Harlequin world where you know exactly what is going to happen after only one or two pages.

Gradually, I began to read more and more Harlequins, until one day, when I found myself about to buy one, I began to suspect I was hooked. I reasoned that anyone who paid 95 cents or $1.75 (or whatever it was back then) for the few often poorly written pages had to be hooked. So I vowed that I would never sink that kind of money into any habit, hoping in that way to limit myself to the occasional read. No sooner had I made my decision, than I discovered a second-hand store two blocks away from my place that sold ten Harlequins for a dollar! My resolve weakened, I became a customer and had to admit that I was a "Harlequin reader."

As soon as I realized this I "came out." As a feminist I know that the personal is political and that we must struggle individually to change ourselves as well as collectively to change society. Yet I didn't want to lose the strange comfort I found in Harlequins and I didn't feel they were terribly destructive or sinful. I could justify making Harlequins a non-struggle area of my life only if I genuinely felt they weren't so bad. And if they weren't so bad I had to be able to tell my friends that I read them. In any case, skeletons in the closet leave you awfully vulnerable, if not to blackmail then to terrible embarrassment, and I wasn't up to living with the risk. I didn't make a public announcement or send cards but I did drop it into conversations whenever I could. This wasn't easy to do, but it got easier as I developed arguments defending women's romantic fantasies as harmless (to others at least, if not themselves), human, and relatively innocent, especially when compared to the pornographic fantasies of men.

No feminist I told ever admitted to me that she read Harlequins or any other kind of romances; it may be alright to watch soaps but no one admits to Harlequins. Not all women are Harlequin readers of course. But many read one or another form of romance novel. Even more have enjoyed such classics as *Pride and Prejudice, Rebecca, Gone with the Wind,* or the film *Moscow Does not Believe in Tears.* It must be a rare woman, heterosexual, or lesbian who does not know, if only from her teenage years, the attraction of the knight in shining armor who will take over her life, give it meaning and take care of all her troubles for ever after.

Yet the fact that the appeal of romance is at least recognized, if not shared by most women including feminists even when it is marginal to their lives and self-image, is not used as a resource by feminist analysts of Harlequins. This departure from one of the basic tenets of feminist research has, I think, weakened much feminist analysis of Harlequins.

Not surprisingly feminists find deeply negative messages in these books. The plots often seem to legitimize general male boorishness and lack of respect for women, to reinforce the sexual double standard, and to infantilize women who are usually younger, more innocent, lower in status, less well established, less sure of themselves, and more vulnerable than the hero. They tend to perpetuate the myth of women's powerlessness and necessary dependence on men. Their central presumption (with a few notable recent exceptions) is that contentment and meaning in life not only can but must be found in love and marriage.

Feminist critics have noted that these messages "betray complexities of life" and "approve and confirm the present structure of society,"[2] they "reinforce the prevailing cultural code [that] pleasure for women is men,"[3] and they are not radical critiques of capitalist patriarchy.[4] All of which is true but unidimensional, for these critics focus on what Harlequins do for capitalist and patriarchal ruling groups without addressing the equally important and more interesting question of what they do for women. For women not only *choose* to buy millions of these books, but have a large and direct input into their shape and content through Harlequin reader panels, survey research, and newsletters.[5] The popularity of Harlequin Romances is as much women's creation as it is Harlequin Enterprises'. In order to understand this we need to know not just how their explicit messages serve "the system" or what the words of the books say, but what they become for the women who read them (or, as some would say, "construct the experience as readers")!

Some feminists have recently begun to treat the woman reader as an active subject and ask this question, but even they tend to treat her as someone completely different from themselves. Janice Radway, for instance, was among the first feminist writers on popular romance to accord the woman reader an active role in the process. On the basis of important original research, including in-depth interviews with readers, she criticizes other feminists for reading Harlequins as simply oppressive myths. But she does so in terms that emphasize the separation rather than connection between researcher and researched, arguing that we should not presume our "own reading [is] a legitimate rendering of the meaning of the genre for those who usually read it."[6] She describes the process of interpretation as: "Trying to render the complex significance of events and behaviours as they are experienced by members of a culture *for others not in or of that culture.*"[7] She also presents her findings as "the product of an interrogation of one cultural system by another carried out through the interaction of ethnographer and informant."[8]

There is no doubt that interpretation is necessary and that there are truths to be discovered that (we) readers have not articulated. There is also little doubt that the language of a scholarly paper or dissertation is not the same as that of Harlequins or of (we) Harlequin readers; but it is a foreign or second language for women researchers also, however proficient we may be in it. We should be sure that our method does not deny us the use of our first and shared language as women, even when we use the second as well. For this shared language and culture is a resource we bring as women to our analysis of women, and romance is an area of our culture that must raise important personal questions for us as feminists, which, in turn, lends itself well to an interrogation from our own lives.

My experience as a feminist and Harlequin reader starkly raised the question "What do they offer me?" I began reading Harlequins before they were even slightly influenced by the values of the women's movement (see below), and as a feminist I often found their message/story offensive. I had to suspend or censor these judgement/feelings in order to enjoy the book. The fact that I could do this suggested that there was another level of meaning for me; something less explicit that appealed to me and presumably to other readers; something that could help to explain why this simple and threadbare formula should so attract women, and how women, who know it to be false, can lose themselves in it; in other words, something that could begin to answer the question "What is the myth of romance for women?"

The Hero as Nurturer

One thing that I saw very quickly as I pondered this was that the hero in Harlequin Romances may be supercilious, arrogant, and patronizing but he is also and above all independent and self-sufficient. This point is often made in detailed contrast to "the other man" who is a common feature of Harlequins. These "other men" are weak, childish, dependent, sullen, and needy. They whine and pout and constantly demand attention and mothering from the heroine:

> Sullenly he pushed her hand away. Briefly Kelly was reminded of a little boy who had been thwarted in a game (*Kelly's Man*, Rosemary Carter, HP362: 5).

> This wasn't the Roger she knew—this man was a stranger, a petulant spoilt boy. Her own anger rising, she said the unforgivable thing. She said, "Roger darling, do grow up!" (*A Very Special Man*, Marjorie Lewty, 2282: 11).

"You're so relaxing Kate," he said happily once. "The one person in the world that I can always rely on completely to look after me. I don't know where I'd be without you." (*Dark Encounter*, Suzanna Firth, 2307: 7).

"Men like me can be lonely, they can sometimes long for a prop—someone near and dear to lean upon. I need you, so please don't be too long in agreeing to marry me." (Needless to say she didn't marry him. *Harbour of Love*, Anne Hampson, 2230.)

The refusal and revolt is sometimes explicit:

The first night ever he had stayed [at her apartment] Gavin had flaked out, with Elizabeth tucking him in like a baby. It even occurred to her then, that a large part of her affection for him was maternal. In many ways Gavin was a huge child, and he would probably require a lot of mothering. "I can't do it!" She said aloud in piteous resignation. (And she breaks off the engagement. *Broken Rhapsody*, Margaret Way, HP549: 102.)

The implicit contrast between these men and the hero is often made explicitly:

Ian was gentle, idealistic, a bit of a dreamer, with one foot in the past like herself. He needed someone practical and hardheaded to look after him; to see that he ate the right food at the right time and didn't spend too many hours bending over his work. Whereas Tearlach was tough and realistic and didn't need anyone to look after him (*Beyond the Sunset*, Flora Kidd, 1732: 131).

Nicholas was all the things she most detested—arrogant, conceited, domineering. She guessed he was self-sufficient and ruthless. But he was not childish (*Kelly's Man*, Rosemary Carter, HP362: 66).

Harlequins are also about *not* to having to mother men, and I think this strikes a strong and pleasurable chord with women who do so much of this. Not only are Harlequin heros grown up (rare birds in women's experience),[10] they are sensitive and considerate and take care of the heroine—something so unexpected that the heroine frequently marvels about it: "What a strange man he was, she thought as she sipped her tea. She had just witnessed in him an unexpected sensitivity. Many men wouldn't even have noticed she was upset" (*The Icicle Heart*, Jessica

Steele, 2297: 106). Whether remarked upon or not, Harlequin Romances are full of heros who take care of heroines:

> "Let's go back to the house," he said, "before you catch cold!" (*Isle of the Golden Drum*, Rebecca Stratton, 1991: 144).

> "Let's get these painkillers down, shall we?" . . . . He held her firmly and gently while she swallowed the capsules. "You don't have to stay with me," she protested weakly..." "I think I'll stay all the same"(*Blue Lotus*, Margaret Way, 2328: 175).

> He walked to the sofa, picked up her shoes sitting on the floor beside it, and carried them back to the heater. "We'll get them warm before you have to put them on," he explained.

> His thoughtfulness sent a warm glow of pleasure through her veins. That combination of indomitable strength and tender consideration was rare. (*A Lyon's Share*, Janet Dailey, HP208: 49).

> As he unwrapped the dripping oilskin, he said, "Now pop up and get into something dry while I make things ship-shape down here."

> With a little sign of contentment Beverley climbed slowly upstairs. It was wonderful to have things taken completely out of her hands. . . . When she came down again it was in warm dry clothes. The fire had been built up and the flames roared and in front of it was placed a basin of warm water.

> As soon as he saw her Alex placed her firmly in the armchair, pulled off her slippers and placed her feet gently but firmly in the warm water (*Lord of the Isles*, Henrietta Reid, 2442: 92).

The same caring scenes are described over and over again in different books, by different authors, sometimes in almost the same words:

> He came into the room bearing a bowl of warm water that smelled faintly of antiseptic . . . . His touch was very gentle as he bathed her grazed hands (*Hotel of Aconandos*, Katrine Britt, 2449: 79-77).

> His hands were so gentle as he bathed her face, she almost
> didn't notice the stinging pain. The water was exactly the
> right heat and he laced it with antiseptic (*Kiss of a Tyrant*,
> Margaret Pagiter, 2375: 179).

Some analysts read the Harlequin hero's involvement in domestic and
nurturing tasks as a symbolic domestication of the male that is satisfying
to women. Others have suggested that it symbolizes a power that women
have won through love. There are surely elements of truth in both of
these related points, but reflection on my own reading experience
suggests that, more importantly, this theme provides the reader not only
with an escape from the constant demand to physically and emotionally
nurture others, but also an access to that same comfort, at least in fantasy.

Janice Radway's interviews revealed this so strongly that she identified
it as the prime attraction of romance reading for women:

> Romance reading is both an assertion of deeply felt psy-
> chological needs and a means for satisfying those needs.
> Simply put, these needs arise because no other member of
> the family as it is presently constituted in this still-patriar-
> chal society, is yet charged with the affective and emo-
> tional reconstitution of a wife and mother.[11]

Her findings support my own sense that part of what women find in the
romance fantasy is someone "who will love them as they wish to be
loved."[12]

Domination, Infantilization, and Resistance

All this is true but it does not explain the undeniably negative and
unpleasant behaviour of the hero which is often also a prominent theme.
He can be domineering, patronizing, dismissive, arrogant, unpredictable, highhanded, bossy, incommunicative, bullying, aggressive, and he
even occasionally uses force. There is also the even more unpleasant
infantilization of the heroine. She often finds herself needing help, and
she often reacts to the hero in silly and childish ways. Why is that an
apparently necessary part of the formula?

When I first began to read Harlequins I couldn't understand the
foolishness of it all. Both hero and heroine behave in unbelievably
ridiculous ways, misunderstand each other all the time, and do things
that in any other context would jeopardize any respect, and therefore
concern, the reader might have. I thought I had solved the problem when
I realized that it was quite a feat to keep two people who are meant to be
together, who are deeply and madly in love, apart for 188 pages. The
authors must have to resort to boorishness on the part of the hero and

silliness on the part of the heroine to do this. But this is not the full explanation.

Ann Snitow[13] and others read the hero's bullying and the heroine's infantilization as a part of the general patriarchal message that women are not full people, are not to be taken seriously, are not responsible and are necessarily dependent on men. But what is in this for women? Some have suggested that portraying negative male behaviour helps women live with this behaviour in their own lives because in Harlequins there is always an explanation for the hero's coldness. Usually it has to do with his love for the heroine. He thinks she is in love with someone else, or is too young for him, or he has been deeply hurt by a woman in the past and is frightened of this dawning love.

It has also been suggested that the uppity, reactive, foot-stamping behaviour of the heroine may give women readers pleasure because they like to see heroines who can talk back to men and give them a hard time. Readers like heroines who do not try to please and impress men, who are, at least at first, indifferent to male opinion.

Certainly, the heroine is *never* looking for a man or thinking of marriage. If she is not indifferent to men and marriage, she has an absolute aversion. Early on she isn't interested enough to use feminine wiles, later she disdains their use. One explanation put forward for this is that the heroine's lack of interest in the hero is required by a traditional code that forbids "good" women to take an active part in initiating sexual relationships. But when I first began to ponder the heroine's unvarying initial indifference or aversion to the hero, it seemed to me that the heroine's lack of initiative is important not primarily because we are bound by an internalized patriarchal morality but because it indicates *genuine love* (whatever that is).

It is important to the reader, who knows that men are easy prey to feminine wiles, that the hero's interest in the heroine cannot be manipulated, that he is one of the rare men who is immune to the temptation of the surface appeal of even a stunningly beautiful women. There is something very satisfying for the reader in a hero's love for an ordinary (though appealing) looking heroine when she has not set out to trap him while another, much more beautiful and sophisticated, woman has. This classic Harlequin scenario signals to the reader that we are seeing "true love." The heroine is loved for herself, warts, tantrums and all.

All these explanations of the appeal of the domineering hero and the infantile heroine are useful; and they are by no means mutually exclusive, but they remain discrete explanations of separate aspects of the formula. They do not, alone or together, provide an understanding of the tight, total Harlequin formula as the seamless whole that it is, and they cannot account for the overwhelmingly powerful emotional impact of "good"[14] Harlequins.

Emotional Power

I first became aware of how powerful the emotional experience of reading a "good" Harlequin is while I was staying at another friend's cabin. We were reading after dinner when someone rudely interrupted me to ask: "Angie, why have you got that silly grin on your face?" I had been reading a Harlequin and had forgotten where I was. I had even forgotten myself. I was, as so many readers have testified, in "another world." When readers say "I feel as if I am in a different world every time I read a Harlequin" and "Harlequins are magic carpets ... away from pain and depression"[15] they are speaking the literal truth about their reading experience.

Readers also frequently and vehemently attest to the importance of a predictable plot, and their reading habits support their claim that this is essential. Despite the almost total guarantee of a happy ending many readers are hesitant to trust it and read the conclusion before they begin the book anyway. Kathleen Gillis [16] says this is because women are *tired* when they read the books and need something relaxing, predictable, and easy to read rather than challenging. Tom Henighen[17] ascribes this desire for a guaranteed happy ending to the middle class housewife's commitment to safe, "straight" love. He deplores her brainwashed willingness to be content with tame and ritualized kisses before an inevitable happy ending. This is so boring to him that he fails altogether to consider that it might be exciting to women readers and instead presumes that it is the result of simple repression on their part.

In fact, a predictable plot and happy ending are important to the reader because they allow her to invest a lot more emotionally than she would otherwise be able to risk and therefore to experience the full power of the reading experience. The obvious question, of course, is where does this power come from? It is certainly not evoked by the words on the pages of the books. The quality of the writing, which varies enormously, cannot account for the unvarying power of the reading experience which must, then, be explained by the reader's interaction with and response to the author's (good or bad; successful or unsuccessful) presentation of the formula. The reader of Harlequins, although intellectually unchallenged, even passive, is enormously active emotionally.[18]

Hero as Mother

Reflections on my own Harlequin reading, combined with a close textual study, leads me to believe that the emotional power of the romance fantasy in general, and the Harlequin formula in particular, comes largely because the hero is in fact a mother figure for women. When we read "good" Harlequins we are re-enacting the emotionally demanding ambivalence of our relationship with an unpredictable, tender, threatening, all-powerful mother.

'True Love,' as an unconditional love which comes unsought and unearned without the heroine actively seeking it and regardless of what she does to antagonize the hero, is like our dream of mother-love. The hero's nurturing and domineering behaviour, two aspects of the childhood experience of mothering, are presented as two constant and interacting themes, often evoked with symbols of mother and child in scenes which echo mother/child images, and involve explicit references to the male as caretaker/mother and the female as a motherless child.

The heroine is usually an orphan or someone who has been neglected as a child. Margaret Jensen, in a survey of 200 Harlequins, found that at least one-third of the heroines are orphans.[19] Most of the others only have a father or an uncaring and selfish mother or stepmother. The few heroines who have an intact family are thousands of miles away from them.

> "My mother died when I was two, a road accident," Elyn said briefly, her smile fading (*Desert Flower*, Dana James, 2632: 22).

> "My mother died when I was three, . . . I can't remember her" (*The Trodden Paths*, Jacqueline Gilbert, 2492: 79).

> Her parents had died within weeks of each other after a car crash and she was virtually alone in the world (*The Rainbow Days*, Jean S. MacLeod, 1719: 5).

> Nicole had never been envious of anyone in her life, not even the girls whose lives held the one thing lacking in her own: a mother (*Walk in the Shadows*, Jayne Bowling, HP247: 19).

> Her mother had died shortly after Stacey was born leaving her globe-trotting husband with the unfamiliar and frightening task of raising their child (*No Quarter Asked*, Violet Winspear, HP124: 6).

Often they long for the mothering they have missed:

> Depression dropped over her like a dark mantle and suddenly all she craved was peace, an end to the hostility between them. She yearned to rest against him, and know him kind and compassionate, cradling and comforting her, giving her the understanding she had not known since her grandmother had died (*Wait for the Storm*, Jayne Bowling, HP505: 138).

> She sat there for a long time, wishing desperately that she had someone to turn to for advice, to confide in, but there had been no one, not since her mother had died, and she suddenly felt as lonely now as she had done in those first terrible months of grief (*Summer Fire*, Sally Wentworth, HP456).

> Tears filled her eyes as she tried to fight off the knowledge that all this beauty and security could have been hers. She could have grown up here, she could have swung in that swing that hung from the lower limb of the silver birch by the gate, as a baby she could have sat in the lovingly preserved high-chair in the living-room . . . . she could have called this wonderful place her home (*Man of the High Country*, Mary Moore, 2349: 64).

Hence, of course the charges that Harlequin Romances deliberately infantilize the heroine to reinforce the sexist message that women are childlike, vulnerable, and dependent. This is a damaging message that is no doubt conveyed by the books, but it does not explain why a childlike heroine is an unfailing feature of the Harlequin formula[20] and why it is appealing to women.

In fact, the emotional power of the "Harlequin experience" requires that the reader regress to childhood in order to relive the vicissitudes of the intense fear and love relationship with the mother. The heroine of a Harlequin usually does not know until the last page that the hero loves her. The other 187 pages take the heroine and reader for an emotional roller coaster ride focused intensely on:

- the heroine's losing fight against inevitable unconditional love for and dependence on the hero/mother;
- her deep ambivalence toward the her/mother with sharp swings between love and hate, admiration, and resentment;
- the thrilling highs when she is noticed and nurtured by the hero/mother;
- the terrible loss when she is not, and fears of loss and separation from him/her;
- the searing pain and jealousy of her sibling rivalry with a woman whom she thinks is preferred by the hero/mother;
- the constant and intense desire for comfort and security through loss of self and fusion with the her/mother;
- the final ecstatic fulfillment of that wish.

All these components of the Harlequin formula are essential parts of the myth/fantasy of fusion with the mother. The emotional power of the tussles and antagonisms, tenderness and rivalry, closeness and distance of the protagonists come from the reader's reliving of the conflicted mother/child relationship in the secure knowledge of its eventual resolution.

For some, the addictive aspect of this reading may come because it provides only a false resolution. The resolution/fusion is always left to the last page of the book because it is the aim of the reading process,[21] but the comfort is tantalizingly brief, gone as soon as the book is closed. Continued release/comfort can only be gained by picking up another book.[22]

Certain types of activities, commonly shared by mother and child, appear frequently enough in different Harlequins to earn the status of themes. The hero and heroine shop for clothes for the heroine together; he comforts her when she has bad dreams; he scolds her for risking illness; he tucks her into bed and gives her medicine; he leads her by the hand; restrains her physically from running away, having tantrums and so on. The hero's maternal role is glaringly obvious in pervasive nurturing scenes like those cited earlier and below:

> [H]e leaned over to see that her door was safely locked (*The Man on the Peak*, Katarina Britt, 2305: 144).

> When she turned to go on, Judy discovered that Charles had come back and was waiting for her. As he saw she was ready to go on, he took her by the hand. Judy made no protest, glad of the assistance as the pull of the hill became even greater (*Spread Your Wings*, Ruth Clemence, 1195: 133).

> It was exquisite relief when they sighted tents and Luke would swing her up into his arms and carry her to the camp fire, propping her round with blankets and sleeping bags for comfort (*Tiger Sky*, Ruth E. Iver, 2244: 115).

> "There, there my love. It's all right. Just a dream." And the arms lost their feeling of constriction as a gentle hand brushed the hair from Verna's sweat soaked brow (*The Sugar Dragon*, Victoria Gorden, p. 138).

> Jason . . . . took her into his arms, as gently as if she'd been a scared child. She clung to him, all the pent-up emotions and tensions of the day breaking in a storm of weeping. He held her closely, stroking her head soothingly without speaking (*Moorland Magic*, Elizabeth Ashton, 1741: 155).

> Later in the dark hours, reliving her ordeal she cried out his name. He was beside her in a flash. She dreamed she was lying in his arms, and when morning came, she found her dream was real (*The Little Imposter*, Lilian Peake, HP206: 190).

With a tremendous effort she opened her eyes staring back at him. "It's a lovely feeling to know I'm safe. Thank you."

"Lie still. You're almost asleep." Strands of her dark red hair clung to her cheek and almost involuntarily he brushed them away. "Now, I don't want to hear another sound out of you," he commanded, as her eyes clung to him and her mouth trembled to say a little more. "Good night" (*Blue Lotus*, Margaret Way, 2328: 24).

The maternal role is also obvious in more impatient infantilizing interactions:

It seemed he was always speaking her name with a marked degree of exasperation (*Kiss of a Tyrant*, Margaret Pargiter, 2375: 160).

"Miss Hurst," he said, and she broke into a run, making for the stairs. But they were so far away and he was so quick in his pursuit of her, he had her by the wrist before she was half way across the hall (*Little Imposter*, Lilian Peake, HP206: 161).

He took her hand, then looked her over. "Look at you, girl. You're covered in sand!" He dusted her down, brushing the sand from her shoulders and arms, turning her and brushing her back and hips (*Ibid.*, p. 136).

He seemed so overpoweringly tall standing over her the way he was, and she was glad when he brought himself down nearer her level, squatting beside her on his heels, his eyes watching her quizzically (*Isle of the Golden Drum*, Rebecca Stratton, 2375: 160).

He lifted . . . the bulky parcel and walked out of the compartment without waiting to see if Judy followed him or not. After a seconds hesitation . . . [she] set off down the corridor after him, her high heels clicking twice to every step he took. Charles turned as she climbed out of the carriage and putting out a hand, helped her down (*Spreading Your Wings*, Ruth Clemence, 1193: 185).

The hero is often bossy and angry in contexts that echo parental discipline. He orders her for her own good; and he gets angry with her because he fears for her safety:

Antonio exploded into anger. "You have the impudence to call me stubborn, and yet you refuse to take the quickest and most comfortable way, even though you are soaked to your skin! *Madre mia*, Francesca, I shall soon lose my temper with you if you do not behave.

Francesca glared at him indignantly and would have objected, but he reached for her left hand and almost crushed her fingers with the hard strong pressure of his. Then giving her a slight shake as he drew her alongside him he started for the village, giving her little option but to go too, and making very little allowance for her shorter stride as she squelched along in her wet shoes (*Trader's Cay*, Rebecca Stratton, 2376: 132).

He took a step which brought him close and he stood over her, tall and lean and formidable." Are you going to do as you're told?" he enquired softly. "I mean what I say, Teri, I'll dump you in that bath, clothes and all unless you obey me" (*Enchanted Dawn*, Anne Hampton, HP132: 83).

He turned to stoop and drop a light kiss on the forlorn little mouth, and said abruptly "Is that tooth bothering you?" "A little bit," she evaded his searching glance . . . . "You'd better make an appointment to have it seen to straight away," he said firmly. "Do that this morning." "Yes Jason," she nodded (*Miranda's Marriage*, Margery Hilton, HQ1742: 116).

"Don't interrupt me!" He shouted his voice hard as flint. "Now drop your stubbornness. Do as I say. Go and rest. It's an order!" With that he strode into his study and shut the door decisively (*Beloved Viking*, Suzanne Lynne, 2007: 123).

The hero's exasperation and anger sometimes extends to threats of violence, in some cases even to violence. Though violence does not feature in what readers have identified as "good" Harlequins.

His breath rasped in anger. "You knew you were going on a journey. Surely the sensible thing to do was eat if only a little. You really are the most irresponsible young woman I have ever known! You ought never to be let out on your own. I could spank you" (*The Spanish Grandee*, Katerina Britt, 1966: 106

"I could bet the living daylights out of you, so go easy, Stacey. What made you run away?" "I'm not running away," She wasn't aware of the tears running down her face, but she did know that she was trembling too hard to be able to speak clearly (*Kiss of a Tyrant,* Margaret Pargiter, 2375: 143).

The Harlequin heroine has extremely ambivalent feelings toward the hero/mother throughout the book. She is resistant to his authority and to her love for him: ". . . 'drink it quietly like a good girl'—he said. 'Must you talk to me as if I'm a child!' she flared. 'I didn't know I was,' he frowned . . ." (*Man in a Million,* Roberta Leigh, HP127: 120). It is clear from the beginning, however, that the struggle is against a more powerful adversary. The power is ultimately the hero/mother's to accept or reject the heroine/child and to command. This is an important given in the formula:

Kyle walked in, and his presence filled the room with sudden vibrant power. I can't fight him, Lola thought—but I'm going to try (*Kyle's Kingdom,* Mary Wibberley, 1836: 133).

Sloan only said her name but Stacey felt defeated: "All right I'll go," she capitulated nervously . . . She could be angry with him, shout at him, cry, argue, and defy him, but in the end it all boiled down to one thing—she obeyed him (*Kiss of a Tyrant,* Margaret Pargiter, 2375: 159).

The hero/mother is portrayed from the child/heroine's point of view as unpredictable and threatening. the heroine's anger, resentment and dislike vie with love for the upper hand. She wants her separate identity and her connection to the mother/hero. The heroine's emotions encompass the ebb and flow of this love/hate, trust/distrust, calm/storm, desire for and fear of separation:

He held out his other hand to her. She went to him and took it almost drowning in the flood of contradictory emotion he aroused in her—resentment, love, challenge, passion—and longing for the giving of his hand to mean more than it did, his fingers the merest light touch upon hers in a clasp which was only guiding her up the stairs (*Pact Without Desire,* Jane Arbor, 2299: 103).

Charles was always unpredictable. She stole a quick glance at his face. In the dim light from the dashboard it was anything but reassuring. Where had the tender lover of last night gone to? Judy sighed as she tried to remember all the wonderful words he had poured into her ears not twenty-four hours ago. It might just have been a dream (*Spread Your Wings*, Ruth Clemence, 1193: 74).

Never before had she been as aware of a man as she was of him: of his animal strength and the sheer physical magnificence of bone and muscle; of his sharp intelligence that one moment could wound and the next could warm (*Man in a Million*, Roberta Leigh, HP127: 123).

As always when they were alone together she had this feeling of completeness, of utter content, as though nothing in the world could hurt her—except himself (*Connellys Castle*, Gloria Bevan, 1809).

She recognized with astonishment that she could openly defy Luke, yell at him and let herself go, yet turn to him in need as if she had known him all her life (*Tiger Sky*, Rose Elver, 2244: 59).

Tania Modleski has also noticed the heroine's ambivalence, particularly anger and rebellion toward the hero in the Harlequin formula. She argues that the heroine's revolt is a fantasy outlet for female resentment, and that the life-threatening accidents which dog the heroine in another fixed component of the formula are the logical extensions of this resentment "in the fantasy of ultimate revenge through self-destruction."[23]

More commonly than not, Harlequin heroines suffer life threatening accidents. They are carried away by the tide, stranded in the desert, hit by falling rocks, cut by sharp knives, run over by cars—all of which serve to show how precious the women really are. Modleski calls these events "the heroines' disappearing act" and argues that they are the only safe way to channel the heroine's (and reader's) anger and frustration. It is true that the wish to harm the other by harm to the self is the fantasy of the powerless against the powerful. Interestingly, however, the original and primal experience of this fantasy is, for us all, in relation to our mother: "She'll be sorry she treated me like that when she finds I'm not here tomorrow"; "If I died tonight she'd be in agony of grief"; or "If she thought I were dying she'd realise that she loves me."

Also, in this particular fantasy, power is not sought solely for revenge but also to be loved, to be treasured, and to feel one's worth to the other— hero/mother. It is no coincidence that the accidents in Harlequins, as in our childhood fantasies, lead to tenderness and nurturing and often, if not always, to avowals of love. The heroine's accident sometimes makes the hero aware of his love for her. It always and primarily gives her and the reader an occasion to revel in that love, concern, and care. The reader can regress to her powerful childhood needs and luxuriate in the wish fulfillment of childish fantasies:

She leaned forward, and at that moment a great wall of green, splintery glass towered over her as she was swept from the rocks and tossed over and over like a rag doll. She was gasping, fighting for breath. There was a roaring in her ears like a mighty wind. She couldn't breathe . . . couldn't breathe . . . . Then she felt herself jerked upwards and she gulped in welcome draughts of air. A voice said: "Take it easy. I've got you. Just relax. . . ." Then a wave swept them both towards the shore, and Scott, picking her up like a child, held her in his arms and he strode up the beach and towards the Land Rover standing on the sand (*Hills of Maketu*, Gloria Bevan, 1309: 184-185).

Slowly consciousness returned and through the veils of mist that swirled before her eyes, she became aware that someone was holding her and touching her head with light, deft fingers to ascertain her hurt. She tried to see who it was, but her eyes would not focus and she closed them again dizzy and sick.

She leaned back thankfully against the stalwart shoulder supporting her, and felt the rough wool of a sweater against her cheek. The man shifted a little to ease her into a more comfortable position, and she felt, or thought she felt, his lips against her uninjured temple, while he murmured in a voice vibrant with anxiety: "Charity, are you all right? Little one. . . ."

She smiled faintly. There was only one person whom her rescuer could be, and she was intensely moved by the tenderness in that low murmur. This was love as she had dreamed of it, kind and compassionate, not fierce and demanding. She had not dared to hope he was capable of such gentleness (*Moorland Magic*, Elizabeth Ashton, 1741: 78).

It is not incidental, either, that the hero has then, like the mother, actually given the heroine life:[24]

Everything that had happened, being lost, then rescued in this beautiful, pitiless, wilderness was strange to her, but nothing more strange than being cradled in this imperious man's arms.

She sighed deeply and brushed the tears from her face. Her head fell back against his shoulder and her melancholy,

deep blue eyes closed. He was strong, the strongest man
she had ever known, and she owed him her life (*Blue
Lotus*, Margaret Way, 2328: 25).

Here one almost expects the hero to begin breast feeding the heroine.
   A rival for the hero's love is another constant in the romance formula.
Ninety-eight percent of the Harlequins that Margaret Jensen surveyed
had a female rival for the hero's love.[25] In earlier Harlequins, these are a
whole species of extremely beautiful, manipulative women who pretend to be all heart and warmth to men but don't bother to hide their
coldness, indifference, and cunning from other women. Your quintessential male-identified woman:

"How clever of you," smiled Miss McGrath, and turned to
the two men. It would always be that way Rachel knew
instinctively. For Fiona McGrath was what is known as a
man's woman (*The Other Linding Girl*, Mary Burchell,
1431: 81).

Rosemary was not genuinely the quiet and womanly sort
. . . Quiet perhaps. But remarkably resourceful in her sly
and secret way. Going almost silently about her business,
despising her own sex and preying on it (*Girl with a
Challenge*, Mary Burchell, Harlequin Omnibus, 37: 242-
243).

Felicia with her own sex made no attempt to be pleasant
(*Blue Lotus,* Margaret Way, 2328: 114).

   In more recent Harlequins, the other woman is much less likely to be
a nasty, male-identified, woman-hating manipulator. She may be kind and
friendly, warm, generous, and gifted, but still breath-takingly beautiful
and a feared potential rival for the hero's love: "It would have been so
much easier to feel right about her feelings for Travis if Miranda was a
witch. But she wasn't. She was nice—and sweet—and offered the hand of
friendship" (*Wonderers Dream*, Rita Clay, Silhouette, 1981[date]).
   This, like other significant recent changes in Harlequin's content (such
as heroines who are older, are not virgins, and will keep their careers
after marriage)[26] is an interesting sign of the impact of feminism in this
unlikely arena. More important for my argument, however, is the fact
that none of these changes alters the basic dynamics of the Harlequin
read. The unwitting, innocent, and even likable rival, is still a rival. Her
presence and the hero's suspected love for her still puts the heroine
through the tortures of the damned and allows the reader to relive her
sibling rivalry in the security of a happy ending: "The pain of unrequited
love was all the more unbearable because she loved him so desperately,

and there was nothing she could do" (*The Man on the Peak*, Katerina Britt, 2305: 139-140). For we readers know all the time that, whether the heroine or even the hero know it or not, the hero is, or very soon will be, madly in love with the heroine: "His gaze went past the glittering figure [of the rival] to the girl in a simple flame colored dress who stood in the shadows" (*The Hills of Maketu*, Gloria Bevan, 1309: 164). This, of course, gives tremendous power to the heroine which a number of analysts have pointed out is pleasurable in itself to women in a male-dominated society. As Margaret Atwood has said:

> Harlequins are about doing the best you can under the circumstances which are not dandy. Harlequins are about Beauty and the Beast. Harlequins are about lion taming: if you can't be a lion yourself you can at least domesticate one. . . . Harlequins are, among other things, how-to books on the fantasy level, for women who experience daily their own lack of power.[27]

The tall, strong, commanding male learns that he needs the heroine although not, of course, in the same way as the weak, dependent other man who leans on her. The hero will never do anything to harm the heroine and he will do everything he can to make her happy because he loves her. Not unvaryingly, but often enough to be noteworthy, the heroine's new sense of power over the hero is noted explicitly:

> "I will give it all up, if you wish;" he told her with such simple sincerity she felt ashamed of her lingering doubts
> . . . .
> He, the most arrogant of the Valdivias, was allowing her to choose his destiny, placing his life, his future and his happiness in her hands (*Valley of Paradise,* Margaret Rome, pp. 187-188).

> "And when you said you'd come with me, down here to find Fleur—to find Philips, I wasn't sure why you were coming, and it took all the strength of will I possessed to say I'd bring you with me, knowing I might have to beg you to come back with me."
> "You'd have begged?" Her voice shook with the turbulent emotions that shook her like a physical shock, and Clary looked down at her with such fierceness in his eyes that she had to believe he meant it.
> "I'd have begged," he said hoarsely, "if I had to, to get you back!" (*The House of Kingdom*, Lucy Gillen, 2026: 187.)

Janet Patterson has argued that, through the hero's love, the heroine/ reader gains access to the male world in the only way open to her.[28] Tania

Modleski and others have also noted the satisfaction for women in vicariously winning power over the male dominator.[29] This is no doubt true but it's not the whole truth.

The Harlequin world is a female world, not a male world. There is *no* male world in a Harlequin. The hero's world is one of beautiful furniture, comfortable beds, magnificent views, delicious and plentiful food, and fine weather; not competition, business, or public power. He, of course, has considerable power and stature in the public world but that is not what he represents in the Harlequins. What the heroine gains access to through him is beauty, ease, and luxury—creature comforts and, above all, security and a home for ever and ever. Her concern is not to impress the hero or to use him in her career. And she is appreciative of women's skills and activities, and supportive of other women who support her in return, and whose woman-identification may be explicitly contrasted to the male identification of the heroine's rival who uses and betrays women in her pursuit of the hero.

The heroine, for one reason or another, usually lives in the hero's beautiful and luxurious home. This, of course, provides lots of opportunity for contretemps, misunderstanding, tension, mutual awareness, and excitement. It also dramatizes the homelessness of the heroine who unfailingly finds herself strongly, even violently attached to this place. The pain of having to leave his home often rivals the pain of losing the hero. The heroine will be totally lost and without a place in the world. The hero's home is her only home, she must be there; it is this home the hero represents, not the male world.

> From being a despotic employer he had become the man she loved, and loved without hope of requitement. Nor had she dreamed that Carne would come to be like a second home. She loved every stick and stone of the old grey house and its terraced garden, and to leave it and its owner was proving a wrench that seemed to tear her in two (*Moorland Magic*, Elizabeth Ashton, 1741: 162-163).

The power the heroine wins through love is also power with a difference. [S]he had the strange sensation of a switch of power, as though she were in command" (*Miranda's Marriage*, Margery Hilton, 1752), but she does not choose to command. Hers is not the power to *do* anything, but the power to abandon herself without risk; to lose herself in another, without any fear that she will be hurt or will suffer. It is the necessary condition for her fusion with the hero/mother and for a truly "happy" and unconflicted ending. She can become one with another and yet have her every wish granted. Paradoxically, the heroine/reader glories in her power because it enables her to luxuriate in a passivity that is anything but masochistic.

Sex and Romance

All these interactions, ins and outs, complications, and even routine daily activities are accompanied by enormously heightened sensual awareness. *Everything* is a thrill: a glance, a touch, a thought, angry or kind words, not to mention closer contact become one thrill after another. The heroine is portrayed in an almost constant state of emotional arousal often erotic, though, as we have seen anger, and resentment feature as well.

This has led some writers to presume that Harlequins are primarily about sex. Male analysts, for instance, have hypothesized that "Harlequin romances are essentially pornography for people [read women] ashamed to read pornography,"[30] or are safe scenarios of vicarious sexual adventure for people (women) without the courage to actually engage in the presumed desirable adventure itself.[31]

Anne Snitow develops a more sophisticated analysis that tries to explain the attraction of sex (or pornography) for women rather than presuming it as these others have done. She argues that one content of pornography, though by no means the only content, in a patriarchal and misogynist society, "is a universal infant desire for complete, immediate gratification, to rule the world out of the very core of passive helplessness . . . . [P]ornography . . . reaches straight down to the infant layer where we all imagine ourselves the centre of everything by birthright and are sexual beings without shame or need for excuse."[32] In a sex divided and male-dominated society, says Snitow

> we have two pornographies, one for men and one for women. They both have, hiding within them, those basic human expressions of abandonment I have described. The pornography for men enacts this abandonment on women as objects. How different is the pornography for women, in which sex is bathed in romance, diffused, always implied rather than enacted at all! This pornography is the Harlequin romance.[33]

Ann Douglas[34] and others have also written about romances as women's pornography and this approach has been widely influential among feminists. Despite the undoubted insights that some of these analyses have to offer, however, there is a deep flaw in an analytical approach which defines women's experience in terms of men's, even in its difference. A very important and hard-won tenet of feminist research and theory is that women's experience must be seen and defined *in its own terms* and not simply in comparison/contrast to men's. This is forgotten here, as it is all too frequently elsewhere, and the resulting insights are limited by the distortion of focus—a distortion which is immediately evident when we reverse the process and call pornography "men's Harlequin's."

Ann Snitow's recognition of the total immersion/arousal of the Harlequin reading experience is acute, but there is an obvious problem in defining pornography apart from its two most noteworthy, and in fact defining, features: explicit sex and the degrading use of women as objects. For our purposes, a more important limitation of Snitow's approach is her own, and others', presumption that Harlequins are about sex even when it is often not "enacted at all" and even though women readers state over and over again that "the books are not about sex but about romance and cite in conversation their preference for novels that lack explicit sexual description."[35]

Analysts who have presumed that Harlequins are about sex have had to deal with readers' claims of lack of interest and with the fact that, though there is constant portrayal of erotic arousal, there is relatively little explicit sex. They have posited as explanation women's lack of sexual courage, their repression due to patriarchal double standards, and lack of social approval of female sexuality, along with their fear of pregnancy in a society in which women are economically and socially dependent on men.

They have not, however, thought to ask whether the arousal and emotional intensity might not come from the dynamics of the fraught hero/heroine relationship itself rather than from the "diffused" sex. Does the sex and sexual excitement perhaps stand for, mirror, and heighten an emotional intensity that is not about heterosexual sex at all? Ann Snitow notices that "the romantic intensity of Harlequins—the waiting, fear, speculating—are as much a part of their functioning as pornography for women as are the more overtly sexual scenes."[36] She does not realize, however, that the power of the male presence comes almost entirely from this intense pattern of "waiting, fear, speculating." The romance *is* that pattern and not the sexual scenes such as they are. The final scene is always a declaration of love, a resolution of the emotional see-saw of fears of separation and loss, not a sex scene.

Janice Radway found that "the hero's protective concern and tender regard for the heroine": is the main thing for readers who care little whether it is portrayed in sexual terms as long as it is "extensively described."[37] I would argue that this care and attention is in itself erotic to the heroine and to the reader. Certainly the two themes of nurture/ security, and erotic and emotional excitement are closely intertwined in the romances.

> He was an exciting person to be with—she couldn't ignore
> him—he was so vital, so attractive, so-so-so comforting
> somehow (*Rata Flowers are Red*, Mary Moore, 1578: 77).

Joan curled tighter in his arms, those strong arms that
would always protect her and thrill her with their caress
(*Alyson's Share*, Janet Daily, HP208: 185).

Radway recognizes a psychological component to much of women's
romance reading when she connects the requisite infantilization of the
romantic heroine with women's "unconscious wish . . . to experience
again . . . that primary love the infant received at the breast and hands of
her mother."[38] But she does not see, as Snitow does, that the emotional
impact comes primarily from powerful infantile desires rather than from
the undeniable need of women for nurture that she has given central role
in her analysis.[39]

The erotic power of the hero is achieved because he is the mother; he
offers the complete gratification of safe total, passive surrender. The
excitement of security:

Julie did not know how to answer him but she made no
effort to pull away again. His strong arms around her made
her feel more secure than she had felt in a long time. But
as his hand moved soothingly across her back, the vague
longings he had always aroused in her blazed into disturb-
ingly intense desires. Suddenly the sense of security
combined with an almost irresistible feeling of dangerous
excitement (*Roses and White Lilies*, Donna Alexander,
McFadden Romances, 98: 67).

The sensuality of nurture:

She held out her hand and he came back and took it in his
hand. "You're cold," he said. She said, "Warm me," and he
sat down on the bed beside her and held her against him,
gently stroking her back and shoulders. Dora snuggled
closer, warmed and comforted by the feel and the smell of
his smooth skin under the rough bathrobe, while a sweet
sensuous languor was draining her consciousness. Her
eyes were closed, her lids and limbs were heavy. She
murmured, "Hold me," as though she was warm so long as
his arms were around her, and then the velvet darkness
covered her like a lover, and she slipped into a deep and
dreamless sleep (*The Black Hunter*, Jane Donnelly, 2187:
159).

The firmly established subconscious identification of the hero as
mother provides heightened erotic intensity to mundane activity as well
as to sexual encounters.

They walked slowly back to where Helen had left her beach robe. Picking it up Leon held it for her to put on and then, turning her round, he began to fasten the buttons . . . . "Hold your chin up." Helen obeyed, blinking rapidly at him as the sun became hurtful to her eyes. His hands touched her throat, he shook his head slightly and gave her an almost tender smile, "I'd kiss you if we weren't being watched," he said, and then, more briskly, "Come, child, its time for tea (*Gates of Steel*, Ann Hampson, HP1: 100).

Strength and tenderness, harshness and gentleness, control and indulgence are erotic in themselves, echoes of the early contradictory experience of the mother:

Suzanne lay against him painfully aware of the strength and tenderness in his arms (*The Man on the Peak*, Katerina Britt, 2305: 84).

He drew her close and once again she felt his great tenderness, and his strength (*Gates of Steel*, Anne Hampson, HP1: 190).

She now sensed in him, the male strength mated with a devastating tenderness (*Northern Sunset*, Penny Jordan, HP508:130).

Nevertheless it is security, belonging and comfort that is the aim of it all, and is, paradoxically, exciting, emotional, and erotic. The resolution of the separation from the mother, the rediscovery of original, sensual and complete fusion is the climax of the romance. The heroine will live happily ever after in the womb provided by the hero. In romantic fantasy loving is mothering; to be loved is to find a mother. The powerful presence of the lover evokes the mother who is everything to the child and the reader's regression to this emotional state is what gives the image of the hero power.

Throughout the book the heroine longs for this release, fears its loss with her separation from the hero, and resents his power over her:

Awakening to sunlight and warmth, she realized that Raoul's personality was powerful enough to enrich everything around her. Listening to the birds in the curly-roofed leaves, she revelled in a feeling of being protected, free from all fear and hurt, although she knew it was sheer fantasy (*Man on the Peak*, Katerina Britt, 2305: 143).

He was so efficient, so reliable, and for a moment Teri allowed herself the pleasure of dwelling on having him for a husband. He would be there always to smooth her path, to treat with amused contempt the problems which from time to time must assuredly come their way. He would be her prop, her secure anchor, her haven in all storms (*Enchanted Dawn*, Annetta Hampson, HP132: 180).

The reader is able to indulge in all the heroine's heightened fear, joy, anxiety, hope, and disappointment because she knows there will be a happy ending. The heroine will, on the last page find her home, a place in which to belong, peace, and security ever after:

She had come home, home to Flint and the safe harbour of his love where she and he would dwell in simplicity and peace. The End (*Harbour of Love*) Anne Hampson, 2230: 186).

She didn't question his understanding but merely sighed happily as she read her future in his eyes and gave herself up to the matchless sensation of being cherished. The End (*Walk in the Shadows*, Jayne Bowling, HP247: 192).

He drew her up into his arms again, while outside the moon clothed the moor and slopes with silver and inside the thick walls of the old house, silence brooded and the shadows gathered in the corners. They were no longer menacing, they represented home and were the promise of deep content (*Moorland Magic*, Elizabeth Ashton, 1741: 190).

Mother—Resource or Neurosis?

My reflections on Harlequins over the years have benefited from a diverse and growing feminist literature attesting to the psychological and social importance of women's relationships to our apparently all-powerful and unpredictable mothers.[40] This is a prominent theme in much experiential/descriptive writing. Jane Lazarre, for instance, notes that the mother-daughter relationship is the most compelling topic of study for the students in her women's studies courses. In writing about relationships within the women's movement Mickey Spencer and her collaborators found "that mother and daughter roles affect many—perhaps most—relationships among women, regardless of blood ties or group size." Feminist writers, film makers, and critics again and again evoke their relationship with their mother when reflecting on their relationship to the female subjects of their work, and feminist literary critics have come to recognize the importance of mother-daughter relationships as they are lived and written about by women authors.[41] It is also an important theme in more theoretical work. Mary O'Brien, for instance, has argued that women's integrated experience of birth as a continuity of mediated labour provides the material basis for a female consciousness, which is more integrated and pro-dualistic than male consciousness, which is rooted in a discontinuous experience of reproduction through the alienation of their seed.[43]

Nancy Chodorow, Dorothy Dinnerstein, and Jane Flax, all, in different ways, explore the social consequences of men and women's different psychological experience of being mothered, respectively, by other and same sex mothers. Chodorow and Flax suggest, for instance, that women, unlike men, develop their sense of self and their relationship to the world and others through a continuous identification with the mother which gives women the basis for a less separative, more relationally defined and connected sense of self than men. Thus women's experience of self and the world is very different from the competitive and dualistic male sense which has been called "the human condition" and which shapes all patriarchal cultures and values. This gives women special emotional, interpersonal and social awareness and capabilities, but it also makes it more difficult for us to forge a strong and secure separate identity.[44]

Much feminist psychoanalytic literature considers men and women's experience of sex, love, and romance in the psychological context of the mother/child relationship. Dorothy Dinnerstein, Nancy Harsock, and Isaac Balbus all include an examination of this part of life in their more general social analyses.[45] Other relevant work includes Diane Hunter's argument that transference wishes link the "unconscious meanings in the doctor-patient relation to the universal craving for the omnipotent mother of early infancy." Louise Eichenbaum and Susan Orbach discuss the lifelong yearning for "mother's support and care [by women who] from girlhood to womanhood . . . live with the experience of having lost these aspects of maternal nurturance," and Ruth Wodak's psycholinguistic findings demonstrate that the "quality of the [mother-daughter] relationship does not depend on social class, . . . [but is] a structurally necessary emotional constellation in women which surpasses the barriers of class time."[46]

This convincing theoretic and empirical testimony to the importance of the mother in women's lives and psychological development lends support to my view that the Harlequin hero is a mother figure. It does not, however, lead me to believe that women's relationship to our mothers' *causes* Harlequin reading, or that Harlequin reading is the result of widespread psychological difficulties of separation among women. Some readers are no doubt addicted and they may be driven to Harlequins by a need to relive an unresolved relationship with their mother or to escape from an uncomfortable separate identity.[47] My own experience, however, and that of many other readers who have shared their experiences with me have convinced me that the vast majority of readers read Harlequins because of social rather than psychological needs.

The powerful early emotional experience of our relationship with our mothers is a *resource* women can call on through Harlequins to provide a much needed escape. For most women, it is not the source of the need for escape. In pointing to the psychological component of the Harlequin experience I am not suggesting that our relationship to our mothers leaves women incomplete or needy in a general sense. I am arguing, rather, that this relationship provides an emotional experience powerful enough to block out the present when women *choose* to regress to it. Most of us choose to do this because our present circumstances are enormously strained, not because we are driven by some persistent psychological need. When our circumstances improve our use of escape through romance ceases.

In my own case, I began reading Harlequins when I was writing my Ph.D. thesis—a time of great pressure when I could not justify taking any time for myself. I got no relief, for instance, from going for a walk or to a movie with friends because I felt that I shouldn't be there. I would, on occasion, find myself longing for a Harlequin because I could count on more sure and total escape from pressure with Harlequins than any other form of leisure could provide. After I completed my thesis I no longer felt that longing to escape into a Harlequin, no longer felt the immense pleasure/relief when reading them, and gradually stopped.

Many women have told me that they, too, have had a "Harlequin period" which gradually came to an end. On hindsight it was a time of particular pressure—for instance, when they were mothering young children,[48] under pressure as an adolescent or in the final year of university. Other women who are intensely pressured and starved for nurture all their lives remain dependent on Harlequins all their lives.

The lack of resources, time, and money for leisure away from home; the lack of social and personal acceptance of women's visible leisure; the nature of many women's lives in which work and responsibility are a constant 24 hour reality, where there is no private place away from these; and the emotional deprivation almost all women suffer in a heterosexually structure society where women are care providers, rarely receivers, and where most women can expect no mothering or nurture after early adolescence, all combine to explain why the fantasy of mothering in the guise of a romantic hero is the predominant form of escape for women.

If even the most emotionally and materially privileged women are deprived of and hunger for mothering, how much more acute the need is for many more women in less than optimum circumstances:

> 1) When I was maybe eight or so, I went to live with my oldest brother. I had to clean the house and do all the hard work there. . . . I used to sit in that

> house and dream about how some day some
> wonderful man who looked like a prince would
> come and take me away, and how we'd live
> happily ever after.

> 2)   Things were so ugly in my family—my father
> drunk and in a rage, hitting one of us or beating
> my mother up. My mother worked most of the
> time . . . She'd come home and fix supper, then
> we'd all sit around that wait. Finally, Mom would
> give us kids our supper. Eventually my father
> came home, and if he was drunk, he'd storm
> around. Maybe he'd knock the pots off the stove
> and make a holy mess. Or maybe he'd take out
> after my mother.

> When I think about it now, it sounds crazy, but
> honestly, the worse things got at home, the more
> I used to dream about how I was going to marry
> some good, kind wise man who would take care
> of me and how we'd always love each other and
> be happy.

These quotations from Lillian Breslow Rubin's account of working class
family life in *Worlds of Pain* show the roots of romance fantasy in
deprivation.[49]

The fantasy is available free in our own heads, or very cheaply in
Harlequins, and it can be indulged at home, even by women with no time
and no power, if they are prepared to read after working a 16 hour day
when everyone is out or in bed—which many do.

More important for women whose pressures are never ending and who
cannot even justify to themselves (let along others) taking time away,
Harlequins provide certain and total escape for the two hours it takes to
read them. When asked why they read Harlequins some readers answer
quite simply, "It beats tranquilizers or alcohol"—an eloquent testimony to
the desperation of their lives and to their self-knowledge. Because we can
literally lose ourselves in the early relationship with our mother it
becomes the ideal vehicle of escape, a catapult into another world that
is as reliable as drugs. This more than anything else is the reason that
Harlequins are such a standby for women who desperately need escape.

The child/parent relationship in Harlequins is so evident that many
writers, without seeing that the hero actually is the mother, have
remarked on various parallels. Jill Tweedie, for instance, has interpreted
the romantic hero as a father figure:

> In my youth, men of the ilk of Max de Winter (Rebecca)
> (and all his other ilks back to Mr. Rochester and beyond)

were generally accepted as love-object, not in spite of but *because* they were old enough to be our fathers and so, to all intents and purposes, were our fathers. And unless we get that straight those personal traits that would be off-putting in a young man only contributed to our turning on . . . . Whatever he did, kind or cruel or rather rude, had to be accepted as a child accepts the vagaries of God the Father . . . . A child's need to be loved is too overwhelming to permit demands on the beloved, the most that could be hoped for was a careful accommodation to paternal whims. We aimed to please.[50]

Ann Snitow notes that what Joanna Russ observed about the heroines of gothic romances—that "they are loved as babies are loved, simply because they exist"—is true of Harlequin heroines as well.[51] Janice Radway also notes that "[B]y emphasizing the intensity of the hero's uninterrupted gaze and the tenderness of his caress at the moment he encompasses his beloved in his still always 'masculine' arms the fantasy . . . evokes a period in the reader's life when she was the center of a profoundly nurturant individual's attention."[52] The idea that the Harlequin hero is a mother figure has almost without exception "clicked" with women readers I have shared it with in public talks. They respond far more often than not with an excited "Ah, yes!" or "Of Course!" People who don't know the books but read a few to check out the idea have been convinced.

This leaves the complex question of why women would fantasize a mother figure as male. It is beyond the scope of this article to offer any but initial observations on this point, but one obvious reason may be that in a patriarchy only men have enough social power to represent the powerful mother figure. Paradoxically, female figures other than mythical ones, do not have the necessary power and resources to stand for the mother.[53] Also, it may be less threatening psychologically to lose oneself in the other sex where persisting difference from the heroine makes the loss of self in fusion less absolute. The maleness of the hero/mother makes him different, also from the feared mother in a way that may further attenuate the threat of fusion. Both these factors may make it easier for women to play with that fusion psychologically.

The erotic aspect of the desire for and experience of fusion with the mother is also much more acceptable in a heterosexually defined and enforced culture when she becomes a male figure. The masculinizing of the mother thus decreases the threat of her attraction for vulnerable women in a patriarchal society. Needless to say it also masks and tames powerful female focused desires in a way that transforms them into a male focused mythical mainstay of patriarchy—the myth of male mothering.

*   *   *

If it is true that women turn to reading romance because our lives are so often barren of nurture and so pressured that we need to feel mothered and we need a quick and guaranteed escape; and if it is true that romance serves both these needs because the romantic hero is a mother figure—what can feminists learn from all this?

First, it shows how important it is to fight the double standards of a culture that devalues women and all that is female if we are to successfully analyze and transform our culture. Formula romance, by far the largest segment of the formula book market, has until very recently been ignored by students of popular culture who have given loving attention to westerns, mysteries, detective stories, ghost stories, and (worse) adventure stories. What writing there is about formula romance is far more critical than writing about other formula forms which are more easily accepted as temporary escapes for otherwise busy, intelligent, well-rounded people who are generally in touch with reality. The "Harlequin reader" outranks bingo player, soap watcher, prostitute, and housewife as a negative stereotype totally defining a woman by one activity or aspect of her life. Readers of westerns are not commonly supposed to live in expectation of a stage coach at the door but Harlequin readers are presumed to believe in the Harlequin world and to live in daily expectation of the hero's arrival. In fact, Harlequin readers are as diverse a group and have as good a grasp on reality as any other formulae readers.[54]

Other negative presumptions drawn about women from Harlequins also turn out to be false. Women are not masochistic and are not reading Harlequins because they enjoy being dominated. The notion that romance is a female neurosis, or even that the female condition is neurosis also proves untenable when we see that romance works as an escape because women use their relationship with their mother as a resource for regression, not because women are actually as male-centred or as successfully brainwashed to believe in salvation through men as might appear at first sight to be the case.[55]

The limits of analyses that do not challenge androcentric expectations and values also become clear. The presumptions that Harlequin romances are 1) power fantasies for people so crushed that they can't even fantasize power, or 2) sex fantasies for people so repressed they can't even fantasize sex, or 3) substitutes for fantasies about individual success for people so limited that they cannot even imagine personal achievement, are insulting.

As soon as we allow women *specific* desires and interests we can see that they are also incorrect. The popularity of Harlequin Romances suggests that most women are not primarily interested in and do not gain satisfaction from power over others or the power to aggress;[56] that most women's erotic pleasure, desire, and potential does not find itself primarily in phallic focused intercourse outside of intimacy, nurture, care, and security;[57] and most women's sense of self and fulfillment requires a rich world of interrelationship and interdependence.[58] Intimacy, security and interrelationship are major turn-ons for women.

It is true that women are largely powerless in patriarchy and are excluded from successful participation in the public world, and our sexuality is far more heavily repressed and denied than men's. Nevertheless, by definition, fantasy involves imagining what is desirable but unattainable or non-existent. Only an exaggeratedly derogatory view of women could underlie the suggestion that we cannot even imagine what we truly desire. If women as a group deeply wanted power over men, or competitive individual success, or easy uninvolved sex with many partners, I'm sure we could fantasize it. In fact, some of us do some of the time—witness the S & M fantasies that apparently please some women. But these fantasies do not constitute major themes in female popular culture because they are not central to women's desires.

To say that Harlequins are no worse than male forms of popular culture (in fact, more benign), that the readers are not necessarily pathetically repressed and masochistic, and that the books must be understood as the product of women as well as Harlequin Enterprises, is not to glorify Harlequins or to imply that they are harmless.[59] Regardless of the positive changes in more recent Harlequin plots as a result of the influence of the women's movement, the plots *do* often infantilize women, justify domineering behaviour from men, and imply that the most glorious destiny of a woman is reciprocal love with a man. Even the least objectionable on these grounds are, in fact, a form of escape which mystifies and hides powerful female connections and female focused needs in a way that is eminently compatible with patriarchy. Harlequins disguise women's powerful homoerotic bond with their prime caretaker and deny women's practical sisterhood of survival. Understanding the deeper psychological dynamics of romance fantasy and checking the androcentric double standards too often involved in its analysis does not change the fact that, while Harlequins help women survive, they do so in the service of what Janice Raymond has called hetero-reality.[60] They are not the simple unidimensional tool of patriarchy that they appear to be on the surface—but they *are*, nevertheless, a tool of patriarchy.

It would be much better if women did not read Harlequins. However, understanding that formula romances are partly women's creation and help women survive makes the question of how we should relate to them as feminists much more difficult. These romances do not deeply influence most adult women's sense of reality and they do not actually lead most women to expect salvation from men or to rely on men. Most adult women who read Harlequins have a pretty good grasp of reality and what their needs are. Women don't look to these books for help in understanding their lives, but for one of the few available sources of escape and comfort. It is hard to see any benefit in denouncing or denying this relief to women.[61]

Harlequin's popularity will decrease as we manage to bring help and support to women and to change social structures in ways that reduce women's stress and our enormous need to escape. Meanwhile, I think one effective way we can combat their popularity is by getting the message out as widely as possible that it is, in fact, women who mother, not men. The little support that women do get actually comes largely from women—sisters, mothers, neighbors, and friends—not from men. Yet the dominant patriarchal ideology is so strong that it hides this from us. In my own pre-feminist days I never named, and therefore never saw, the support I got from other women and the love I felt for them. The sisterhood I was actually living, if only in truncated form, remained invisible to me. Yet I know, from teaching women's studies classes as well as from my own responses, that women are open to recognizing the truths about their lives when they are articulated—especially when those truths are affirming women and our strengths and connections.

A sense of the complexity of the Harlequin phenomenon can help us resist any tendency to too easily echo the patriarchal contempt for women who read them. It can help us use this distorted, but nevertheless real, expression of female popular culture to learn more about women's desires, needs, and strengths, as well as weaknesses. Harlequins are obviously not an autonomous cultural form and are therefore limited as a source of information about autonomous women's needs. But they are still better for this purpose than entirely male defined and controlled institutions and cultural forms. Used in conjunction with research and reflection on other aspects of our lives, and with feminist theory, Harlequins should provide useful new questions for research and throw additional light on questions we are already examining in different contexts.

For instance, the books' international, cross cultural, cross racial, and cross class appeal lends support to the view that despite the obviously important diversity among women, much of what it means to be a woman is shared at a very deep level.[62] Also, suggestions by feminist theorists that women's sexuality and sense of power and relationship to the world are different from men's seem to be born out by Harlequins.

Harlequin romances reveal female needs for nurture that should not be dismissed as mere products of women's dependence and neurosis. They suggest that escape from our oppression as women does not lie simply in denying our eternally giving mothers and our needs for nurture in an identity as 'free spirits' who do not nurture. I requires, instead, the much more complex and difficult struggle:

> to accept and integrate and strengthen both the mother
> and the daughter in ourselves, [this] is no easy matter,
> because patriarchal attitudes have encouraged us to split,

to polarize, these images, and to project all unwanted guilt, anger, shame, power, freedom, onto the 'other' woman. But any radical vision of sisterhood demands that we reintegrate them.[63]

The psychological dynamics of the "Harlequin experience," in fact, lend weight to the growing sense among feminists that our relations with our mothers and our children, and women's needs for mutually "mothering" behaviour are central areas for feminist reflection and struggle.

Revaluing women's relational and connective capacities and world view, and recognizing the concomitant vulnerability of our separate sense of self leaves us with the enormous task of redefining and creating, in our personal lives and in society as a whole, new reciprocal, mutually affirming and interdependent definitions and expressions of strength, autonomy, justice, power, and eroticism. The mother-daughter relationship, and the "mothering" needs and abilities of women are (like Harlequins) both a resource and a barrier in this struggle:

> It was too simple, early in the new twentieth-century wave of feminism, for us to analyze our mothers' oppression, to understand "rationally"—and correctly—why our mothers did not teach us to be Amazons . . . . [Yet] there was, is, in most of us, a girl-child still longing for a woman's nurture, tenderness, and approval, a woman's power exerted in our defense, a woman's smile and touch and voice, a woman's strong arms around us in moments of fear and pain . . . . It was not enough to *understand* our mothers; more than ever, in the effort to touch our own strength as women, we *needed* them. The cry of that female child in us need not be shameful or regressive; it is the germ of our desire to create a world in which strong mothers and strong daughters will be a matter of course.[64]

If the Harlequin hero is a mother figure, the Harlequin phenomenon, paradoxically, testifies to this longing among women for women, and its political importance. It also suggests that the female bonding and friendship that must be central to any transformation of the patriarchy has hidden expressions even in the most unlikely of patriarchal institutions.

Notes

1. Tatiana Tolstoi, "Hints from the heart on romance writing," *The Guardian Weekly*, 27 June 1982.

2. Audrey Claire Swafield, "Paperbacks Promoting Passion! What is Harlequin Really Presenting?" *Canadian Woman Studies* 3, 2: 6.

3.   Ann Barr Snitow, "Mass Marketing Romances: Pornography for Women is Different," *Radical History Review* 20 (1979): 150.

4.   "The reader is not made aware that her solution is, in actuality, the problem. [S]o . . . . no questioning of, or action against, the capitalistic structure that puts her place outside the mode of production, will take place." Swafield, p. 5.

5.   In 1982 Harlequin Enterprises sold 218 million books in twelve languages in 98 countries. In Canada twenty eight percent of the paperbacks sold were Harlequins. Romances of all kinds, taken together made up fifty percent of paperback sales in the U. S. From Margaret Jensen, *Love's Sweet Return: The Harlequin Story*, (Toronto: Women's Press, 1984), p. 34.

     Harlequin's exhaustive market research, pre-testing, and reader surveys are described fully by Janice Radway in *Reading the Romance: Women, Patriarchy, and Popular Literature*, (Chapel Hill and London: University of North Carolina Press, 1984).

6.   Janice Radway is one of the few analysts of Harlequins who stresses, as I do, the importance of women's active role in interpreting the text "whose literary meaning is the result of a complex, temporally evolving interaction between a fixed verbal structure and a socially situated reader." Radway, "Women Read the Romance: the Interaction of Text and Context," *Feminist Studies* 9, 1 (Spring 1983): 54-55. Her study provides valuable data from women themselves about how they see their Harlequin reading. This information is enhanced by her sensitive interpretation which I refer to later.

     Where I differ from Radway is her presumption that feminists make up an entirely different "interpretive community" than Harlequin readers, that there is no overlap that can be called on to aid analysis. She says that "we have no evidence that we even know how to read as romance readers do" (*Reading the Romance*, p. 11). I argue, on the other hand, that feminist analysts, as women, potentially share an interpretive community with readers which we could explore and use as a resource (though not the only resource) in analysis. The lack of reference to certain aspects of their experience (as much as the false generalization of other aspects of their experience that Radway has criticized) is a weakness in feminist analysis of Harlequins.

7.   Ibid., p. 9.

8.   Ibid.

9.   Harlequin's two main lines are the classical Harlequin Romance and a series of slightly longer format books with the same basic formula called Harlequin Presents. Books in both series are numbered. I have included the identification numbers of the books, and in order to distinguish books from the Harlequin Presents series from those in the other series I have put HP before the numbers of the former.

10. Harlequin heroines and writers seem to agree: "Experience had taught Chloe that ordinary men were a sadly selfish bunch. So she conjured up an ideal. He would have to be rich and generous; tall, dark, and handsome; kind to children and animals. And he would possess a sense of humour. She and her sister had a good laugh over the requirements. They both knew full well that such a man could never really exist: At least that's what Chloe thought—until she met Benedict Dane . . . " (*A Very Special Man*, Marjorie Lewty, 2282: 9).

11. Radway, "Women Read the Romance," p. 61.

12. Ibid., p. 57.

13. Snitow, p. 150.

14. By "good" Harlequins I mean those in which the formula is used to maximum impact.

Janice Radway has documented the important point that, contrary to the presumptions of most analysts of Harlequin's, formula books are not all the same to the readers. They are not interchangeable. Readers have preferences and distinguish between "good" and "bad" samples of the genre. She has also done valuable work in identifying, through detailed questionnaires, the characteristics of "good" Harlequins.

This part of her work (see Chapter 4 of *Reading the Romance*) is particularly interesting to me because my preferences agree so closely with those of the women she interviewed. Her findings provided support for my sense that my own experience as a reader is comparable to that of others and can serve as a source of insight into the "Harlequin experience" in general.

15. These are two quotations from Harlequin publicity material. Their gist is reported over and over again by women interviewed about their experience of Harlequin reading. See, for instance, comments by readers interviewed by Claire Harrison for the CBC Ideas series "Love at First Sight: Romance Novels and the Romantic Fantasy." Transcript available from CBC Transcripts, Box 500, Station A, Toronto, M5W 1E6.

16. Cited by Claire Harrison, "Love at First Sight."

17. As interpreted by Claire Harrison.

18. Janet Patterson is another one of the writers who recognizes that "women are not consumers but active readers; novels are not commodities but cultural experiences" (p. 23) and asks "why women want to read Harlequins" (p. 22). She is the only writer I know who has dealt with the emotional nature of the Harlequin experience and the power of the ritualized repetitive experience in her answer to that question. See Janet Patterson, "Consuming Passion" *Fireweed* 11 (1981): 19-33.

19. Jensen, p. 88.

20. Childlike moments/allusions persist in those recent "successful" Harlequins which downplay women's dependence and inequality in general.

21. Janice Radway's survey of the reading habits of forty-two regular romance readers confirms that the impact of the plot requires the shaping of the final resolution/fusion and that the satisfaction attained is only momentary. Most readers read the books from beginning to end at one sitting. "Once immersed in the romantic fantasy [they] do not like to return to reality without experiencing the resolution of the narrative . . . . [Their ingenuous strategies] for avoiding disruption or discontinuity in the story betoken a profound need to arrive at the *ending* of the tale and thus to achieve or acquire the emotional gratification they already can anticipate" (*Reading the Romance*, p. 59).

22. Over half the women Radway surveyed read more than sixteen hours a week and another 24 percent between eleven and fifteen hours a week (*Reading the Romance*, p. 59). One-third read from five to nine romances weekly, another fifty-five percent completed between one and four romances weekly. She interviewed regular customers at a romance bookstore so her sample is probably skewed toward the heavier readers. According to Rosemary Griley in *Love Lines: The Romance Readers Guide to Printed Pleasures,* (New York: Facts on File Publications, 1983), cited by Jensen (p. 142), "light" readers of romance read up to 25 books a month and "heavy" readers devour eighty or more books a month. The "heaviest" reader that Margaret Jensen interviewed read sixty Harlequins a month and the "lightest" reader read two per month (p. 143). Most read between twelve and sixteen per month and would therefore qualify as "light" readers. Other sources confirm that romance readers are generally not occasional readers. See Yankelevitch, K. Skelly and White, *The 1978 Consumer Research Study on Reading and Book Purchasing,* (Darien, Conn.: The Group, 1978), prepared for the Book Industry Study Group, and cited by Radway, *Reading the Romance*, p. 59.

While there are clearly women who are addicted to Harlequins, whose reading habits are excessive their number can be grossly overestimated if one forgets that it takes only from one and a half to two hours to read the books. Four or five books a month amount to between six to ten hours a month—not a large commitment of time when compared to other leisure forms such as fishing or watching TV sports.

23. Tania Modleski, "The Disappearing Act: A Study of Harlequin Romances," *Signs* 5, 3 (1980): 442.

24. "The fact that she owed her life to Luke Van Meer didn't tie her to him" (*Tiger Sky,* Rose Elver, 2244: 47).

25. Margaret Jensen, "Women and Romantic Fiction: A Case Study of Harlequin Enterprises, Romances, and Readers," Ph.D. Dissertation, McMaster University, 1980, cited in Radway, *Reading the Romances,* p. 122.

26. For a description of those changes see Gail Hamilton, "Romancing the Bookshelf," *Resources for Feminist Research* 13, 3 (November 1984): 46-4, and Jensen, *Love's Sweet Return*, Chapter 6, "Strange Bedfellows: Feminism and Romance."

27. Margaret Atwood, "The Story of Valerie Vapid," *Broadside* 6, 4 (February 1985): 10.

28. "One of the specifications of the Harlequin guidelines is an exotic setting . . . . *The exotic setting is the male world.* Clearly the setting is exotic socially and sexually as much as it is geographically" (Patterson, "Consuming Passions," p. 27, emphasis in the original). But the "exotic" setting is *not* exotic. She is out of her depth but enormously and absolutely at home. It is *her* place, essentially domestic and offers comfort and security and peace if she could only stay there.

29. "A great deal of our satisfaction in reading these novels comes, I am convinced, from our conviction that the woman is bringing the man to his knees and that all the while he is being hateful, he is internally groveling, groveling, groveling" (Modleski, p. 441).

30. Peter Parisi, lecture delivered 6 April 1978, Livingston College, Rutgers University, cited in Snitow, p. 151.

31. Tom Henighen cited by Claire Harrison.

32. Snitow, p. 154.

33. Ibid.

34. Ann Douglas, "Soft Porn Culture," *New Republic,* 30 August 1980.

35. Radway, *Reading the Romance*, p. 104.

36. Snitow, p. 157.

37. Radway, *Reading the Romance*, p. 105.

38. Radway, *Reading the Romance*, p. 145.

39. In contrast to my own understanding of the romance fantasy as essentially a psychological fantasy of mothering, Radway sees it as an expression of women's struggle "toward individuation and actualization of self . . . embodied within the language and forms of patriarchy . . . [that is] a particular kind of female self, the self-in-relation demanded by patriarchal parenting arrangements" (p. 147).

Therefore, she notices the reader's "wish to be protected by an all-powerful parent" (p. 254), only in passing, and deals with it as one part of her fantasy reliving of "a woman's journey to female personhood *as that particular psychic configuration is constructed and realized within patriarchal culture*" (p. 138, emphasis in the original), rather than the central dynamic that I argue it is.

40. For a review of this literature and its significance see Marianne Hirsch, "Mothers and Daughters," *Signs* 7, I (1981): 200-222; and Heather Jon Maroney, "Embracing Motherhood: New Feminist Theory" in *Feminism Now: Theory and Practice*, eds. Marilouise and Arthur Kroker et al.(Montreal: New World Perspectives, 1985): 40-64.

41. Jane Lazarre, "Restoring Lives at City College," *The Village Voice* 26, 20 (18 May 1982): 5, 32; Mickey Spencer et al. "Mother/Daughter Roles in the Feminist Movement," *Quest* 5, 3 (1978): 71-80; the relationships of feminists to the female subjects of their work is examined in *Between Women: Biographers, Novelists, Critics, Teachers, and Artists Write About Their Work on Women*, eds. Carole Ascher et al. (Boston: Beacon, 1984). Marianne Hirsch reviews literary sources. In *The Ideology of Mothering: Disruption and Reproduction of Patriarchy*, (special issue of *Signs* 15, 3 [Spring 1990]), two articles read classics through the mother/daughter relationship. See Shuli Barzilai, "Reading 'Snow White': The Mother's Story" (pp. 515-534); Ann B. Murphy, "The Borders of Ethical, Erotic, and Artistic Possibilities in *Little Women*" (pp. 562-585).

42. For a fuller discussion of this literature see my monograph *Feminist Radicalism in the 1980s*, (Montreal: New World Perspectives, 1986).

43. Mary O'Brien, *The Politics of Reproduction*, (London: Routledge Kegan Paul, 1981).

44. Nancy Chodorow, *The Reproduction of Mothering*, (University of California Press, 1978); Dorothy Dinnerstein, *The Mermaid and the Minotaur*, (New York: Harper and Row, 1977); Jane Flax, "The Conflict between Nurturance and Autonomy in Mother/ Daughter Relationships and within Feminism," *Feminist Studies* 4, 1 (1978): 171-189. This socio-psychoanalytical work has been very influential and its insights have been used in formative feminist analyses of such diverse topics as war and peace, philosophy, bureaucracy, patriarchy, power, politics, and revolution. See, for instance, the special issue of *Atlantis* on peace studies, eds. Barbara Roberts and Michlene de Seve; Jane Flax, "Political Philosophy and the Patriarchal Unconscious: A Psychoanalytic Perspective on Epistemology and Metaphysics," in *Discovering Reality*, eds. Sandra Harding and Merril B. Hintikka, (Reidel, 1983); Nancy Hartsock, *Money, Sex and Power*, (Essex: Longmann, 1983); Sara Ruddick, "Maternal Thinking," *Feminist Studies* 6, 2 (Summer 1980); Isaac D. Balbus, *Marxism and Domination*, (Princeton, N. J.: Princeton University Press, 1982).

45. All op. cit., note 55.

46. Diane Hunter, "Hysteria, Psychoanalysis and Feminism: The Case of Anna O," *Feminist Studies* 9, 3 (Fall 1983); Louise Eichenbaum and Susan Orbach, *Understanding Women: A Feminist Psychoanalytic Approach*, (Basic Books, 1983); Ruth Wodak, "The Language of Love and Guilt: Relationships Between Mothers and Daughters from a Socio- and Psycholinguistic Point of View," *Resources for Feminist Research* 13, 3 (November 1984): 21-25.

47. The relationship with the mother has been identified by feminists as the source of some of women's neurotic behaviour in heterosexual love relations. See, for instance, Ilene Philopson's claim that "a daughter who has experienced faulty maternal empathy can gain self-worth through acting as an extension of her mother . . . [and as an adult], can choose a love object who [*sic*] she views as omnipotent . . . and achieve self-valuation through her identification of 'fusion' with this person." "Heterosexual Antagonisms and the Politics of Mothering," *Socialist Review* 12, 6 (November-December 1982): 55-77. This literature would obviously be relevant in considering the minority of obsessive readers (see note 22). But I very much resist the presumption that Harlequin reading is by definition neurotic.

48. It seems that Harlequin Enterprises knows this, for their marketing strategy includes free distribution of Harlequins to new mothers in hospital.

49. Lillian Rubin, *Worlds of Pain: Life in the Working Class Family*, (Basic Books, 1976): 40-41. The same deprivation and its link to romantic fantasy is evident in such other accounts of working class family and community as in Basil Henriques et al., *Coal is Our Life: An Analysis of a Yorkshire Mining Community*, and Meg Luxton, *More Than a Labour of Love: Three Generations of Women's Work in the Home*, (Toronto: Women's Press, 1980). The women interviewed by Radway and reported in *Reading the Romance*, and those by Margaret Jensen, op. cit., themselves give eloquent direct testimony to this.

50. Jill Tweedie, "Beautiful and Doomed," *The Guardian Weekly*, (28 March 1982).

51. Snitow, p. 154, citing Joanna Russ, "Somebody's Trying to Kill Me and I Think It's My Husband: The Modern Gothic," *Journal of Popular Culture* 6, 4 (Spring 1983): 666-691.

52. Janice Radway, *Reading the Romance*, p. 84. (See note 40 for a brief indication of the role Radway ascribes to this evocation of infancy in her overall analysis of Harlequin reading.)

53. It would be interesting to see if romance fantasy generally plays a different role for lesbian than for heterosexual women. If my analysis is correct, it may be that romance fantasies play a less important role for lesbian women both because, paradoxically, a female "hero" is a less convincing representative of the powerful mother, and because more lesbian than heterosexual women may have mutually nurturing relationships.

    I have lesbian friends who read Harlequins, which is in itself an interesting indication that they are about something more than heterosexual love and sex. Further research on lesbian women's relationship to romance would doubtless provide valuable insights into the romance phenomenon.

54. Profiles of romance readers from different surveys vary somewhat but all indicate that "[the readers] mirror the general population in age, education, marital, [employment], and socio-economic status." Carol Thurston, "The Liberation of Pulp Romances," *Psychology Today*, (April 1983): 14-15. (Bracketed word added on the basis of information from other surveys.)

55. This helps make comprehensible the fact that women brutalized by men often read romances or even begin to read them when things get bad. They are under no illusion that real life or real men in any way resemble the Harlequin world or the Harlequin hero. The comfort from escape is nevertheless enormous because it does not depend on any expectations of a male saviour or male comfort.

56. For feminist theoretical literature which supports the notion that women have a special relationship to power see: Nancy Hartsock, Sara Ruddick, both op. cit.; Berit As, "A Materialist View of Men's and Women's Attitudes Towards War," *Women Studies International Forum* 5, 3: 355-364; and articles in *Reweaving the Web of Life: Feminism and Non-Violence*, ed. Pam McAllister (New Society Publishers, 1982).

57. The theoretical study of women's specific sexuality is less developed than the study of our specific relationship to the world and to power. But circumstantial evidence from a number of sources supports the implications from Harlequins that intimacy, nurture, and security are central to women's erotic pleasure. When Ann Landers asked her readers "Would you be content to be held close and treated tenderly and forget about 'the act'?" 72 percent of the 90,000 women who responded said "Yes" and 40 percent of these were less than 40 years old (Shere Hite, *Women and Love: Cultural Revolution in Progress*, [New York: Knopf, 1987]).

Those with the inveterate androcentric assumption that men's experience and desires are necessarily women's have predictably presumed that these women are all very sad cases of repression or stunted sexual development or have never experienced the "real thing." At a certain point, however, it becomes perverse not to use women's responses to understand women's desires. Once we do this we are led unavoidably to the question of whether sex and the erotic are the same for men and women.

58. The theoretical bases of women's more connected sense of self and the world and greater capacity for mutually affirming interdependence are described by Mary O'Brien, Nancy Chodorow, Dorothy Dinnerstein, and Jane Flax (all op. cit.). Influential studies of this specific female experience and its psychological and social importance have been done by Jean Baker Miller, *Toward a New Psychology of Women*, (Boston: Beacon, 1976) and Carol Gilligan, *In a Different Voice: Psychological Theory and Women's Development*, (Cambridge: Harvard University Press, 1982).

59. Some writers who rightly challenge the extremely negative stereotyping of Harlequin readers and point out that we are active participants in the process and not mere passive victims, have moved from this to a representation of Harlequins as more benign than I think is warranted. See, for instance, the defense of Harlequins and Harlequin reading in Margaret Jensen, Gail Hamilton, Tatiana Tolstoi, all op. cit.; and Emily Toth, "Who'll Take Romance?" *Women's Review of Books* 1, 5 (February 1984): 12-13.

60. Janice G. Raymond, *A Passion for Friendship: Toward a Philosophy of Female Affection*, (Boston: Beacon, 1986).

61. Unless you are of the school that believes the objective should be to make life as difficult as possible for as many women as possible so eventually "they" will rise up—a sort of feminist version of the hope with which some leftists have been watching the cost of the recession on ordinary people, waiting for the time when the "crisis of capitalism" becomes its collapse and things get so bad that people finally rebel and the revolution arrives!

There is a hint of this position in some of the critiques of Harlequins that suggest that they offer an escape which prevents women from struggling to change their lives. It seems, however, that women's lives are hard enough even with Harlequins. A social critique and a commitment to social change seem to come when women get the support that gives us the power and the space to question and to act. That should surely be what we are aiming to provide, not additional pressure.

62. The dominant patriarchal cultures in Arab countries and in Japan, for instance, do not encourage romantic fantasy or the myth of male mothering, and yet women in these countries and the Caribbean seem to find them enormously satisfying.

63. Adrienne Rich, *Of Woman Born: Motherhood as Experience and Institution*, (New York: Bantam, 1977), p. 257.

64. Rich, p. 225. There is, in fact, a well developed feminist practice which recognizes our relationships with our mothers and our relational needs as both barriers and resources which must be consciously embraced and transformed in our personal/political struggle for a more human and freer world. See also: Sara Ruddick, "Maternal Thinking," and *Between Women*, op. cit., especially the chapters by Bell Gale Chevigny, Jane Lazarre, Jane Marcus, Sara Ruddick, and Martha Wheelock; Jane Lazarre, op. cit; Baba Copper, "Mothers and Daughters of Imagination," *Trivia* 11 (Fall 1987): 8-20; and Judith Arcana, *Our Mothers, Ourselves*.

8

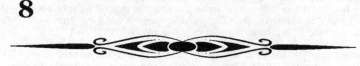

SPATIAL ENVY
YVONNE RAINER'S
THE MAN WHO ENVIED WOMEN

Peggy Phelan

Near the end of Yvonne Rainer's recent film, *The Man Who Envied Women*, the frame is filled for the second time with Donald Judd's large grey concrete sculptures luxuriating in an open Texas field.[1] The camera walks across these sculptures like fingers over a piano: they seem to hold a kind of tune half hidden, half audible. The sculptures are concrete outlines of squares the color of tombstones. The heaviness of their frame accentuates the hollowness of the air they embrace. Like a Wittgensteinian word game, or better still, like Mark Strand's witty poem "Keeping Things Whole", Judd's sculptures suggest that "space" is that which negotiates between airy fields (infinite possibilities) and concrete architecture (finite facts), while not residing entirely in either the one or the other. As Strand puts it anthropomorphically: "When I walk/I part the air/and always the air moves in/to fill the spaces/where my body's been". Filling in the spaces created by departing persons, places, and things is the central concern of *The Man Who Envied Women*. Judd's sculptures, with their refusal to locate or define a spatial point of origin or termination, are the objective correlative for the difficult idea of space that Rainer's film alternatively vigilantly argues for, and whimsically hopes for. In this combination of argument and hope Rainer's film resembles some of the best work of Jean-Luc Godard.

More interesting than the visual absence of the image of Trisha the female protagonist, is Rainer's innovative expansion of the possiblities of the surface of the film. Using video transfers as kind of windows (frames-within-frames), grainy super-8 as an interruption of the smoother surface of the film, the fragments from classic Hollywood and avant-garde films as Jack's interior mental landscapes, Rainer disallows the pleasurable illusion of a visually polished art piece and forces in its stead a reconfiguration of the traditional architecture of the frame. Rainer describes her attempt to break down the frame as a: "disruption of the glossy, unified surface of professional cinematography by means of optically degenerated shots within an otherwise seamlessly edited narrative sequence... . I'm talking about films where in every scene you have to decide anew the priorities of looking and listening."[2] This refusal to maintain a "unified [visual] surface" mirrors the film's disdain for traditional narrative coherence and progression. In place of the spatial and temporal homogeneity we expect in narrative films, Rainer creates a much more difficult unity.

The Man Who Envied Women's subject is not so much "a week in the life of Trisha," although it is partially that; the film is mainly interested in chronicling the manifestations and consequences of the pervasive malaise of spatial envy. This subject makes issues as apparently diverse as the politics of Central America, the Manhattan real estate crunch, the vicissitudes of sexual and social relations, the virility and impotence of poststructuralism, and the medicalization of women's bodies, seem deeply intertwined. Imperialism in Central America and New York love affairs are similar, for example, in that they are each motivated, in part, by the desire to gain space. In Rainer's film the latter is wryly represented by the only half-funny one liner: "When are we getting married so I can have your apartment when we get divorced?" The Central American situation, as we shall see, is treated much more somberly. Using a collage of "moving pictures" as a kind of collective interpretive Rorschach, Rainer is able to swing a wide and fluid net over these seemingly unrelated topics. These moving pictures function as a kind of classical Chorus which punctuate the drama Rainer's film unfolds. Initially assembled by the visually absent but-very-present Trisha, they are recreated and rearranged no less than six times in the film; their spatial rearrangements parallel the shifting spaces and stories of spatial envy which animate *The Man Who Envied Women.*

Rather than beginning with a "feeling for form," Rainer's film begins by underlining the incoherence of form. Postulating that form always involves the possession (imaginative or actual) of space, Rainer begins her narrative proper with Trisha's double loss of space. After moving out of the apartment she shares with Jack, she is evicted from her studio. Trisha, the mysteriously elusive artist, begins between "spaces"; she is dis-possessed. She can create only in fragmented images, in cut-outs that she must—perforce—leave behind. This is the parable of loss, of always fragmented and interrupted formal concentration that the film slowly unfolds. Rainer's consistent disruption of the frame's space technically mirrors Trisha's cut up "home" and her cut-out art.

Trisha's opening monologue is just the first layer of Rainer's associative meditation on the implications of losing and gaining space:

> It was a hard week. I split up with my husband of four years
> and moved into my studio. The water heater broke and
> flooded the textile merchant downstairs. I bloodied up a
> pair of white linen pants. The Senate voted for nerve gas
> and my gynecologist went down in Korean Airlines flight
> #007. The worst of it was the gynecologist. He used to put
> booties on the stirrups and his speculum was always
> warm.

Although these events are linked in time, they are linked in other more subtle ways was well. To put it simply, albeit crudely: splitting up with Jack sets off a series of dismissals and departures. Trisha's flooding menstrual blood and her studio's flooding water heater are alike in their fits of unruliness against their spatial confines. This private and individual unruliness moreover, finds its public and political image in the dark drama of Korean Airlines flight #007. Overstepping, overflowing, or flying over the boundaries of space, no matter how visible or invisible such boundaries might appear, can have tragic consequences.

Trisha's overflowing menstrual blood is crucial; Rainer's title plays on the Freudian notion that women are beset with penis envy. Part of Rainer's aim is to turn the tables: she wants to suggest that men envy women in part because of their internal biological space. (Women, as it were, carry their "air space" inside them. To employ this metaphor psychoanalytically, and from the woman's point of view, violations of "air space" are acts of power: the physiological and social arrangments of heterosexuality combine to maintain women in a subordinate position to men. To suggest that male sexual desire is motivated at least partially by spatial envy, a country and western song might phrase it "hunger for a home", rape becomes not only a logical, but an inevitable consequence of the psychological-physiological architecture of heterosexuality.) Rainer uses the woman's body and the functions of its still mysterious spaces as a kind of lens through which contemporary "problems" can be evaluated. She tries to link the mind that thinks and the body that feels in a specifically womanly way. One might say she attempts to reinvestigate the traditional oppositions of Western metaphysics, in the wake of Derrida, from a feminist point of view.

Part of her correction to the story poststructuralism tells is stylistic. Metaphysics in Rainer's view cannot go too long without a joke; the film's most serious moments (with the exception of the last ten minutes or so) are continually undercut with a joke. In what J. Hoberman thinks is the best line in the film, Rainer, in a distorted off-center close-up reminiscent of Hitchcock, invites "all menstruating women [to] please leave the theatre."[3] This invitation is symptomatic of Rainer's most congenial habit of mind. Her most consistent impulse, and her most comfortable perspective, is from a distance—almost over her shoulder. This is not a film that asks the spectator to like the characters, to enjoy the scenery, to laugh heartily, or to nod one's head knowingly at all the familiar conversation. The effort at the heart of this film is as engaged in throwing you out as it is in settling you in.

I

Returning again to the enabling fiction of the analyst/analysand which she explored in *Journeys from Berlin/1971* (1980), Rainer's troubled and troubling male protagonist Jack Deller begins the film "on the couch." Deller's doctor is off-screen and voiceless (perhaps the ultimate representation of Rogerian client-centered therapy), and his confessions are actually the ponderously sounding words of Raymond Chandler's letters and diaries. Rainer's frequent tendency to have characters quote from other texts is part of her larger argument with narrative, and specifically with her sense that narrative constructs (inevitably) singular characters and singular points of view: by disallowing her characters singular linguistic habits she prohibits as well a singular habit of mind and a singular point of view. In a 1985 article in *Wide Angle*, Rainer comments that her indefatigably quoting characters help "foreground not only the production of narrative but its frustration and cancellation as well...Words are uttered but not possessed by my performers as they operate within the filmic frame but do not propel a filmic plot." Deller sees himself as a man more gifted and blessed than troubled and cursed. He is a university professor—he teaches film theory, sort of—with Leftist leanings who uses words to seduce everyone (especially himself) into a cocoon of babel more hypnotic than revelatory. During his "sessions" Jack sits in a chair facing the camera. He sits on the left side of the frame, and continually gazes beyond the left vertical end imposed by the frame. This invisible space is acutely present in his monologues, just as the visually absent Trisha is acutely present in the narrative texture of the film. Jack, more than any other character in the film, is desperately dependent upon an audience. That the audience for his intimate meanderings turns out to be "the spectator" who is forced into the position of "the doctor," is just one overt example of Rainer's obsessive tendency to suggest that film's effort to address is, absolutely, dependent upon an erasure. The first word of the film, "doctor," addresses someone who is not there. The standard critical claim that the spectator always identifies with the camera requires that the camera become a surrogate spectator. The camera, in so becoming, literally effaces the spectator. The power of the camera's eye (the potentially ideal I/eye) in addition to showing us objects and lending us its gaze, also shows us up. The space of the frame can be rented or leased but it can never be owned. The camera's vision is presented but not possessed in much the way Rainer's characters "utter but do not possess" their own language. The illusion of cinema's visual realism is radically denied by Rainer's meandering and deliberately disunified visual frames. Her most sustained investigation of the ontology of the filmic image occurs, suitably, in Jack's struggle to separate and make coherent his parcelled past: that is, in Jack's sessions with the invisible doctor.

At one point, Jack sits in his chair facing the doctor/spectator to the left, and the camera moves back to reveal an audience completely absorbed in watching the film clips playing next to his head. The scene is unsettling. The film clip is from *The Night of the Living Dead*, and the spectators begin to attack each other as the film images grow more chaotic and the sound track more discursive (in a three way phone conversation Trisha summarizes Chodorow's and Dinnerstein's arguments and ruminates on the associations between the name "Jack Deller" and fairy tales). Despite all the aural and visual ornamentation, this sequence forces the spectator to reexperience the acute psychic discomfort that comes from the recognition of the profound connection between voyeurism and cinema. There is nothing original about this connection of course, but what is original (and awful) is the disturbing connection this particular sequence demands. The mayhem produced by the images of *The Night of the Living Dead* literally incites the audience to perform its own aggressive mayhem. Given that these clips are in the same spatial frame as Jack's "confessions," the underlying connection implicitly suggests that psychoanalysis, like cinema, in relying on "projection" as its paradigmatic principle, is inherently voyeuristic. To discover that the only position one can take in this "long shot" is the role of the doctor is to discover as well that one's interest in Jack (cinematically and psychoanalytically) stems from a desire to "treat" him. More uncomfortably, it is to realize that one's interest in the similarities between the "cinematic apparatus" and the psychoanalytic paradigm stems from the spectator's own desire to be "treated".

Jack's central concern in these sessions is his relationship to women, a relationship that undergoes a radical change after the death of his first wife. Trisha, his second wife, has left him after four years, in part because of his inability to be faithful. His well-designed explanations for his lack of fidelity essentially consist of his belief that after his idealized first wife died, he became incapable of seeing women as anything other than sacred gifts. To turn down such a gift verges on the sacrilegious—and our Jack is no heretic. One gift he has inherited from Trisha, a gift he did not ask for, is her "art work." Jack asks Trisha to take it with her when she moves out. She says she'll return for it. Insofar as *The Man Who Envied Women* has a narrative "plot," it is this early promise of return that the film uses as its departing point. Like everything else, the meeting is interrupted, even superseded, by the promise of another meeting between Jack and Jack-ie (Raynal), who are also ex-lovers. This meeting actually does occur, and it is from the unsettling perspective of their relationship that almost all of the varied threads the film unwinds come together. But as we wait for the party, the "meaning" of the art that is left behind, the hieroglyphics of an unreachable—both visually and romantically—artist, consume more and more of Jack's attention.

This art work is a collage of magazine clippings; three come from *The Sunday New York Times* and two come from *Mother Jones*. They include: an "About Men" column written by a priest, an ad for a Central American cigar which features a rich man and his dog as the Barthesian "sign" of success, and a gruesome photograph of decapitated bodies with a caption which seems to identify one of the victims as a six month old Guatamalean child. The spatial arrangement of these images is continually revised. Off-screen voices create narratives of coherence about them. The connection between the cigar ad and the mutilated bodies is described allegorically: the successful cigar-selling man profits, both directly and indirectly, from the mutilation and death of Salvadorean peasants. The United States' interest in Central America is read as an imperial lust for the control of geographic space.

The plea for the "emotional" space of men represented by the "About Men" column is seen both economically (guess who profits?) and socially. That the space for this column occupies the Sunday paper, while the "Hers" column is put in the "Home" section of Thursday's *Times* ("among the latest sofas") is seen as an ideological manifestation of the privilege of space. More subtly, as the woman's voice narrates her objection to the partitioning of column space in a slightly whining way, the column becomes another source of spatial envy as well.

The ad for the menopausal drug is seen as part of the larger treatment of "women's problems" historically. It is linked to the themes of sexual difference in poststructural discourse. The precise relationship of the (by now) axiomatic connection between the textual body and the sexual body is explored with a twist that would make Roland Barthes cringe. Rather than seeing this connection as the source of Barthes' *jouissance*, a kind of perpetual foreplay which teases one to contemplate a mental and spiritual communion so intense it holds the potential for infinite ecstasy, Rainer suggests that the link between the mind that thinks and the body that feels is one of loss—a kind of permanent grief. Early on, Trisha makes a provocative connection between the ovaries and the brain: "The ovaries of a seven month old fetus contain almost 1,000,000 egg cells. From then on, the ova constantly decrease in number without replenishment. The only other cells to do this are those of the brain." The mutual process of dropping eggs and losing brain cells, neither of which are regenerative, revises the traditional (masculine) "mind/body split" into a more radical affinity. The body that feels and the mind that thinks are unified in their similar physiological movement from abundance to loss. The brain and the ovary then are the physiological kernels which sow, or so it would seem, a metaphysics not to acquisition, but of inevitable depletion.

The horrific image of the decapitated bodies (the split between the body and the mind so complete as to make Western metaphysics a

pathetic understatement), is the image that elicits the deepest meditation. In one of the only moments of unification between the sound track
and the image track, the voice of one of the off-screen commentators
(Martha Rosler's) breaks off as Deller's hand trails away from the wall
after shifting the images around in an effort to bury the gruesome image
(and the naked bodies) under all the other clippings. It is a moving
sequence, not only because Deller at last seems "in sync" with the world
of the film, but also because one of the questions of "owning space"
hinges—apparently absolutely—on someone else losing it.

This relationship is explored with a poignant befuddlement as Rainer
follows the sequence of public hearings called to consider Manhattan's
recent proposal to allocate housing funds to artists moving into the
Lower East Side. The idea behind this plan was to keep New York City as
a congenial "space" for art and artists—a cynical observer might say that
the idea exposes New York's own imperial lust for cultural supremacy—
but no matter: contemplating "moving to Jersey" is viewed with equal
horror by all members of the hearings. One of the unfortunate consequences of this proposal was that it pitted the artists against the ethnic
working-class whose very presence in Rainer's overtly theoretical film,
calls into question the efficacy of art and the aesthetic impulse to
manipulate and re-order space for some artistic good. The immense
space of Donald Judd's sculptural field and the huge canvases of Leon
Golub suddenly seem absurd: do "images" and "representations" de-
serve/need to consume so much space? Do we participate in the
construction and maintenance of a world in which "representation"
literally dominates our lives, and robs some people of four walls? "Almost
overnight we met the enemy," Trisha declares, "and it was us."

II

If the spatial arrangements and rearrangements of Trisha's abandoned
art work (work that has fallen under the gaze of hyper-articulate eyes)
constitute the melody of the film, part of its rhythmic structure comes
from Jack's magic headphones. Like some fantastic state-of-a-future-art
walkman, Jack's oversized mechanical ears make him privy to the
conversations of Manhattan street-strollers. It is perhaps the triplicate
repetition of these scenes that prompts Hoberman to dub Rainer "the
Purple Rose of Soho," and to compare her films to Woody Allen's.
Rainer's one-liners are dry and infectious. They are also obsessively
concerned with sex. The space between Jack's ears, by implication,
seems overloaded with sexual puns: his head selectively receives the
world from a sexual point of view.

In the first issue of *Motion Picture*, Rainer writes that the purpose of
these scenes is to convey the idea that the city, for Jack, is a "place full

of sexual anxiety, obsession, and verbal assault, litanies of sexual distress...[It is] a barrage—a veritable eruption—of ordinarily repressed material." But the problem is that the conversations are all in one-key: if it is a jungle it specializes in one animal. More importantly, these jokes are all about sexual stereotypes: gay men as housewives, feminism as a badge of admittance for politically correct men to a wider set of women's bedrooms, and so on. If these cliches are supposed to frighten a man who spouts off the subtle seductions of Foucault and who speaks of the cinematic apparatus as an intimate echo of Lacanian subjectvity, then he is in really sorry shape. But I think Rainer's aim and its effect are quite different. We tend not, I think, to take these lines as symptomatic of Jack's fear: we tend to take them as welcome comic relief.

Jack's "character" is a literal embodiment of Bakhtin's "heteroglossia" in that it comes to us only through other texts.[4] Rainer refuses to have him cohere. Played by two actors (Bill Raymond and Larry Loonin) and with little or no laughter, he seems a strange bird indeed. His psychic "revelations" are the machismo fantasies of Chandler augmented by Hollywood films playing next to his forehead. In one exceptional exception, instead of seeing one of these clips, we see a slow motion black and white clip of Trisha Brown's riveting performance of *Water Motor*. The dance floods the frame within the frame; Brown's movements are enchantingly suggestive of the body as water; her body flows with an eroticism that is seemingly incorporeal.

To see this lyrical moment as part of Jack's world (either his imaginative dream or his hallucination of his first wife) is to reassess his own position therein. One wants to credit him, however, marginally, with some dignity: if he can talk in a way which evokes this woman dancing, he might have once moved in circles which once touched her. His incredibly nostalgic descriptions of his first wife, which initially seem like one more layer of defense about the failure of his second marriage to Trisha, are rearranged and reconfigured as Brown dances; his descriptions of her turn into something much less defensive, something verging on an accurate testimony of a real gift. That his response to the evocation of this world also includes masturbating while clutching *Playboy* and seducing students with his many tongues makes our response to his several selves more complicated.

The ambivalence of our response to Jack is most strongly felt in the climatic hallway scene. At last Jack and Jackie meet; at last *The Man Who Envied Women* fulfills one of its narrative promises. They meet, suitably, at the edge of the party—in the hallway facing the elevator (and its promise of exit) and perpendicular to the door leading to the exuberant party (and its promise of social entry). Shot in this claustrophobically narrow hallway, Jack and Jackie start draping each other with words. Like children with their parents' clothes, they dress each other in disguises one can only half believe they believe. And again, they quote. He quotes Foucault—mainly on the ubiquitous locales of power; she quotes Meaghan Morris—mainly on the impotence of theory.[5] The way the words are spoken is unbelievably erotic: their voices seem to dot i's with their own winking eyes and t's are crossed with thick tongues. The words and the voices seem visceral: one is intoxicated both cerebrally and physically. But the scene is more than rhetorical Olympics (first prize: The Other); it is a sort of Joycean epiphanic moment: not for the characters (who are by this time almost completely peripheral to the "coherence" of Rainer's plots) but for the film itself.

Jackie is not speaking *to* Jack: she addresses a different spectator altogether. She seems to be addressing on/off-screen Trisha. Or at least, it would seem that Trisha hears Jackie more clearly than Jack does. Jackie's voice, thick with a French accent, is passionate and sounds half sleepy. She wears a kind of shimmering gown that half reveals her breasts. The camera scrutinizes her with a pleasure it simply cannot find in Jack. She rolls her tongue around these amazingly large words with the strange wonder of a French woman speaking English as if for the first time; the sounds of the words resonant with the confidence of their own originality, they are sure they have never been spoken in quite this way before. As I watch this scene I feel as if the theatre will collapse under all these words; as if there should be a rating for films based solely on the number of words spoken into little rooms; as if seduction is made up of nothing but words.

This slow seduction underscores Jack's ironic insistence on repeating Foucault's axiom: "There is no opposition between what is said and what is done." As Jack and Jackie move intellectually further and further apart, their bodies move closer and closer together. As Jack continually repeats Foucault's arguments about the ubiquitous dispersion of power, Jackie categorizes and delimits differences in the power to discriminate power. Jack is content to ignore "what is said" for what might "be done." He seems not to hear a thing she says. Jackie is, in almost a literal sense, speaking a different langauge:

> Only the naive humanist feminist thinks she can change something by changing her consciousness; the rigorous feminist plumbs the hidden depths of subjectivity, studies its construction in language…winds through the labyrinth to find not a monster but a new position of the subject…One awkward consequence of the freudo-marxist marriage presided over by language, is to open up an inviting space for marxist and feminist laborers which can only be defined by the hystematic evacuation of certain questions—political,economic, and above all historical questions…Theory as a watchdog is a poor creature: not because it is nasty or destructive but because for attacking the analysis of confrontation it simply has no teeth.

As if this is the permission Rainer has been waiting for, the remainder of *The Man Who Envied Women* moves steadily away from the theoretical pronouncement (the world of Jack) to a more personal, and more tentative meditation. We move more comfortably and more completely into the world of the imagination. This world, entered only through the portal of the feminine, is formally invoked (evoked?) by Jackie, who again borrows Morris' words:

> Passing from the realm of the theory of the subject to the shifty spaces of feminine writing is like emerging from a horror movie to a costume ball...Feminine writing lures with an invitation to licence, gaiety, laughter, desire and dissolution, a fluid exchange of partners of indefinite identity.

Underscoring this change in mental space Rainer cuts to Trisha's narration of a dream. She dreams her mother and Jack are lovers. Both mother and daughter are played by Rainer. Just as Trisha seems to accept that her mother is Jack's lover, the mother watches Jack and Trisha (disguised behind a paper mask) in bed together. Now Trisha is furious. But the dream is so obviously funny, so clearly a willful Oedipal reconfiguration that Trisha's refusal to laugh seems hilarious. Trisha's eyes are so completely disguised she is apparently unable to see herself. Fittingly, slinking through this "Oedipal extravaganza"—the phrase is Rainer's—is a one-eyed cat. Cut back to the hallway. Jack and Jackie are embracing all the rhetorical possibilities of physically embracing.

And then again Trisha's voice: "If a girl takes her eyes off Lacan and Derrida long enough to look she may discover she is the invisible man." That the film's invisible woman, Trisha, says this only heightens the irony; the film abandons the poetics of theory and individual masculinity for a more persuasive look at Trisha's moving pictures.

As it happens when theory is not the loudest voice in the room, what the eye sees when it looks again is a different image altogether. Trisha's concluding ruminations, unlike Jack's initial confessions, are tentative and groping:

> Lately I've been thinking yet again I can't live without men but I can live without a man. I've had this thought before, but this time the idea is not colored by stigma or despair for finality. I know that there will sometimes be excruciating sadness but I also know something is different now, something in the direction of unwomanliness. Not a new woman, not non-woman, or misanthropist, or anti-woman, and not non-practicing lesbian. Maybe un-woman is also the wrong term. A-woman is closer. A-womanly. A-womanliness.

I must admit that I'm not sure what Trisha means by this. She seems willing and ready to bury Jack's hold on her. And ready to bury something larger as well. Among the more enigmatically haunting sequences in the film is an early one in which Trisha complains that her father chose this week to "pop out." In Trisha's various retellings of her stories of "life with Jack" there is a feeling that she is telling the story of life with Pop as well. Trisha's exasperation with the way the memory of her father intrudes upon her recollection of "life with Jack" speaks to the doubleness of the pain of mourning. The father, like Jack, intrudes on Trisha—both as a maddeningly inadequate presence and as a persistent and unwelcome absence. This is all in the realm of speculation—there is little direct reference to this in the film. But what is germane to Trisha's announce-ment of "something different now" is the persistent hope that if a-womanliness means anything at all, it might have some impact on Trisha's Oedipal dreams. With Pop and Jack tucked back in the suitcase, maybe Trisha, her mother, and the one-eyed cat can create a new dream. One that may well be filled with "excruciating sadness," but one that might yet be allowed the representation of a dream-text, one that might raise the hiterto repressed.

We return again to the art work—for one last rearrangement. This time Rainer asks, "If this were an art work how would you critique it?" The answer brilliantly recasts the connections between the images and susggests that spatial arrangements, artistic and rationalistic, are inher-ently political. I quote just briefly from Rosler's long argument:

> I would feel I was being tricked into trying to deal with things that have become incommensurable as though they weren't incommensurable. That I was being told that the myths of civility at home and the problems of daily life are only a veneer over the truth that the state destroys people. It is as though I were being told that when dealing with the ultimate, my worries about how I live my life in America are not important.

She then goes on to elucidate the ways in which the arrangements of the images tell political and visual stories. The uncaring emotional facade of men that the "About Men" column argues against, "determine[s] how we conduct our foreign policy. It isn't only a matter of economic interest, but of how we choose to pursue that interest. If we're willing to grind up other people because we can't be bothered to feel about them then it does matter." What she argues for then is a new notion of spatial privilege—an anti-privilege; or maybe that's the wrong term—privilege-lessness is closer. A world in which the space one occupies (publicly and privately) is not subject to or the object of envy; a world that Judd's sculptural embraces create when their spatial beginnings and endings cannot be defined or located.

The fact that the sculptures themselves dominate a wide open field in Texas underlines the distance we need to traverse before such an ideal spatial arrangement might occur. Judd's sculptures, in other words, demand a second look. Rainer's film proposes a democracy of spatial equality so radical that its very proposal requires a continual rearrangement not only of the images in the frame but of the frame itself.

III

I said earlier that the identification between the camera and the spectator inevitably effaces the power of the spectator and that implied within this effacement there was a failure of address. Jack's sessions which address an absent doctor and are augmented by films addressed to an audience alert to other texts, underscore the difficulty of filmic address. The spectator is the film's invisible hearer, its unseen doctor and deliverer of catharsis. At the "Narrative Poetics Conference" at Ohio State University, Teresa DeLauretis argued that Rainer's film encouraged her to feel addressed as a women spectator and that the success of this fulsome address was one of the greatest achievements of *The Man Who Envied Women*. DeLauretis contended that the film saw as a woman sees and that it did not bow to the conventions of the male gaze (conventions that DeLauretis has long beeen skeptical about but are nonetheless recognized by most feminist film critics) and thus advanced both feminist film theory and film practice.[6] Insofar as the distinction between gender specific points-of-view has any validity, it is certainly true that *The Man Who Envied Women* is animated from and for a women's eye. My earlier point was more concerned with underlining the challenge of Rainer's film in terms of address itself. By upsetting the conventions of filmic point of view (e.g.: not showing Trisha at all and thus making it impossible to follow her gaze; the conflicting narrative angles of the plot(s) et al.), Rainer also challenges the conventions of filmic address. By "address" I mean not only the complicated and complicating processes of identification between "character" and spectator, but also the more simple feeling of belongingness—as if one is invited and encouraged to be engaged. More than simply saying post-Brechtian film, and avant-garde film in particular, makes the spectator feel alienated—makes the spectator recognize the gap between the technical camera eye and her own eye, I'm trying to say that what Rainer's film suggests is that film's deep dependency on point-of-view (gender specific or otherwise) as the primary means by which the spectator is given intimate access to a kind of knowledge, no matter how relative—as in the elegant equivocations of *Roshomon*—is what needs to be dismantled and understood as a seductive fiction. Insofar as Trisha's concluding remarks about "a-womanliness" can be seen as an abandonment of gender as a shorthand notion of identity, it would seem that Rainer is trying to abandon the ownership of (and perhaps film's conspiracy in the maintenance of) single identity itself.

The relationships between language, image, and character are individually and collectively rearranged in *The Man Who Envied Women*. Rainer's ambitious film underlines the ways in which narrative coherence demands and creates a spectator alert to a too simple coherence. The project of the film is not to delineate the reasons and motivations for Jack's envy of Trisha or Jack-ie; nor is it the story of Jack's transformation from bully to lover; I don't even think it's about the way in which film theory informs film practice although that is sort of distractingly interesting. I think the film is actually about the appetite to rearrange and reconfigure the connections between image, language and character in film, the desire to rearrange and reconfigure sexual relationships in "Life" and economic-political-spatial relationships in "Art" and in "The World," and I think it is about Rainer's own appetite for a new aesthetic of filmic architecture. (I ought to stress that I believe there is a difference between delineating an appetite for something and delineating the thing itself. *The Man Who Envied Women* is much more of a proposal and speculative dream than it is a programmatic manifesto; this too is in keeping with Rainer's witty metaphysics and Trisha's wide ruminations).

"Filmic architecture" borders on the oxymoronic: architecture tends to connote stability and the fixing of and within space. It tends to connote sculptural fields like Judd's and towers like Trump's. Rainer's *filmic* architecture takes flexibility and flow as defining principles, and film's inevitable failure to meet the desire to fix or possess space itself as its philosophic spine. *The Man Who Envied Women* rejuvenates the political/aesthetic agenda of the avant-garde film in its method, and it challenges contemporary critical theory's thralldom with masculinist modes in its argument. *The Man Who Envied Women* challenges theory's own desire for possession and coherence. Theory's panting after discursive space is perhaps not only a logical but an inevitable consequence of the desperation and parcelling out of "space" in critical discourse itself. Film studies, feminist or otherwise, exists in a discursive space that encourages (even demands) "possession." The bitter irony, of course, is that film's most radical potential lies in its resistance to being possessed or owned.

Film's ability to move pictures continuously, to endlessly rearrange the cut-outs by which and through which we come to see and project identity and ownership, and through which we come to desire them both, demonstrates as well the importance of challenging our own comfort with the conventions of coherence. In film, the particularly comfortable conventions are sharply delineated points of view (owning stories) and the modes of address typical of narrative and documentary film. From the first ten minutes of super-8 film, through the video "documentary" of the housing hearings, Rainer constantly manipulates the surface of her film. We, like Jack, are left with cut-outs whose "meaning" lies in its potential to be endlessly rearranged. What makes this film more than a smart leftist manifesto, is the innovative way in which Rainer matches her political vision of privilegelessness with the aesthetic possibilities of interrupted and shared filmic space. Rainer degrades the values of the ownership of ideas, discourse, and Manhattan lofts, by continually rearranging what we expect film to own: the space of its frame.

Notes

1. *The Man Who Envied Women*. 16 mm, color, 125 min., 1985. Distributed by First Run Features, 153 Waverly Place, New York, New York, 10014, CFDC, 67A Portland St., Toronto, Ontario, M5V 2M9. All quotes unless otherwise noted are from the film. Art Simon discussed this paper with me with admirable patience and insight. I thank him and hereby absolve him of responsibility for what follows.

2. Rainer, "Some Ruminations around Cinematic Antidotes to the Oedipal Net (les) while Playing with DeLauraedipus Mulvey, or, He May Be Off Screen, but..." *The Independent*, April, 1986: 25.

3. J. Hoberman, "The Purple Rose of Soho," *The Village Voice*, April 8, 1986:64. Hoberman lucidly summarizes the feminist theoretical implications of Rainer's decision not to show Trisha's image.

4. See M.M. Bakhtin, *The Dialogic Imagination*, ed. by Michael Holquist, trans. by Holquist and Caryl Emerson (Austin: University of Texas Press, 1982). See especially, "Discourse in the Novel," the final essay. "Heteroglossia" is defined and discussed on p. 263 and following.

5. Most of the Foucault comes from *Discipline and Punish* translated by Alan Sheridan (Random House: Vintage Books, 1974).; the Morris quotes are taken from, "The Pirate's Fiancé" in *Michel Foucault: Power, Truth, Strategy* (Sydney: Feral Publications, 1979), edited by Meaghan Morris and Paul Patton.

6. DeLauretis' talk was delivered with humor and polemical zeal. Rainer was present at the conference, and *The Man Who Envied Women* was shown the night before DeLauretis' talk. Rainer answered questions after the screening but did not comment publicly after DeLauretis' talk.

III

PHALLUS OF MALICE

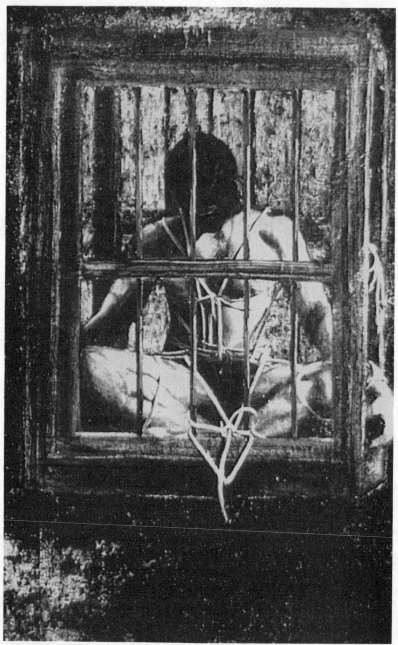

Attila Richard Lukacs, *Still*

9

PARADING THE MASCULINE:
FIGURES, DECOYS AND OTHER CANARDS

Chris Tysh

Father can't you see I'm burning?

In the garden of enunciation an explosion shatters daddy's house. Tantamount to a surrender, deafening cries, glass debris accumulate around what is left of the paternal store, other substitutes. Many are said to have seen the thing itself, summoned from the night like a spectral evidence, speak in a stage whisper. Lights, inseparable from representation, dim and jam the view. At curtain rise, faintly rouged and nude he reads from a text.

> He remembered the moment of his birth and how he had been pulled gently from his mother's womb. He remembered the infinite kindness of the world and all the people he had ever loved. Nothing mattered now but the beauty of all this. He wanted to go on writing about it, and it pained him to know that this would not be possible. Nevertheless, he tried to face the end of the red notebook with courage. He wondered if he had it in him to write without a pen, if he could learn to speak instead; filling the darkness with his voice, speaking the words into the air, into the walls, into the city, even if the light never came back again.[1]

Fawn-lily in his mouth, he repeats the account with the insincere tone of amazement.

> The timber present in plenty from top to bottom of the building (the furniture, the old-style parquet flooring, the ceilings with no thermal insulation, the panelling, and even the carcasing of the walls) subsequently enabled the fire to spread with incredible speed through every part of the edifice, which for its stately appearance was constructed entirely in lightweight materials, as was common practice at the time. The firemen, after a long struggle, managed only to inundate with great streams of water a few charred remains *forming a paltry heap, as if all that had burned there had been a very small shed.*[2]

                                        Lordship error.

Outside, flowers of speech already direct the rescue operation. Gazing is allowed its ruined bonus.

                    * * * *

dear luce:
   Translate my name, God said. First begin with the kiss you owe me, a debt magnified by our discursive tatters, riven by schisms. How much longer will I be able to duck the fenced carnival booths, the imperturbable logic of appropriations, sliding the ring, choking up on their new fault lines? This little pig went to market.

> Here there is a question, let us call it historical whose *conception, formation, gestation*, and *labor*, we are only catching a glimpse of today. I employ these words, I admit, with a glance toward the operations of childbearing—but also with a glance toward those who, in a society from which I do not exclude myself, turn their eyes away when faced by the as yet unnameable which is proclaiming itself and which can do so, as is necessary whenever a birth is in the offing, only under the species of the nonspecies, *in the formless, mute, infant and terrifying form of monstrosity.*[3]

                              Ah, the lovely colonnades,

tether, law, solace, the din of language which both writes and wounds, screens and opens to the possibilities of fashioning a new space, hammered out the way she is observed removing a hair from her tongue, suppressing an involuntary spasm. How easily the hymen is pressed to the margin, posted far away from us, the logical *destinaires*, to supplement and console for the recent bootlegging and pillage.

> Loss of legitimation, loss of authority, loss of seduction, loss of genius—*loss*.[4]

Far from seeing in these various deperditions a shift to a new topography aligned with a libertarian collapsing of the old master narratives, one cannot help reading a certain punitive rhetoric, constructed upon the demands of naming culprits.

> From the critical theory of the Frankfurt School to the pop-critique of Christopher Lasch, the discussion of loss of authority inevitably comes around to women, who return, empirically, as among those principally to blame for this loss.[5]

P.S. Dear maleman, if it is true that *une lettre arrive toujours à sa destination*,[6] return to sender after five days, your signature will be my charge of pleasure, my wound yours, name and leader.

> Woman's destiny is to be wanton, like the bitch, the she-wolf; she must belong to all who claim her.[7]

Under the current banner of delegitimation of the phallus (and the obligatory determining and determined effects) we give in to a particular fallacy by subscribing to a gift scenario in which the up till now unrepresentable female, the faulty, delinquent fringed other is being bequeathed to those mostly discredited by the postmodern regime of fatherlessness. Whereas what is closer to the real and what motivates this reinscription of the masculine is certainly not a sense of generosity on women's part but the imaginary distortion (as in Althusser's famous definition of ideology) which posits a female *méconnaissance*, a not-seeing that under the new discursive economy canonized on suppressing paternal authority the wolf's paw is still holding fast to the proffered bite. The heavily financed crisis in masculine subjectivity—which some commentators in a tell-tale sign of obeisance to cultural nostalgia have dubbed hysteric—interpellates the logic of disinheritance with the most cunning, most recuperative twist possible under the circumstances. One could suture at this precise juncture a well known mechanism derived from the mourning economy in order to read this production of surplus value where normally loss is warranted.

> alors éclatait le désespoir, ce moment le plus étrange du deuil, lorsque dans la chambre mortuaire, *les plus proches*

s'ajoutent celui dont ils sont diminués, se sentent de la
même substance, aussi respectable que lui et même se
considèrent comme le mort authentique, seul digne de
s'imposer à la tristesse commune.[8]

The preposterous canard consists of this monumental reversal by
which the male hysteric "adds onto himself that by which he is diminished," in effect purchasing another site to appropriate (and collect his
rent). What was indexed as negative in us is reconstituted as a plus factor
after this, *somme toute*, painless crossing of gender boundaries, or
"papa's got a brand new bag."[9]

Commodities cannot themselves go to
market and perform exchanges in their
own right.[10]

Stamped with new ideological configurations (where an unmistakable
odor di femina replaces priority of the phallus as purveyor of meaning
and value), the masculine subject is caught rehearsing the double game
of hysteria or what Derrida calls *écriture à deux mains*.

The hysterical symptom, in fact, is the expression of a
double unconscious fantasy: the patient simultaneously
and contradictorily, in terms of logic of consciousness
plays both roles, masculine and feminine.[11]

The politics of this practice take on the manner mirror of the hysteric
who, not content "to experience both the woman's and the man's
sensations in the situation he conjures up for himself,"[12] has the supreme
audacity to *capitalize* on a self marked by a spot where desire is worn out
by the memory of all losses.

* * * *

somebody almost walked off wid
alla my stuff[13]

Did somebody almost walk off wid alla my stuff? Or what? Did you say
that? My différence (anse quand tu nous tiens) is spread out over there
and Messieurs the Innkeepers of Logos can just amble by, smell and
rummage my fluidity, finger your oh so carnavalesque heterogeneity, fist-
fuck her utopian indecidability and for kicks drape our fragmentation,
gap, contradictions, on their very male selves. Mind you, they're not
really buying, "just trying them on" to see if they fit some possible
scenario, up there on the stage of the 21st century Symposium on

Philosophy for the Future, or The World of Difference, partaking of a little illicit frisson of masquerade, a license to rouge up without blushing or losing their aplomb: a ceremony of last resort, a flight of hysterical fancy one could call philosophical slumming. Curiously this transitivism (cf. Freud's notion, according to which the child who beats says he is beaten) or transvestism, bears no resemblance to the outrageous drag queens we have become familiarized with in the productions of Genet, Selby, or Fassbinder. One has only to bring to mind Divine in *Notre Dame des Fleurs* crowning herself with her dental plate in a mad riot to overturn the tables, or yet follow Elvira Weishaupt, the tragic hero/ine of *In A Year Of Thirteen Moons*, into the dirty dawn of Kaiserstrasse thus to measure the incontrovertible distance that exists between these feminized males, spread, abused, humiliated, and the wolfish *figurants* of the hysteric theater busy with their fin-de-millennium pantomimes. The only way the current philosophical slumming could result in a tangible, durable transformation is, if, in the process of this theatricalized hysteria, the male subject were to become contaminated for a given lapse of time, in the optic of the traditional shamanistic rituals of "making ill in order to cure."[14] As for now, in the panic scrambling towards postmodern constructs of gender, these are merely power patterns on seamed stockings.

* * * *

Resting on the etymological bric à brac of hysteria, I summon a scene (faithful to Freud's dictum that hysterics suffer mainly from reminiscences) like the sound of mother tongue, the return of the wandering womb. Listen to the beggar woman.

> She walks all through the night, and the whole of the following day. Through rice-fields, rice-fields. The sky is low overhead. . . Under the white, searing sun, with the child still in her womb, she leaves her homeland. She is fearless now. Her way is clear before her. Her mother has pronounced sentence of exile, from which there is no appeal. Tears stream down her face, but she pays no heed to them. She is singing at the top of her voice, one of the songs she learnt as a child in the village of Battabang.[15]

Notes

1.   Paul Auster, *City of Glass*, (New York: Viking Penguin, 1987), p. 200.

2.   Alain Robbe-Grillet, *Recollections of a Golden Triangle*, (New York: Grove Press, 1986), trans. J. A. Underwood, p. 145: my emphasis.

3.   Jacques Derrida, *Writing And Difference*, trans. Alan Bass, (Chicago: University of Chicago Press, 1978), p. 293: my emphasis in the last two lines.

4.   Alice Jardine, *Gynesis*, (Ithaca and London: Cornell University Press, 1975), p. 68.

5.   Ibid., p.67.

6.   Jacques Lacan, "Le Séminaire sur *La Lettre Volée*," Ecrits, (Paris: Les Editions du Seuil, 1966), p. 41. (A letter always arrives at its destination).

7.   Marquis de Sade, *Philosophy in the Bedroom*, (New York: Grove Press, 1966), p. 219.

8.   Maurice Blanchot, *Thomas L'Obscur*, (Paris: Gallimard, 1950), p. 109: my emphasis, my translation:

"Then despair would break out, that strangest moment of mourning when in the mortuary chamber the relatives *add onto themselves the one by whom they are diminished*, feeling they are of the same substance, as respectable as he and even consider themselves to be the authentical dead, the only one worthy of commanding general sadness."

9.   James Brown

10. Karl Marx, *Capital*, quoted in Gillian Beer's "Representing Women: Representing The Past," *The Feminist Reader*, (New York: Basil Blackwell, 1989), p. 74. A quotation which cites Luce Irigary, *This Sex Which Is Not One*.

11. Sarah Kofman, *The Enigma Of Woman*, (Ithaca: Cornell University Press, 1985), p. 123.

12. Ibid. p. 124.

13. Ntozake Shange, *for colored girls who have considered suicide when the rainbow is enuf*, (New York: Collier Macmillan, 1977), p. 49.

14. Catherine Clément, "The Guilty One," *The Newly Born Woman*, (Minneapolis: University of Minnesota Press, 1986), trans. Betsy Wing, p. 15.

15. Marguerite Duras, *The Vice-Consul*, trans. Eileen Ellenbogen, (New York: Pantheon, 1987), pp. 15-17.

10

FEMINIST EJACULATIONS

Shannon Bell

For Gad, my partner in cum, with love.

This text is about the ejaculating female body. How did it cum to be that male ejaculation has never been questioned, debated, analyzed; just accepted as a given feature of the male body and male sexuality? An odd question. Yet it is no more odd than what has actually happened to female ejaculation throughout history. There are two questions that have not been raised about female ejaculation, from its discussion by the early Greeks to the most recent. The first is how can women have control over ejaculation; the second, and more recent question, is: why have feminist voices failed to speak about and embrace female ejaculation?

These questions will be backgrounded while I trace the theorizations and writings on female ejaculation conducted by philosophers, physicians, and sexologists, and as recorded in the documentations kept by anthropologists. In Western philosophy and society female ejaculation has been framed five ways: as fecundity, sexual pleasure, social deviance, medical pathology, and as a scientific problem. These frames will become more defined during the discussion.

Traces of Female Ejaculation in Patriarchal Texts

The expulsion of female fluids during sexual excitement was thought by a number of Greek and Roman doctors and philosphers to be a normal and pleasurable part of female sexuality, the debate evolving around whether female fluids were or were not progenitive. Aristotle argued against the general belief that female seed was produced by women; Hippocrates and Galen were the most well-known of those ancients who argued that women emit seed. Hippocrates (460-377 b.c.) advocated a "two semen" theory of generation based on the belief that both male and female fluids contributed to conception.[1]

In *The Generation of Animals*, Aristotle (384-322 b.c.) argued against the two semen theory of generation and connected female fluid with pleasure:

> Some think that the female contributes semen in coition because the pleasure she experiences is sometime similar to that of the male, and also is attended by a liquid discharge. But this discharge is not seminal ... The amount of this discharge when it occurs, is sometimes on a different scale from the emission of semen and far exceeds it.[2]

Galen, supporting the theory of female seed, made a distinction between female fluid that was procreative and female fluid that was pleasurable. He identified the source of pleasurable fluid as the female prostate.

> ... the fluid in her prostate ... contributes nothing to the generation of offspring ... it is poured outside when it has done its service ... This liquid not only stimulates ... the sexual act but also is able to give pleasure and moisten the passageway as it escapes. It manifestly flows from women as they experience the greatest pleasure in coitus ...[3]

Western scholars and doctors throughout the Middle Ages remained faithful to Hippocrates's and Galen's notion of female sperm, which came to them through Arab medicine. In fact, the theory of the female seed survived long after the Middle Ages.[4]

De Graaf, a seventeenth-century Dutch anatomist, in his *New Treatise Concerning the Generative Organs of Women*, outlined the Hippocratic and Aristotelian controversy over female semen. He sided firmly with the Aristotelians and denied the existence of female semen. In describing the pleasurable ejection of female fluid, De Graaf wrote: "it should be noted that the discharge from the female prostatae causes as much pleasure as does that from the male prostatae."[5] He identified the location and source of the fluid as the "ducts and lacunae ... around the orifice of the neck of the vagina and the outlet of the urinary passage [which] receive their fluid from the female 'parastate', or rather the thick membranous body around the urinary passage."[6] De Graaf also describes the fluid as "rush[ing] out," "com[ing] from the pudenda in one gush."[7]

In the nineteenth century, female fluids were linked with disease. Alexander Skene, who in 1880 identified the two ducts inside the urethral opening, was concerned with the problem of draining the glands and the ducts surrounding the female urethra when they became infected. The Skene glands and urethra became important to the medical profession as potential sites of veneral disease and infection, not as loci of pleasure. The emphasis shifted to disorders and treatment. Evidence of female fluid was linked with disease. Male discourse entered the ejaculatory female body that was viewed as the grotesque body; the object of analytic scrutiny.

Krafft-Ebing, in his mammoth study of sexual perversion, *Psychopathia Sexualis*, identified female ejaculation as the pathology of a small (albeit sexual) portion of a pathological group. Under the heading of "Congenital Sexual Inversion in Women," Krafft-Ebing discusses sexual contact among women, and contends that:

> [t]he intersexual gratification among ... women seems to be reduced to kissing and embraces, which seems to satisfy those of weak sexual instinct, but produces in sexually neurasthenic females ejaculation.[8]

According to Krafft-Ebing ejaculation only occurs among women who suffer neurasthenia—body disturbances caused by weakness of the nervous system. Krafft-Ebing therefore relates female ejaculation to a nervous disability.

Perhaps this is to be expected from a Victorian sexologist; what is unexpected is the manner in which this passage has been appropriated by a well-known lesbian feminist historian, Shelia Jeffreys. Jeffreys, in *The Spinister and Her Enemies. Feminism and Sexuality 1880-1930*, marks female ejaculation as an "invention" of the male imaginary: "There are ... examples in the sexologocial literature of men's sexual fantasies about lesbian sexuality. Krafft-Ebing invented a form of ejaculation for women.[9]

Freud, in his analysis of Dora, followed the medical conventions of his time and made a connection between Dora's hysterical symptoms and the secretion of female fluids.

> The pride taken by women in the appearance of their genitals is quite a special feature of their vanity; and disorders of genitals which they think calculated to inspire feelings of repugnance or even disgust have an incredible power of humiliating them, of lowering their self-esteem, and of making them irritable, sensitive, and distrustful. An abnormal secretion of the mucous membrane of the vagina is looked upon as source of disgust.[10]

Female ejaculation also came to be considered a figment of the male imagination. References to female ejaculation can be found in *The Pearl*, a two volume Victorian journal (reprinted in 1968), which contains short stories, poems, ballads, and letters. These and other references in late nineteenth-and early twentieth-century erotic literature have subsequently come to be marked figments of the male imagination. Steven Marcus, for example, states in The Other Victorians: A Study of Sexuality and Pornography in Mid-Nineteenth Century England (1966) that in pornographic writings

> there is first the ubiquitous projection of the male sexual fantasy onto the female response—the female response being imagined as identical with the male ... and there is the usual accompanying fantasy that they ejaculate during orgasm.[11]

There have also been positive depictions of female ejaculation. The ejaculating female body can be found in the love discourse of two women at the margins of the patriarchal order; women who, according to Krafft-Ebing's contention, would have been considered "neurasthenic," at least to him. Eleven years after the first publication of Dora, a love letter was written, by a triply bad girl, Almeda Sperry, who was a lesbian prostitute anarchist, to a doubly bad girl Emma Goldman, an anarchist bisexual:

> Dearest, it is a good thing that I came away when I did ...At this moment I am listening to the rhythm of the pulse coming in your throat. I am surging along with your lifeblood, coursing in the secret places of your body. I cannot escape the rhythmic spurt of your love juices.[12]

Female ejaculation was marked a common and normal occurrence by Van de Velde in his marriage manual, Ideal Marriage: Its Physiology and Technique. (1926).

> It appears that the majority of laymen believed that something is forcibly squirted (or propelled or extruded) or expelled from the woman's body in orgasm, and should so happen normally, as in the man's case.[13]

Female ejaculation was documented in passing by anthropologists. Two-well known anthropological studies, Malinowski's The Sexual Life of Savages (1929) and Gladwin's and Sarason's Truk: Man in Paradise (1953), contain references to female ejaculation. Malinowski notes that the Trobrianders use the same word, "momona," for both male and female discharge. Momona means "it squirts out the discharge."[14] Malinowski documents that the Trobrianders believe this discharge lubricates and increases pleasure. The Trukese, a matrilocal society where women are considered "domineering and assertive, sexually provoking and aggressive"[15] and where the female genitals are considered "in several respects intrinsically of more importance and interest than are the male genitals",[16] describe intercourse as

... a contest between the man and woman, a matter of the
man restraining his orgasm until the woman has achieved
hers. Female orgasm is commonly signaled by urination
[sic] ... If the man ejaculates before this time he is said to
have been defeated ...[17]

Anthropology has also revealed that female ejaculation is a part of the
puberty rites of the Batoro of Uganda. The Batoro have a custom called
"kachapati" which means "spray the wall." The older women of the
village teach the younger females how to ejaculate when they reach
puberty.[18]

Despite the descriptions of female ejaculation in medical, anthropological, philosophical, and popular literature from time to time throughout Western history, female ejaculation has been practically ignored
until the late 1970s and 1980s.

De-eroticizing Female Pleasure:
Female Ejaculation and Sexual Science

The clearest and most complete description of the physiological
process and anatomical structure of female ejaculation was published in
The International Journal of Sexology (1950) by Grafenberg, a German
obstetrician and gynecologist. In his "own experience of numerous
women," Grafenberg observed that:

An erotic zone always could be demonstrated on the
anterior wall of the vagina along the course of the urethra
... Analogous to the male urethra, the female urethra also
seems to be surrounded by erectile tissues ... In the
course of sexual stimulation, the female urethra begins
to enlarge and can be felt easily. It swells out greatly at
the end of orgasm ... Occasionally the production of
fluids is ... profuse ... If there is the opportunity to
observe ... one can see that large quantities of a clear
transparent fluid are expelled ... out of the urethra in
gushes ...[19]

Despite Grafenberg's clear description, female ejaculation was ignored
and/or denied by the dominant scientific discourses defining female
sexuality from 1950-1978. Kinsey, Pomeroy, and Martin (1953), writing
three years after Grafenberg, mention female ejaculation only to deny its
existence.[20] Masters and Johnson (1966) note that "female ejaculation is
an erroneous but widespread concept."[21] As recently as 1982, Masters,
Johnson, and Kolondy continue to refer to female ejaculation as "an
erroneous belief"[22] and suggest that the fluid could be the result of
"urinary stress incontinence."[23]

Grafenberg's analysis remained in obscurity until Sevely and Bennett reintroduced it into sexological discourse in their review of the literature on female ejaculation, "Concerning Female Ejaculation and the Female Prostate" (1978) published in *The Journal of Sex Research*. Their review originated the contemporary debate among sex researchers, gynecologists, urologists, and sex therapists regarding the existence of female ejaculate and its source. This debate has focused on three areas of concern: efforts to prove that women do or do not ejaculate; analysis of the chemical composition of ejaculate to determine whether or not it is urine; and, the potential of ejaculation for constructing a new theory of sexuality.

A listing of some of the titles of the articles defining the contemporary discourse on female ejaculation should be sufficient to indicate the de-eroticization of female ejaculation and the ejaculatory organ. "Concerning Female Ejaculation and the Female Prostrate" (1978); "Orgasmic Expulsions of Women: A Review and Heuristic Inquiry" (1981); "Pelvic Muscle Strength of Female Ejaculators: Evidence in Support of a New Theory of Orgasm" (1981); "Female Ejaculation and Urinary Stress Incontinence" (1982); "Concentrations of Fructose in Female Ejaculate and Urine: A Comparative Biochemical Study" (1988); and, "Female Urethral Expulsions Evoked by Local Digital Stimulation of the G-Spot: Differences in the Response Patterns" (1988). An excerpt from "Female Urethral Expulsions Evoked by Local Digital Stimulation of the G-Spot: Differences in the Response Patterns" reveals subjects who do not have control over the activity of ejaculation.

> Stimulation was administered to each woman by both the female and male members of our medical team ... During the administration of stimulation, the subject was in the dorsal recumbent position required for vaginal examination ... digital palpation of the anterior wall of the vagina, using one or two fingers, was begun ... When urethral expulsions occurred, one member of the team placed a small porcelain vessel under the urinary meatus to collect the outflowing liquid.[24]

The subjects here do not have power over their body. The body is "confiscated" and "turned into the uncanny stranger on display"[25] for the knowledge of "scienta sexualis."[26]

Male sexologists still have an investment, perhaps an investment in holding onto a sexually privileged position where sexual activities revolve around their "spending" or "withholding" of ejaculate, in questioning whether women can ejaculate. Female ejaculation is, for some, a matter of belief, rather than a physiological response. Alzate, who conducted a clinical study of twenty-seven women, disregarded what he termed a subject's "emphatic" affirmation that she often ejaculated and discounted his recorded observation of her doing so, to claim that "the ignorance and/or confusion still prevalent among women about the anatomy and physiology of their sexual organs may make them mistake either vaginal lubriaction or stress urinary incontinence for an "ejaculation."[27] There is a recurrent tendency for researchers to disregard, reinterpret, and overwrite women's subjective descriptions of ejaculation. Sex researchers Davidson, Darling, and Conway-Welch, in the most extensive social survey of a female population regarding their experience of ejaculation (1289 women responded), state that anecdotal data suggests that the physiological sensations associated with the expulsion of fluid are very similar to those physiological sensations associated with voiding of urine.[28] I was presenting a paper in a session on "Female Ejaculation" at the World Congress of Sexology in December 1989 in Caracas, Venezuela. I discussed representations of female ejaculation and showed slides of the ejaculating female body; a Spanish medical team showed vaginal photographs of the glands and ducts surrounding a woman's urethral. An older hegemonic male member of the audience, publically contended that "we have just seen pictures of this fluid shooting out of the female body and slides of its location but he would believe women ejaculated if one pathologist declared that they did."

The composition of female ejaculate was analyzed in six studies in which the subjects' ejaculate was chemically compared with urine and male ejaculate. The fluid was tested to determine whether it contained higher levels of glucose than urine did and whether or not prostatic acid phosphatase (PAP)—a major constituent of male semen and of prostatic origin—was present. The urea and creatinine levels of the fluid were tested against urine. If the fluid had a chemical content similar to urine, as two out of the six studies contended, it didn't count as "real" ejaculate.

Female ejaculation was legitimated and popularized for the first time in *The G Spot and Other Recent Discoveries About Female Sexuality* (1982). A large protion of the chapter "Female Ejaculation" is composed of self-reports from, and case vignettes of, female ejaculators. Some of the women had been diagnosed by their companions and by the medical profession as suffereing from urinary incontinence. Other women depicted the act of ejaculation as an experience of pleasure and a regular part of their sexuality. The authors of *The G-Spot* suggest that because "female ejaculate can only serve one purpose: pleasure"[29] and that women have historically been absented from the realm of pleasure, the knowledge of ejaculation has not been accepted and socially appropriated by professionals or the public.

Josephine Sevely, *Eve's Secrets. A New Theory of Female Sexuality* (1987), has provided the most comprehensive study of female ejaculation. Her theory not only sexualizes the urethra but also emphasizes the simultaneous involvement of the clitoris, urethra, and vagina, which function as a single integrated sexual organ. The implications of Sevely's theory are threefold. First, a woman's sexual organ ceases to be fragmented into clitoris and vagina: it is an integrated whole composed of clitoris, urethra, and vagina. Second, this integrated whole is a multiplicity "full of things," all alive with sensation. The [w]hole is an active w[hole]; no more clitoral activity versus vaginal passivity. Third, the "anatomical difference" between male and female genitals upon which phallocentric culture and society is premised is challenged by an alternative construction of anatomical symmetry. Both male and female bodies have prostate gland structures and both have the potential to ejaculate fluids during sexual stimualtion. The female body, free grom the limiting economy of the male psyche-libido, reveals physiological difference within anatomical symmetry. The female body can ejaculate fluid from thirty-one ducts; with stimulation can ejaculate repeatedly; can ejaculate more fluid than the male body; and, can enjoy a plurality of genital pleasure sites: the clitoris, urethra, vagina, the vaginal entrance, the roof of the vagina, the bottom of the vagina, and the cervix.

Feminism and Ejaculation

The ejaculating female body has not acquired much of a feminist voice nor has it been appropriated by feminist discourse. What is the reason for this lacuna in feminist scholarship and for the silencing of the ejaculating female subject? It has to do with the fact that the questions posed, and the basic assumptions about female sexuality, are overwhelmingly premised on the difference between female and male bodies: "the most visible difference between men and women, and the only one we know for sure to be permanent ... is ... the difference in body."[30] The most important primary differences have been that women have the ability to give birth and men ejaculate. Women's reproductive ability has been emphasized as a central metaphor in feminist critiques of patriarchal texts and has been theorized into a "philsophy of birth" and an economy of (re)production. Feminists, in their efforts to revalorize the female body usually devalued in phallocentric discourse, have privileged some form of the mother-body as the source of écriture féminine: writing that evokes women's power as women's bodily experience. Mary O'Brien, for example, in *The Politics of Reproduction* (1981), provides a feminist model for interpreting masculinist political philosophy. O'Brien begins her project by posing the question: "Where does feminist theory start?" She replies: "Within the process of human reproduction. Of that process, sexuality is but a part."[31] O'Brien names her reappropriation and theorization of the mother-body as a "philosophy of birth." Luce Irigaray writes that "historically the properties of fluids have been abandoned to the feminine."[32] The fluids, reappropriated in feminine sexual discourse and theorized by French feminist philosophers such as Luce Irigaray and Julia Kristeva, have been the fluids of the mother-body: fluids of the womb, birth fluids, menstrual blood, milk: fluids that flow. Ejacualte—fluid that shoots, fluid that sprays—has been given over to the male body. To accept female ejaculate and female ejaculation one has to accept the sameness of male and female bodies.

Contemporary femininsm, however, has rejected sameness as being defined from the perspective of the male body, as conformity with the masculine model. To avoid identification with a male phenomenon, women have suggested that the term "ejaculation" should not be used. I argue that the term should be kept while using the distinctive characteristics of female ejaculate to redefine and rewrite the meaning of the term: female ejaculate is not "spent"; with stimulation one can ejaculate repeatedly; and, a woman in control of ejaculation may ejaculate enormous quantitites.

The second factor in feminists' failure to embrace ejaculation as a powerful body experience is their understandable concern regarding possible male control over female ejaculation in the context of a masculinist and heterosexual script in which ejaculation is presented as something men do to women's bodies. The Boston Women's Health Collective, editors of *Our Bodies, Our Selves* (1984), warn women that the G-Spot and female ejaculation could be "used to re-instate so-called 'vaginal' orgasms as superior" and could "becom[e] a new source of pressure" to perform.[33] Ehrenreich, Hess and Jacobs, in *Re-making Love. The Feminization of Sex* (1986) misconstrue the emphasis in *The G-Spot* on the urethra as a return to Freud's primacy of the mature vaginal orgasm. Ehrenreich et al, argue that Chapter Four of The G-Spot, "The Importance of Healthy Pelvic Muscles," which links strong pubococcygeus muscles (PC muscles) with ejaculation and G-Spot orgasms and provides case vignettes of women who discuss the merits of strenghtening their PC muscles, encourages women to strengthen "the muscles that hold the penis in place."[34] In my experience these muscles do not in fact hold the penis in place; rather, they push it out and spray the ejaculate. The penis (if one is around) may then re-enter until the glands and ducts surrounding the urethra become so enlarged in size through stimulation that they expel the penis and spray again. Ehrenreich et al, also claim that "the acrobatics necessary to achieve the 'new' orgasm" privilege male-dominant sexual positions.[35] This criticism is odd since Ladas et al provide case vignettes of ejaculation in many different positions: woman on top, rear entry, man on top, partner using his/her hand, and woman using her own hand. They provide case histories from lesbians and note that "preliminary reports indicate that there may be a higher incidence of female ejaculation in the lesbian population than there is among heterosexual women.[36]

Female ejaculation is about power over one's own body. For many women who do experience ejaculation, however, it is a passive experience—something that happens, not a capacity and process they control. If feminists are going to appropriate and reclaim the female body, it is very important that women provide feminist scripts of the ejaculating body in *control* of ejaculation. The following are two examples of such scripts. The first representation is a short film segment, which is part of a larger lesbian erotic film, "Clips," produced by Blush Entertainment Group (1988). In this clip, a fem woman wearing white lace masturbates with a dildo icicle while watching the TV news which shifts to lesbian porn; she is watched by her butch lover who reads the newspaper, smokes a cigarette, walks around. The fem reaches orgasm, removes the dildo, and ejaculates toward the TV set, appearing to wet the screen with her body fluid. She then ejaculates again, this time without orgasm and she and her lover then make love. This feminist pornographic representation provides quite a contrast to The Grafenberg Spot, a popular feature porn flick, produced by the O'Farrell Theatre in San Francisco. Its positive feature is that the male star discovers that female ejaculation is "normal"; he goes from disgust to delight. The film, however, presents ejacualtion as something that a man in the know can make a woman do. There are two releases of the film for distribution, one has additional footage of the making of the film. This footage includes shots of the vaginas of the ejaculating females being filled by a syringe; the implication is that the camera shots of ejaculate are not actual female fluid, thus putting into question the womens' ability to ejaculate and also contextualizing the ejaculation scenes as merely pronographic fantasy.

The second script is a written vignette that involves only one person. After stimulating or having her clitoris and urethra stimulated by a mouth, a hand, a vibrator, the woman, positioned on her knees with legs wide apart and pelvis tilted forward, begins to masturbate; when she feels she is ready (when her ducts feel full), she contracts her vaginal muscles and pushes her urethra out at the same time using her other hand or her friends hand to press on her pelvis and stomach, pressing the liquid out of her ducts; the fluid sprays out; she laughs and repeats; she laughs and repeats.

A Woman's Ejaculation Guide

Okay, so now I know you are saying to yourself "How do I do this?" "How can I help my partner(s) do this?" "What will it do for me sexually?" "How does it empower me?" The answer to the first question, "how do I do this," is almost nowhere to be found in the sexologist literature. After attending a 1985 workshop in New York given by Alice Ladas, first author of *The G-Spot*, (the workshop was on the vaginal myograph and strengthening pelvic muscles), I headed for a bookstore to purchase *The G-Spot*. I read the chapter "Female Ejaculation" and I read it to Gad, my partner then and now my partner in cum. Then I started to practice. It was really difficult to figure out how to do it from the descriptions of ejaculators' experiences. For them ejaculation was primarily something that happened not an action that they controlled. I practiced and practiced and by the time we left New York I was so sore from masturbating that I could hardly walk or pee. This was not the thrill I had expected. So I sat down again with these women's experiences and took notes. And I realized that they had not emphasized the crucial aspect about ejaculating: it is necessary to *PUSH OUT*.

Step One: Find what has come to be known as your "G-Spot"; don't call it that, it is named after Grafenberg, a man. It is the muscle and spongy tissue around that part of your urethra that is inside your vagina. It begins about a finger (more or less) inside your vagina and is about a finger long and a finger wide. If the muscles that go around your vagina (the pubococcygeus muscles) have not been used much, they have to be built up. The muscles can be built up by doing contractions: contracting the top of your vagina against the bottom and releasing. This is fun and you could have an orgasm or two. You could start by doing twenty-five contractions three times a day for one week, then fifty three times a day, then one hundred.

Step Two: Using whichever hand you usually masturbate with, take two or three fingers and rub them against the part of your urethra inside your vagina. Press hard and notice the feeling which may seem like having to urinate. This is a signal that you are ready to ejaculate. Now, place the middle finger slightly below the external part of your urethra and begin to masturbate the same way you rub your clitoris. (I begin with a slow firm up and down motion, increasing the speed and pressure as I approach ejaculation.) As you are masturbating you will notice that the two ducts, one at each side of your urethra feel full and perhaps somewhat painful. There are another twenty-nine ducts scattered over the top of your vagina and once you identify the body sensation you will be able to locate them on your lower abdomen. They are located in a pyramid from your clitoris to just above your ovaries.

Step Three: Take your other hand and press down on one or more of the ducts from the outside. Push your urethra out and push, the way you do when you urinate. A crucial aspect about ejaculating is that *it is necessary to PUSH OUT*. Liquid will come shooting out of your urethra in a steady stream or in a jet.

I can ejaculate only in positions in which I can push my entire pelvis out and up: on my knees with legs a foot and a half apart; on my back with my pelvis raised up; weight distributed on my feet and shoulders, and knees at least two feet apart; and, squatting or standing, again with feet far enough apart so I can push my urethra up and out.

If your partner is female, you may be able to help her ejaculate. As you stimulate her anterior vaginal wall and the exterior part of her urethra, get her to push out when she is ready. You will both feel the glands and ducts around the urethra swelling and filling with liquid. If the muscles have atrophied, as mine had, contraction exercises may be required.

What ejaculation will do for you sexually is to give you a powerful pleasurable kinesthetic, visual, and auditory experience—a total body

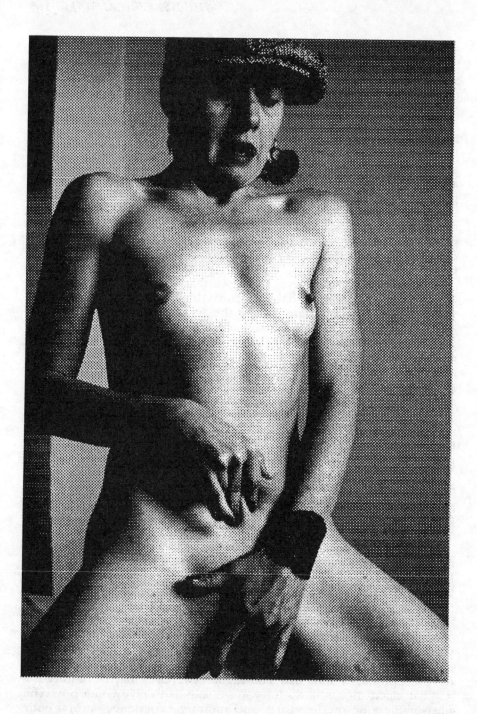

experience. You can repeat it almost indefinitely once your body awakens to it.

Ejaculate: The ejaculate changes in amount, color, odor, and taste during your menstrual cycle. At ovulation the fluid is very hot (it corresponds to your vaginal temperature), thick, yellow, and pungent. Following ovulation the fluid is thinner, there is more of it, it is clear, and plesantly salty. It remains this way until bleeding starts, at which point it is again thick for the first day or so. It then returns to being clear.

Health: I have found that ejaculating during ovulation—because it reduces vaginal temperature—reduces yeast infections that result from the increase in vaginal temperature at ovulation.

Safer Sex: The same safe sex rules apply for girl cum as boy cum: keep it out of all mucous membranes and your blood stream; keep it our of your partner's eyes.

Ejaculating Picture: The picture is meant to be pornographic, erotic, and educational. It is of me—the author of the text. It is encoded in traditional pornographic genre—shaven pussy—because I like it and I think ejaculating serves to deconstruct the image itself as well as the "Women Against Pornography" reading and critique of the image. This is not a young pussy, but for the viewer who equates hairlessness with the pre-pubescent girl and the girl with powerlessness, the visual inscribes an active sexual organ and a powerful sexual organ. The indiscretion of the author showing her own genitalia (the lived body) subverts the written body, transgressing "writing the body," and transgresses her own written text.

Notes

1. Hippocrates, *De geniture*, eds. and trans. W.C. Lyons and J.N. Hattock, (Cambridge: Pembrooke Press, 1978), chap. 6 (7.478).

2. Aristotle, *De Generation Animalium*, trans. Arthur Platt, in *The Complete Works of Aristotle*, eds. J.A. Smith and W.D. Ross, (Oxford: The Claredon Press, 1912), II 728a.

3. Cited in Josephine Sevely, *Eve's Secrets. A New Theory of Female Sexuality*, (New York: Random House, 1987), p.51.

4. Danielle Jacquart and Claude Thomasset, *Sexuality and Medicine in the Middle Ages*, trans. Matthew Adamson, (Great Britain: Polity Press, 1988), pp. 66-74.

5. Rainer de Graaf, *New Treatise Concerning the Generative Organs of Women* (1672), annot. trans. H.B. Jocelyn and B.P. Setchell, *Journal of Reproduction* and Fertility, Supplement 17, (Oxford: Blackwell Scientific Publications, 1972), p.107.

6. Ibid., p.141.

7. Ibid., p.141.

8. Richard von Krafft-Ebing, *Psychopathia Sexualis*, trans. Franklin S. Klaf, (New York: Stein and Day, 1965), p.265.

9. "Shelia Jeffreys, *The Spinster and Her Enemies. Feminism and Sexuality 1880-1930*, (London: Routledge and Kegan Paul, 1985), p.110.

10. Sigmund Freud, "Fragments of an Analysis of a Case of Hysteria" (1905), *The Standard Edition of the Complete Psychological Works by Sigmund Freud*, Vol. VII, trans. and ed. James Strachey, (London: The Hogarth Press and the Institute of Psycho-analysis, 1953), p.84.

11. Steven Marcus, *The Other Victorians: A Study of Sexuality and Pornography in Mid-Nineteenth Century England*, (New York: Basic Books, 1966), p.194.

12. Candice Falk, *Love, Anarchy and Emma Goldman*, (New York: Holt Rinehart and Winston, 1984), p.175.

13. T. Van de Velde, *Ideal Marriage: Its Physiology and Technique*,Second Ed., (London: Heinemann Medical Books), 1965, p.138.

14. Bronislaw Malinowski, *The Sexual Life of Savages*, (New York: Harcourt Brace and World, 1929), p.167.

15. Thomas Gladwin and Seymour B. Sarason, *Truk: Man in Paradise*, (New York: Wenner-Gren Foundation for Anthropological Research Inc., 1956), p.233.

16. Ibid., p.253.

17. Ibid., p.109.

18. Alice Ladas, Bevely Whipple, and John Perry, *The G Spot and Other Recent Discoveries About Human Sexuality*, (New York: Dell, 1983), pp.74-75.

19. Cited in Sevely, pp.85-6.

20. Alfred J. Kinsey, Wardell B. Pomeroy, and Clyde E. Martin, *Sexual Behavior in the Human Female*, (Philadelphia W.B. Saunders Co. 1953), pp.634-5.

21. William H. Masters and Virginia E. Johnson, *Human Sexual Response*, (Boston: Little Brown, 1966), p.135.

22. William R. Masters, Virginia E. Johnson, and R.C. Kolodny, Masters and Johnson on *Sex and Human Loving*, (Boston: Little, Brown, 1982), p.69.

23. Ibid., p.70.

24. Milan Zaviacic, et al, "Female Urethral Expulsions Evoked by Local Digital Stimulation of the G-Spot: Differences in the Response Patterns," *The Journal of Sex Research* 24 (1988): 312-13.

25. Helene Cixous, "The Laugh of the Medusa," *New French Feminisms*, eds. Isabelle De Courtivron and Elaine Marks, (Amherst: University of Massachusetts Press, 1980), p.250.

26. Michel Foucault, *The History of Sexuality*, Vol.1, (New York: Vintage Books, 1978), Part Three.

27. Heli Alzate, "Vaginal Eroticism: A Replication Study", *Archives of Sexual Behavior* 14 (1985): 530-33 and Heli Alzate and Zwi Hoch, "The `G-Spot' and `Female Ejaculation': A Current Appraisal," *Journal of Sex and Marital Therapy* 12 (1986): 217.

28. J.K. Davidson, Sr., C.A. Darling, and C. Conway-Welch, "The Role of the Grafenberg Spot and Female Ejaculation in the Female Orgasmic Response: An Empirical Analysis," *The Journal of Sex and Marital Therapy* 15 (1989): 120.

29. Ladas et al, p.79.

30. Elaine Showalter, "Feminist Criticism in the Wilderness," *The New Feminist Criticism: Essays on Women, Literature and Theory*, ed. Elaine Showalter, (New York: Pantheon Books, 1985), p.252.

31. Mary O'Brien, *The Politics of Reproduction*, (London: Routledge Kegan Paul, 1981), p.8.

32. Luce Irigaray, *This Sex Which is Not One*, (New York: Cornell Press, 1985), p.116.

33. The Boston Women's Health Collective, *Our Bodies, Our Selves*, (New York: Simon & Schuster, Inc., 1984), p.171.

34. Barbara Ehrenreich, Elizabeth Hess, and Gloria Jacobs, *Re-Making Love. The Feminization of Sex*, (New York: Anchor Press, 1986), p.185.

35. Ibid., p.184.

36. Ladas et al, p.84.

Whither

the

Phallus?

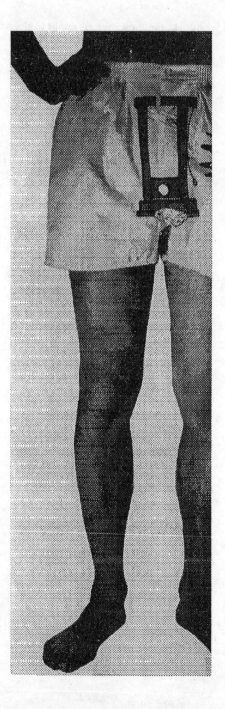

11

THE FETISH IN *SEX, LIES &VIDEOTAPE*: WHITHER THE PHALLUS?

Berkeley Kaite

While in Paris last summer, I picked up a copy of *Paris Passion*, the anglo guide to Parisian cultural life. Within its bulging middle section full of "The Best" of Paris (an annual tribute) was the "The Best Bicentennial Buy." The featured revolutionary souvenir was a snapshot from the waist down of a pair of men's boxer shorts worn by a model. The graphic on the front, from waist to crotch, is a silkscreen of a guillotine. The blade of the machine has descended and claimed another victim: the tip of a recently dismembered penis beneath the blade is visible at the level of the model's crotch. The intersection of the guillotine—surely the most potent symbol of the masses under seige, of dismemberment, and of a little death to the bourgeoisie—with contemporary castration suggests a cynicism and an emergent hysteria around "the uncoding of men as men?"[1] A phallic signifier? Hardly. Witty? Very. Overdone? To anchor the visual image the caption is offered: "Tired of that unsightly bulge? Buy the man in your life these souvenir Bicentennial boxer shorts. Guaranteed to cut a fine figure. 100 percent cotton. Cost (a snip at): 139F."

It does suggest, as per the "panic thesis[2]", that men may be the ones who are panicking ("No longer the old male cock as the privileged sign of patriarchal power... but the postmodern penis which becomes an emblematic sign of sickness, disease, and waste. Penis burnout, then, for the end of the world"), and that the phallus (or at least the penis) is under seige. If nothing else, the way we think about sexual difference is changing: strategies of the representation, negotiation, and containment of sexual difference are, in the late eighties/early nineties, undergoing a radical renunciation. Consider the following three examples: Unlike Norma Jean Baker who tried to become Marilyn Monroe, Madonna is not only saved by the politics of cynicism but knows that the image is radically separated from the real. She also presents the video, "Open Your Heart," as an indictment of spectatorship and the prerogative of the male gaze. As she performs a Gilda-like striptease on stage, surrounded by several male onlookers, these same men are exposed as incapacitated by the spectacle: they look at their peril. One is trapped in eyeglasses as thick and blurry as coke bottles (and we appropriate his point of view when we are offered a look through those lenses); another cannot look long or well enough: the black screen descends and cuts off his viewing pleasure; others are mere cardboard cutouts whom Madonna shoots "dead" with an imaginary gun.[3] As the great spoiler of the voyeur's pleasure, her capacity to command the gaze is the small death or emasculation of the spectators in the video.

A second example can be found in the television ads for Black Label beer, which also recode difference in the way they fetishize and phallicize the female body; make a spectacle of the male body; and display the "negative" image of the black and white film so that the final visual narrative is a reversal of what it should be—all in the service of seduction. Thirdly and in another vein, Pee-wee Herman "himself" is symptomatic of contemporary disturbances around the negotiation of sexual difference. Constance Penley writes that when Pee-wee and the other characters on the "Playhouse" television show oscillate between male and female personas, it constitutes an "oscillation without anxiety... a postmodernist stage of camp subjectivity, one distinguished by a capacity for zipping through sexual roles that is as fast and unremarkable as zapping through the channels."[4]

In what follows I will isolate one element in the signification of difference, notably fetish objects and relations. At the risk of making a fetish of fetishism, I will explore the election of the fetish in the service of seduction, particularly the way it stages a play of differences, or cuts a fine line between affirmation and denial. And, I will also address the question, Does this play of fetishism have something to do with contemporary hysterical inscriptions that serve to recode masculinity?

Sex, Lies & Videotape

The unfortunate victim-penis of the revolutionary boxer shorts shares the same epoch as the award-winning film *Sex, Lies & Videotape* in which another penis may just as well have suffered the same fate as its dismembered counterpart in *Paris Passion*. The film works with, and through, the triangle of Ann and her husband John, and Cynthia (Ann's sister with whom John is having an affair). What destabilizes that already precarious arrangement is not only the arrival of an out-of-towner, John's old college friend, Graham, but Graham's proclivity for videated sex. He does not wish to film and/or watch sexual activities; instead, Graham interviews women *about* sex. His subjects (all women) talk about sex. He then uses these videotapes, later, for fantasmatic and solitary gratification.

Soon after Graham and Ann meet they challenge each other to reveal secrets. Ann paraphrases something she has already mentioned to her therapist: "I've never really been that much into sex," and offers a small and familiar treatise on how men and women attach a different importance to sex. Ann, the traditionalist, wants us to believe that women do not want it as much, or at least not for the same reasons as men think they do. Graham follows this with the stunningly nonchalant declaration that he is impotent, at least "in the presence of another person." This fact consolidates an uncanny interest in Graham on the part of both Ann and Cynthia (and John, though in a slightly different vein). They independently seek him out in his apartment and both succumb to the allure of the technology and the man and agree to talk about sex in front of the camera. Cynthia, with a libido that eventually ruins John (he calls her "Cyn/sin" a couple of times in the film), is the first to partake of video pleasures. The videotapes then become the pivotal and privileged object around which all fantasies, questions, desires, and fears revolve. And they are the perfect metaphor for fetishized sexuality and fetishized relations of difference.

But Graham's impotence also elects a curious signifier—a limp penis— as a cental organizing metonym for the film. Graham's video equipment is the proletariat of the body politic: it does the body's dirty work. The unabashed impotence is proclaimed (the limpness of the signifier, as it were). As a fetish, the videotapes recuperate absence (through presence); power, but at the cutting edge of disempowerment; and, the body's part-object but at the price of disembodiment. As fetish, the videotapes remove the diegesis from the realm of pure psychodrama and sends it into the orbit of seductive technologies and the technology of seduction.[5] In *Sex, Lies & Videotape,"* as with other cultural technologies, "difference" and seduction are a discourse of objects, relations, and a statement on the prevention of narrative closure. More on these below.

The Fetish

The term "fetish" in this paper will primarily correspond to certain psychoanalytic assumptions. Fetish objects are metonymically affiliated with 'part-object' status: they are substitutive in nature, seductive in aim, simultaneously threatening and erotic, and with a precarious balance of knowledge and disavowal, presence and absence and corporal plenitude and loss. The association with castration (loss) is as indelible as the hyper-coding of fetish objects in visual terms. The fetish is elected to disavow "knowledge" of feminine "loss" and allay the perceived threat this perception brings. Freud writes that "the horror of castration has set up a memorial to itself" in the creation of objects that substitute for the missing female penis.[6] The castration complex, and its attendant representational apparatus, is the attempt at reconciling knowledge of girls' "loss" with the "conviction ... energetically maintained" that this cannot be the case.[7] Stand-ins for the missing penis take on a fetishistic character and endow the female body with textual features, or they re-write the body. The negotiation of sexual difference based on possession/non-possession of the penis is first a visual investment.[8] The construction or endowment of the female body as an erotic spectacle and the tensions between the pleasure and the threat involved in looking are all managed through the performance of the fetish. The (typically) male subject, implicated in the scopic moment, stands in relation to the signifying power of the female textual body and, in encountering the fetish, believes in it or allows it to work for him.

In the "society of the spectacle," however, fetishistic transactions may be characteristic of signification in the scopic economies, rendering somewhat "normal" the "perversions" that preoccupied Freud (although he also noted that a "disposition to perversions is an original disposition of the human sexual instinct"[9]. Marx significantly used an optical metaphor—the camera obscura—to illustrate ideological relations: wherein a fetishism of objects in turn implicates a fetishism for subjects.[10] The paradox of the camera obscura is that in its aim to capture and re-present a referent it distorts it by its very medium (Marx's phrase, from *The German Ideology*, is "in all ideology men and their circumstances appear upside-down... this phenomenon arises just as much from their historical life-process as the inversion of objects on the retina does from their physical life-process").[11] Later, in *Capital*, the visual scenario is invoked again in an indictment of the "magic and necromancy" of commodities, specifically their imputed power to "socialize" (make social) humans' relationships with objects.[12] He writes that:

> ...the products of labour become commodities, social things whose qualities are at the same time perceptible and imperceptible by the senses. In the same way the light from an object is perceived by us not as the subjective excitation of our optic nerve, but as the objective form of something outside the eye itself. But in the act of seeing, there is at all events, an actual passage of light from one thing to another, from the external object to the eye. There is a physical relation between physical things. But it is different with commodities. There, the existence of the things *qua* commodities, and the value–relation between the products of labour which stamps them as commodi-

ties, have absolutely no connexion with their physical properties and with the material relations arising therefrom.[13]

What one wants to retain from Marx on commodity fetishism is the emphasis on the phantom images of ideology (and it is not hard to see the slide from a theory of the hieroglyphics of idolatry, with its mockery of ideas, artifice and illusion, to a polemic—at the very least—of the aesthetics and politics of objects); the notion of exchange relations; and the processes of exchange, whereby objects (commodities) simultaneously embody "dead labor" *and* are vitalized by the way they are invested with properties beyond their physicality, i.e., are given value in exchange relations. Marx, when he writes of the "magic and necromancy" of fetish objects, points to how they are at once an investment in death, difference, and simulated indifference. I will return to this.

But, in his scathing indictment of commodity fetishism and the inauthenticity of appearances or the appearance of things, Marx does not take us far enough in understanding how trafficking in symbols is actually seductive, how, through generalized exchange value, producers are simultaneously consumers (and how there can be no radical separation between subjects and objects; an 'essence' and its obverse; presence and absence), and finally, how the sign fascinates and entices? How does the commodity, "at first sight, a very trivial thing," wield so much power in a "mist-enveloped" system of worship?[14] Or in the words of the pleasure "theorists", what of the ambivalence around the "convergence of commodity and meaning" into *signs* of pleasure?[15] In spite of establishing sexuality at the center of subjectivity and locating the fetish within distinctly sexual origins and scenarios of difference, the logic of eroticism within the orthodox psychoanalytic narrative lacks the precision necessary to account for the problematic of sexual difference, the role of the fetish in the refusal of difference, and thus its role in seductive economies. Why is difference, and/or its effacement (fetishistic relations seem to straddle this negotiation which refuses closure) enthralling and seductive?

The fetish is always a play on difference(s). Baudrillard's critique of the "metaphysic of alienated essence," which characterizes the Marxist denunciation of the subversiveness of objects, challenges the unyielding base- superstructure model whereby use-value (the question of "truth") is a reflection of an anterior reality.[16] The privileging of exchange value—whereby objects signify only within a generalized and abstract system of differences—emphasizes the "labor of signification" and (with the obscuring of use-value) the negotiations of differences (and indifferences) in the gaps between signifiers and signifieds. Only now, what seduces is the machinations of the signifier searching for its signified(s). This indictment of the inherently bourgeois penchant for visibility and measurement (a reductive fetishism of the "seen") allows us to consider that the fetish is as much about ambivalences around absence and the repressed as it is about the immediately apparent. It is not that the signified cannot be measured: the problem is not one of locating and measuring meaning. The problem in the age of the camera obscura is finding and measuring the signifier. In *Sex, Lies & Videotape* this is problematized in rather interesting ways. The fetish is about simulated absence; and absence in this instance recalls a limp signifier. Thus, in any fetishized transaction (especially in the visual imaginaries) the drive to visibility is simultaneously about repressions, gaps, absences—what cannot be witnessed, what cannot be spoken. Any fetish, combining both presence and absence, is more than just an alibi for the "real": the fetish is about simulated relations, and, as with any simulation, it offers an indictment of the boundaries between the visible and the repressed, the subject and the object, the signifier and its referent. In short, the fetish prevents closure, but it does this through partially effacing difference, not by exacerbating it.

Baudrillard argues that the abstractions of ideological labor, the seemingly endless substitutions that are elected in relations of generalized exchange, means that any object is randomly affiliated with fetishism, not for its absolute but for its relative value. But I think that there is a problem with the assumption of the "relative autonomy' of objects (no different than the perils of asserting the relative autonomy of authors). For one thing, there are favored fetish images that circulate within a number of cultural discourses. The spike heel shoe, for example, is a staple feature in soft and hard core pornographic magazines, in representations that confer "sexiness" (and/or phallicism and sometimes murderous evil) on the female image. The fact that it is not just any shoe, but the stiletto heel, indicates at the very least that particular meanings converge (sometimes with a vengeance) in a simulated relationship of difference and indifference: not just any object can be sexualized in the name of difference. The suggestion of an equivalent exchange among signifiers (or that the object is one signifier among many) overlooks the exchange relations which coalesce on the object and through the ways in which it negotiates difference. These negotiated relations are dramatic plays on difference and simulate symbolic exchange. There is no "copyright" with any simulation. "Simulation" (from the Latin) is to copy, represent or feign, and stems from "same", with etymological connotations of "at the same time" and "together". An object held in simulation at once refers tofference and sameness, or difference and indifference, or difference and its denial (or postponement—at the root of "differ"). This is not unlike the fetish—simultaneously there/not there.

If *any* thing were capable of becoming a fetish object, then people and bodies (male and female) can be fetishes, subjects can become objects,and objects, subjects. While I agree strongly, with D.N. Rodowick, that subjects and objects cannot be held in radical separation,[17]) I want to emphasize the problematic of fetish *relations*. If the fetish is a particularly reliable, and erotic, compromise, and if as part-object it recalls an anterior "whole", it is caught in a web of relations of difference (not just embodied objects which mark a static difference) which serve to simulate something that does not exist in the real. In the case of the shoe, the compromise is between its obvious cultural location among feminine accoutrements (of the last few hundred years at least). (Elizabeth Wilson writes that in the 14th century shoes became "exaggeratedly long and pointed"[18]) and its import as a phallic symbol, complete with stiletto, a dagger-like heel (a heel is always a man.) We might say the spike-heel shoe is poised in ambivalence, or activates an erotic theft.[19]

The Fetish, the Camera, the Videotape

How can the video camera and videated image be fetishized? And how does this fetishization relate to difference? Neither the camera nor the moving picture, in themselves, are sexual. But they have been sexualized in *Sex, Lies & Videotape* and other cultural technologies. Susan Sontag, in her memorable *On Photography*, writes of the camera's "inescapable (sexual) metaphor... named without subtlety whenever we talk about 'loading' and 'aiming' a camera, about 'shooting' a film."[20] Christian Metz has outlined with precision the relationship between the filmic lexis and fetishism.[21] While it is the photograph, according to Metz, that *is* a fetish, or can be fetishized, a film and cinema negotiate fetishism. Metz's commentary about absence, loss, fragmentation, and death is pertinent here. Recall that fetishism is structured around a number of metaphoric and metonymic transactions: based on the substitutive power of part-objects, the fetish operates through suspended belief (and disbelief), an investment (frequently visual) in simultaneous absence and presence. Like photography, the fetish overlays with death and loss in the way it captures and ossifies a moment that is highly condensed and ultimately mis-represented or misquoted and "cut" out of its referent. Of equal importance here is what the fetish does not say (or cannot say), in other words what it summons in absence or the absence—loss—that it evokes. What Phillippe Dubois calls "thanatography", or photography's affiliation with death, is the subversive phantasy/fiction that challenges, or gives new meaning to, the "presumed real."[22] This harkens back to Marx's comment about the "magic and necromancy" in the subversive power of the fetish: it combines the dead labor of commodities and the death of the referent in the photograph. The indexical authority of photo and moving image suspends both time and space. The power of mastery and captivity, which the representation bestows on its referent, is a frozen moment. People and objects are, in the words of Metz, instantaneously abducted from one world and re-presented in another. (As with death), the photo preserves the past; the moment is forever held for closer scrutiny, and always suggests an appropriation or excision out of another referent (pointing again to a part-object). The image preserves the fragment (the quotation) in its death—it recaptures and reactivates absence, loss, and the protection against that loss (or the melancholic illusion of protection/presence.) The redemption of the lost and absent past, through this dominent fiction, is at once phallic endowment and a phallic death wish. Metz refers to the fetish as a "pocket phallus": the spectacle of terror and seduction that plays on a missing element (in the text or in any dominant narrative), and recalls dispossession (of the subject): because the fetish in any account is a metaphor for forfeiture and dismemberment. The fatality of the fetish does not lie exclusively with its part—and dead—object status. Fetish objects, especially in the photographic discourse, structure and capture the gaze. They also figure castration in the way they metonymically embody loss (or death) within narratives of sexual difference, and desire, and subjectivity (if we believe they metaphorically quote the penis they also foreground castration as well). They always recall something that is not there—a small death by any other name. However, the subversiveness of fetishization resides with the virility of objects, precisely the way productive relations vitalize objects, infuse them with their own contradictions, tensions, ambivalences, and frissons. It is this vitality, the process of "ideological labor,"[23] that liquidates any sense of absolute value, objectivity, or subjectivity. Objects are exchanged for subjects and vice versa. This simultaneity—presence and absence—is what elects certain objects to fetish status, hence their s(t)imulation and excitement.[24] They are, in short, at the cutting edge of fictive coherence and dispossession.

Metz's point about *film* is that it activates fetishism through endlessly displacing "the look" (he calls this a primal displacement).[25] He refers to the manipulation of framing, the way film depends on the "constant and teasing displacement of the cutting line which separates the seen from the unseen."[26] Films work, he writes, "like a striptease of the space itself," creating and sustaining instability, flux, and the ambivalence around terror and pleasure. The important difference between films and photos is that whereas the former combines multiple juxtapositions, photographs focus on a petrified surface.

Metz's point that the fetish, in order to work, ideally must be isolated and ossified, can be applied to the home video, in the sense that video cassettes (like photos) can be touched, handled, re-played, and its frames frozen and isolated. The aesthetic of the music video is frequently that of a rapid succession of still images, interspersed with the obviously fabricated singing and acting poses of the performers (the image then being one performer among many). Andrew Ross notes the increasing popularity of VCR technology in the home, accompanied by the domestication of video consumption, and precisely this potential to isolate segments for viewing pleasure.[27] Any fetishized transaction works through the illusion that it is there for the solitary pleasure of the individual, that it is captured by the eye of the voyeur, and his eye alone. The domestication of the fetish entertains this notion.

The Technology of Seduction

In *Sex, Lies & Videotape* the camera is given full screen space in various diegetic sequences; we watch it filming Cynthia and later Ann, heightening the investment in, not just the surface of the look, but also what takes place behind the look. The "technology" of seduction is not just machinery; although surely part of the allure of videated images is found precisely in their mediation—whatever happens with light, colour, illumination, shadows, as well as what is missing or left out, happens imperceptibly. These technologies ask that we invest belief in operations of significance that we cannot see. The elusive combination of presence and absence, the faithful investments in an (imaginary) off-space (the preoccupations of Freud, Marx, Baudrillard), are the seductive *machinations* of the fetish. Fetishistic relations are the tensions and frictions that shimmer.

In *Sex, Lies & Videotape* the videotapes themselves ultimately threaten, disturb, traumatize and seduce. The two female characters in the film are driven by intrigue, enough to want to be filmed, and one to the point of voluntary exhibitionism. But Ann's husband, John, isolates the power of the fetish when, with considerable vehemence, he demands if Ann had made "one of those videos." His anger, fear, and fascination are removed from wondering if Ann and Graham had any carnal contact. His wife's engagement with the technique of seduction, and not the sexually retiring Graham, incites John to violent extremes. In his outrage and his desire to view Ann's video himself, he drives to Graham's late in the evening, wakes him, and tosses him out of the house, finds Ann's video, and watches it. This, I think, suggests an excess of presence; John does not really get the private viewing he wishes for, as Graham, although evicted, can hear the re-played video from outside. This radical exposure is the destructive moment seized by Graham to indict the tapes: after John leaves, Graham returns to his living room to destroy the tapes and the video camera. What threatens Graham's phantasmatic relation to the videotapes, and what causes him to renounce the power and pleasures of them, is the challenge of closure in the phallic economy, put by John. John's viewing of the video, for different purposes and under circumstances contrary to those of Graham, opens up the fetish and fetish relations to the possibility of multiple readings, not just absence recalled, but an excess of presence.

Still, the question of visibility and the off-screen problematize the referent, which is what makes *Sex, Lies & Videotape* the curious venture that it is (and aligns it with the same mood connoted by the boxer shorts mentioned above). If the fetish is a double-play of absence and presence, if it involves forfeitures and divestments, then the "uncanny and traumatic"[28] moment of perception and disavowal evokes and retains a limp penis. In this case the fetish is literally a stand-in for a corporal signifier, but a deflated one at that. Not only do the videated images surpass any potency in the real; they elect the fetish as the site of hysterical significance, foregrounding ambiguity in relations of subject and object, absence and presence, voyeur and narcissist. Whither the phallus?

Does Graham Have Penis Envy?

I want to retain the argument that the fetish, in any transaction, is tied to a destabilizing construction of otherness, and that this construction operates in a whole network of relationships throughout the film. This precarious working through of the domestication of the threat of otherness, at once negotiates a simulated difference and indifference; it both empowers and emasculates. This is evident in other areas of the film's discursive and dramatic plays on the management of identity in the framework of "images" of separation and collusion. Frequently, for example, the soundtrack is juxtaposed with visuals that do not exactly contradict the speaking voice of the narrative: that is the point. The claustrophobia of the fetish—the over-coded endowment, metaphoric and metonymic, of the object through its exchange value—is indicated in the way characters and their symbolic properties are interchanged for one another or, at least, in the way they coalesce to suggest that the boundaries between lies/truth, men/women, the real/representation, are blurred and contested.

The first instance of such a visual and verbal paraphrase occurs when Graham drives into the city. All we see, and this is the first scene of the film, is the shadow of the front of his car as it traverses the ashphalt. It comes to a sudden stop and we hear a voice-over of Ann saying (to her therapist): "Garbage." As she discusses, without any reflection upon what she is expressing, her concern with "what to do with all the garbage." She puts her hands to her forehead and extends them outwards as if to suggest her head will explode—from all the garbage. Her voice is paired with our visual introduction to Graham. We soon discover that he too is no stranger to garbage of his own ("Garbage: animal entrails"; "entrails: bowels, intestines, meaning 'interior' or 'internal'").

This fetishistic hyper-coding whereby the object embodies (in exchange) both "one" and the "other", or when it is an indictment of the referent, is underscored very early in the film, beginning with Ann's and Graham's shared, repressed "garbage." When Graham arrives and is met at the front door by Ann (their first encounter), he immediately asks if he can use the bathroom. After he reappears in the living room Ann remarks, "That was quick." Graham replies nonchalantly, "False alarm." After a brief chat with Ann he announces with a nervous laugh: "I'm ready to use the bathroom now." These non-normative comments first establish Graham as merely an oddball. But the oblique references to anality (or at least to Graham's internal functions: what else can they be?) implicate Ann and Graham in an anxious circularity. They share the same universe (via these visual and verbal associations to "garbage"), and the seductive machinery of the film is set in motion by the metonymic displacements of the characters. Indeed, later that evening Ann visits Graham asleep on the couch upstairs and gazes at him as though in a narcissistic trance.

At various points there is an equivalence between other characters; the film's fluidity is achieved through these narcissistic overlaps and exchanges. Ann and Cynthia are also implicated in a confusion of identities. As Ann talks to her therapist about her relationship with her husband John, the sound-track of her voice is accompanied by a scene in which John and Cynthia are engaged in sexual foreplay. Later, after Cynthia announces that she would like to "do it" in her sister's bed (with of course her sister's husband), John and Cynthia meet for an afternoon tryst at his home. It is during this illicit exchange that Graham and Ann share secrets over lunch. However, the editing of these two scenes confuses who is speaking. While Cynthia approaches John in bed, so that her hair covers the side of her face, Ann asks Graham, in their off-screen dialogue, if she can reveal "something personal." At that moment it is not clear who posesses the speaking voice. It could also be Cynthia's, in fact there is a strong illusion that it is. The phenomenon of disembodied voices occurs several times throughout the film and of course underscores the castrating transactions of the fetish; that is, the boundaries around categories of difference are susceptible to a seductive dissolution.

Disembodied voices are also a characteristic of Graham's videotapes. His "talking heads" are the substitute for carnal knowledge. And carnal knowledge in this fetishized universe of representation refers us back to the limp signifier and auto– erotic self-referentiality. These would seem to compete or contrast with the lustful and fully illicit liaisons between Cynthia and John. But the videotapes and the video camera are what fascinate and disturb, thus supplanting and dispersing any "real" referent. They do this because like all videated production they aspire to a perfection, as Hal Foster notes, subsuming all signs of labor in their own regime.[29] In *Sex, Lies & Videotape* the videos are also implicated in scenarios of loss and displacement: sex for Graham is removed from the laborious as he loses himself in the images, or is consumed by them.

The "talking heads," and Graham's subversive relationship to phallic sexuality, stand outside the laws of sexual difference and other, official, discourses on sexuality and the law. There are, for example, references to auto-eroticism (which in the case of women, after all, is exclusive of phallic donorship), the first made in the context of Ann's therapy. On one of Graham's videotapes we hear him ask a woman the "most unusual location" she's masturbated in; he later reveals that sometimes his subjects "do things for the camera." And Cynthia masturbates "for the camera" as well. Prior to that confession (made to her sister), and during her videotaping, Cynthia invokes a disembodied penis with the following account of the first time she saw a penis:

> The organ itself seemed like a separate thing, a separate entity to me. I mean, when he finally pulled it out and I could look at it and touch it I completely forgot there was a guy attached to it. I remember literally being startled when the guy spoke to me.

The camera then sustains a prolonged shot of Graham, expressionless, vacant, supine. Because the fetish involves a simulated exchange and combines properties of the voyeur *and* the narcissist, it can never be purely phallic. One can argue, I think, that there *is* a self-referential component in Graham's "talking heads" and auto-eroticism (via Irigaray). But because it conjoins with vulnerability, and Graham's inability to "speak" himself (he used to be a pathological liar; now his body is relegated to a kind of corporal silence), fetishized relations seduce by recalling what cannot be represented, or by the simulated other (while reflecting narcissism). (Is this not the secret to Madonna's "blond ambition"?)

The film is framed by institutional discourses that are challenged by the fetishized transactions, from within or auto– referentially. I am referring to psychotherapy and marriage whose laws, in some cases, are summarily broken. *Sex, Lies & Videotape* opens with psychotherapeutic dialogue between Ann and her therapist. This "talking cure" is quickly supplanted by another, that of the fetishized "other" in the videotapes, whose confessional impulse is further consolidated through the gaze. Ann's psychotherapy and the therapist are dismissed after she discovers Graham.

The second scene in the film is of John in his office, talking with a male friend on the phone about the friend's impending marriage. The conversation centers on the institutional aspects of marriage, particularly how married men (symbolized through the wedding ring John spins around on his desk), are more alluring to or have a cachet with other women. As John says, "It's critical." (And this is a phrase later appropriated by Graham when he interrogates Ann about what it is she likes about marriage: "I don't mean to be critical." This further underscores the shared ambivalence of both men towards "the law," neatly focussing on their eventual sharing of Ann. We later discover that this is at least the second woman they have had in common.) The precarious uncoding of the masculine in a marginal placement to phallic sexuality occurs, as well, in the second-to-final scene of the film. Two events conspire to disturb John's privileged relationship to marriage *and* the discursive fellowship of men. In telling a colleague that his wife wants to be freed from the marriage, John protests a little too loudly that he does not really care and that it is his wife's problem that she will not accept his commitment to his work. He however immediately receives the shattering news that he has lost the big account (due to his philandering with Cynthia and continually deferring appointments with the client) and is doomed to severe disapproval from his colleagues, and the terminal position of junior partner. In this scene, he also looks like "junior" in his white suit, vest, bow-tie and glasses, and little boys' clothes (like Pee-wee Herman, one notes). He has been emasculated in more ways than one.

Like the ear in "Blue Velvet," the fetish opens multiple narratives, preventing closure: not unlike Graham who stirs up the bourgeois complacency of the triangular relationship. It unsettles in its seduction and is one route to prying open the tensions and frictions in any text. In terms of contemporary affect, *Sex, Lies & Videotape* may point to a de-centered gaze and, at the risk of sounding too optimistic, a politics of sexual dislocation.[30] For Graham, the videos are a substitute for a limp signifier, at least within the semantics of the film, recall the loss of his own phallic potency. Rather than inscribing a "map of erotic significance on the woman's body,"[31] fetishistic negotiations more appropriately suggest that strategies of the male gaze indict the male body, and its representations, and of course eroticize castration. Kaja Silverman interprets the "great masculine renunciation," which occurred with the relaxing of sumptuary laws in the eighteenth century, as the repression of exhibitionism and narcissism in the male subject, with the consequent male identification with "woman-as-spectacle." The consequences arising from the contested terrain of the representation is the female form endowed to cover up male loss, the flaw of the real.[32] Whether a willful injunction to dispossession, or the discursive construction of difference which straddles the negation of difference, the fetish and fetish relations work to fictionalize coherence. In spite of Graham's "looking at women," he is in fact looking at a deflated representation of his disembodied self. Can men have penis envy? Or, what's "pee-wee" about Herman?

Notes

1. Lynne Kirby, "Male Hysteria and Early Cinema," *Camera Obscura* 17 (May 1988):126. The issue entitled "Male Trouble" contains articles that re-work theory (oedipal identifications, malemasochism) and popular culture (Pee-wee Herman, "Three Men and a Baby," Jerry Lewis). See also the *Canadian Journal of Politicaland Social Theory* 13:1-2 (1989), for the development of arguments for "the hysterical male."

2. Arthur Kroker, Marilouise Kroker, and David Cook, *The Panic Encyclopedia*, (Montreal, New World Perspectives, 1989).

3. Charles Acland, "Look what they're doing on TV! Towards an appreciation of the complexity of music video," *Wide Angle* 10:2 (1988). Acland discusses music videos, in particular Madonna's "Papa Don't Preach," and urges "intertextual" and "inter-media

considerations" (p. 9). See Lisa A. Lewis, "Female Address in Music Video," *Journal of Communication Inquiry* 11:1 (Winter 1987) for a rather different emphasis: "Madonna... rewrites the tragic Marilyn Monroe image she references, into a decidedly female image of recognition and power" (p. 78). E. Ann Kaplan's analysis of Madonna videos is as celebratory as Lewis's although she advances a more complex, and not unproblematic, understanding of seduction and the video in *Rocking Around the Clock: Music Television, Postmodernism & Consumer Culture*, (New York: Methuen, 1987).

4. Constance Penley, "The Cabinet of Dr. Pee-wee: Consumerism and Sexual Terror," *Camera Obscura* 17 (May 1988):149. See also, in the same issue, Ian Balfour, "The Playhouse of the Signifier"; Henry Jenkins 111, "'Going Bonkers!': Children, Play and Pee-wee"; and Scott Bukatman, "Paralysis in Motion: Jerry Lewis's Life as a Man." The last essay studies the perverse appeal of Jerry Lewis and his films, as figured through their "disruptive polylingualism" and the Lewis "persona of the female hysteric, (who) acts out his own ambivalence towards an inscribed and proscribed social position (masculinity)" (p. 196).

5. Edmond Grant suggests that the film is inaccessible and unsatisfying because the character of Graham is merely a "space cadet who never quite turns into a flesh-and-blood being with realistic sexual troubles," *Films in Review* (October 1989). Writing in *The New Yorker*, Terrence Rafferty also localizes the idealistic "problem" of Graham within the "pop-psychology truism, 'Get in touch with your feelings'," in "Lies, Lies, and More Lies," (7 August 1989). Both reviews put the film within the pale of an "auteur's" quirkiness; enigmas that cannot be explained; characters who are simple, if repressed; and a story with an "outrageous plot device" (Grant). What is left begging and unexplored is the question of the film's appeal; how it seduces (it is merely acknowledged that Soderbergh offers some "topflight visuals" [Grant] and a "slick, eclectic technique" [Rafferty]); the role of seduction in the film itself (and its attendent discourse on "truth"); and the repressions in the text, not just in the characters. Harlan Jacobson, in his review of the film, "Truth or Consequences," *Film Comment* (July-August, 1989), is concerned with Soderbergh's potential as a director and the baffling fact that he is only 26. In "Video Love: Sex, Lies and Videotape," Greil Marcus, in a review which waffles between the appreciative and the dismissive, argues that it is "pointless to look for meaning" anywhere in this film notable for its "off-market funkiness," *ENclitic* 11:3 (1989). Haven't these people ever watched MTV or MuchMusic or experienced videos and their seductive pleasures? In this same issue of *ENclitic*, there are commercial advertisements which is justifiable for specialized publications that are continually threatened by small circulation numbers and a low return. (One advertisement for example, is for Delmonico's Seafood Grille—"If it swims, We've got it!"—and underneath, in small letters: "We welcome the American Express Card"). But two other advertisements on page 5 suggest that video-appeal has purchase, even among intellectuals, which locates the film culturally (rather than as the project of a "relatively autonomous author," or a flawed study of a character (Graham) who places himself "so far outside of everyone else's normality, outside of the politeness that keeps life level, that he no longer even recognizes his transgressions" [Marcus, p.30]). The ads are for "EZTV," "LA's Premiere Video Gallery" with a screening room; and "Channel One Video."

6. Sigmund Freud, "Fetishism," (1927) in *On Sexuality*, trans. James Strachey; ed. Angela Richards, (Harmondsworth: Penguin, 1983 [1927]) p. 353. See also Sigmund Freud, "Three Essays on the Theory of Sexuality," in *On Sexuality* [1905]; and "Splitting of the Ego in the Process of Defence," *Standard Edition*, Vol. 23, trans. James Strachey, (New York: Norton, 1940). Other sources are: Robert C. Bak, "Fetishism," *Journal of the American Psychoanalytic Association* 1 (1953); Michael Balint, "A Contribution on Fetishism," *International Journal of Psychoanalysis* 16 (1935); J.C. Flugel, "Polyphallic Symbolism and the Castration Complex," *International Journal of Psychoanalysis* 5 (1924); Angel Garma, "The Meaning and Genesis of Fetishism," *International Journal of Psychoanalysis* 37 (1956); W.H. Gillespie, "Notes on the Analysis of Sexual

Perversions," *International Journal of Psychoanalysis* 33 (1952); Phyllis Greenacre, "Certain Relationships Between Fetishism and Faulty Development of the Body Image," *The Psychoanalytic Study of the Child* 8 (1953); Phyllis Greenacre, "Further Notes on Fetishism," *The Psychoanalytic Study of the Child* 15 (1960); Bela Grunberger, "Some Reflections on the Rat Man," *International Journal of Psychoanalysis* 47 (1966); Henry Lihn, "Fetishism: A Case Report," *International Journal of Psychoanalysis* 51 (1970); Alan Parkin, "On Fetishism," *International Journal of Psychoanalysis* 44 (1963). George Zavitzianos, "The Object in Fetishism, Homeovestism and Transvestism," *International Journal of Psychoanalysis* 58 (1977). These authors indicate that the object-choice of the fetishist frequently recalls a visual moment; however the olfactory sometimes plays a role in the structure of fetishism. See Bak, Balint, and Parkin.

7.   Freud, "Fetishism," p. 113.

8.   Kaja Silverman, via Lacan, argues that linguistic castrations precede the perception of anatomical threat in *The Acoustic Mirror: The Female Voice in Psychoanalysis and Cinema*, (Bloomington: Indiana University Press, 1988).

9.   Sigmund Freud, "Three Essays on the Theory of Sexuality," in *On Sexuality*, p. 155.

10. Karl Marx, *The German Ideology*, ed. C. J. Arthur, (New York: International Publishers, 1970 [1846]). See also Marx's essay, "The Fetishism of Commodities and the Secret Thereof," *Capital*, Vol. 1, ed. Frederick Engels, trans. Samuel Moore and Edward Aveling, (New York: International Publishers, 1967 [1867]). W.J.T. Mitchell discusses fetishism and ideology in Marx's rhetoric in *Iconology: Image, Text, Ideology*, (Chicago and London: The University of Chicago Press, 1986). Linda Williams compares and contrasts Freud and Marx on fetishism, with special emphasis on the sexual fetish in hard-core pornographic films, in "Fetishism and Hard Core: Marx, Freud, and the `Money Shot'," *For Adult Users Only: The Dilemma of Violent Pornography*, ed. Susan Gubar and Joan Hoff, (Bloomington: Indiana University Press, 1989)

11. Marx, *The German Ideology*, p. 47.

12. Marx, *Capital*, Vol. 1, p. 76.

13. Marx, *Capital*, Vol. 1, p. 72.

14. Marx, *Capital*, Vol. 1, pp. 71, 72.

15. Colin Mercer, "A Poverty of Desire: Pleasure and Popular Politics," in *Formations of Pleasure*, ed. The Formations Collective, (London: Routledge, 1983), p. 93.

16. Jean Baudrillard, *For a Critique of the Political Economy of the Sign*, trans. Charles Levin, (St. Louis, Missouri: Telos, 1981), p. 91.

17. D.N. Rodowick, "Vision, Desire and the Film Text," *Camera Obscura* 6 (1980); and, "The Difficulty of Difference," *Wide Angle* 5, 1 (1982).

18. Elizabeth Wilson, *Adorned in Dreams: Fashion and Modernity*, (London: Virago, 1985), p. 20.

19. Berkeley Kaite, "Reading the Body Textual: The Shoe and Fetish Relations in Soft and Hard Core," *The American Journal of Semiotics* 6, 4 (1989).

20. Susan Sontag, *On Photography*, (New York: Dell, 1977), p. 14.

21. Christian Metz, "Photography and Fetish," *October* 34 (Fall 1985).

22. Quoted in Metz.

23. Baudrillard, p. 94.

24. Jacques M. Chevalier, *Semiotics, Romanticism and the Scriptures*, (Berlin and New York: Mouton & de Gruyter, 1990).

25. Metz, p. 87.

26. Metz, p. 88.

27. Andrew Ross, "The Popularity of Pornography," *No Respect: Intellectuals & Popular Culture*, (New York: Routledge, Chapman and Hall, 1989).

28. Freud, "Fetishism," p. 354.

29. Hal Foster, *Recodings: Art, Spectacle, Cultural Politics*, (Port Townsend, Washington: Bay Press, 1985).

30. On these see *inter alia*, Kaja Silverman, "Fassbinder and Lacan: A Reconsideration of Gaze, Look and Image," *Camera Obscura* 19 (January 1989); Sharon Willis, "Seductive Spaces: Private Fascinations and Public Fantasies in Popular Cinema," in *Seduction and Theory: Readings of Gender, Representation and Rhetoric*, ed. Dianne Hunter, (Urbana: University of Illinois, 1989); Dana Polan, "Brief Encounters: Mass Culture and the Evacuation of Sense," in *Studies in Entertainment: Critical Approaches to Mass Culture*, ed. Tania Modleski, (Bloomington: Indiana University Press, 1986).

31. The phrase is from "The Legs of the Countess," by Abigail Solomon-Godeau, in which the author writes of the appropriation of fetishistic scopophilia by the Countess de Castiglione. *October* 39 (Winter 1986).

32. I would emphasize "loss" rather than "lack," the former being more dialectical and recuperative. See, Kaja Silverman, "Fragments of a Fashionable Discourse," in *Studies in Entertainment*; J. C. Flugel, *The Psychology of Clothes*, (New York: International Universities Press, 1931); for an elaboration of male "lack," see Kaja Silverman, *The Acoustic Mirror* and "Fassbinder and Lacan."

12

MY FIRST CONFESSION

Stephen Pfohl

I recall a time in which I wanted a baby sister but would settle for a doll, a simulacrum of a girl to play boy with. It was my third birthday and I insisted. My parents bought me the doll, a cute girl doll, frilled and feminine.

At first I was pleased with this gift, a delight to my eyes. Then I heard the sound of my parents moving about in the garden. I had become the subject of inquisition: worried eyes wondering and troubled voices that asked, "Well now that you have a doll to play with are you really sure that's what you truly want?" Eyes upon me, judging my desire, they waited for signs of a normal self. A strange unease overtook me, I hid within myself, transformed. Some other me excluded, silenced, made abject. "No," I confessed, "the doll I had desired, it's what girls want. This I want no longer." Smiles burst the tension and ease returned to the body of a young boy, hugged by adults. It was America in the early nineteen-fifties and it was no time to play boy with a cute girl doll. There were imaginary Indians on television, snakes in the jungle electric and communists behind the curtain. Back to the toy store went my baby sister, an uncertain double replaced by a six shooting gun. Many wild savages did I slay, each recording a continuous count notched upon the handle of my weapon; and each day felt better, the further I progressed from the shame of my first confession.

13

SIMULATIONS

Andrew Haase

I

Under the gaze I am "transformed into something cold and dead."[1] Transformation is not without repercussions. Signification ricochets off a privileged visionary apparatus and takes its revenge: my body is mutilated.

The pleasure, the pleasure of psychoanalysis, begins with philosophy's refusal to crawl in scum and shit.

"Perspective is the triumph of an artificial view of things, an illusion built upon a specific preconception, a way of seeing that is more the work of the brain than of the eye."[2]

"We are living on the violent edge between ecstasy and decay; between the melancholy lament of postmodernism over the death of the grand signifiers of modernity—consciousness, truth, sex, capital, power—and the ecstatic nihilism of ultramodernism; between the body as a torture-chamber and pleasure palace; between fascination and lament."[3]

When I can no longer pick the crabs from my pubic hair I am forced to shave. My penis appears skinny, flat. My body arches over to me-see. My penis is a raw chicken. My penis is thin.

Postmodern masculinity is the formulation of desire as androgyny.⁴ Historically maintained by the authority of a nature/culture split, collapsing gender distinctions proposition us on every channel. Released from "Don Juan" categorical imperatives by the equivalence of machismo and wimpiness, male desire transposes itself at full velocity. A choice of chains rather than a cynical emancipation. Men without faces, men without phalli, participate in chameleon identities. The pleasure game: Russian roulette with multiple masks and all chambers loaded.

I do not see Keri until she asks for my order. It's 90°. "I'd like a turkey club and an iced tea. No make that a beer. St. Pauli Girl." I watch David watch the waitress as she approaches our table. Keri wears a name tag. Her legs are the same color as her hair. Her sneakers are the same color as her shorts. I watch her black t-shirt curve around her tits. "Hello what can I get you?" I will say, "What's good?" David says, "What's your name?"

Not only an exclusive game for bourgeois men but a play of imagos. Dressing up is now available for the whole family.

"Of the three metamorphoses of the spirit I have told you: how the spirit became a camel; and the camel, a lion; and the lion, finally, a child."⁵

"The eye interprets everything...in terms of seeing."⁶

I become conscious of Keri's presence only as she leaves to put in our order. David squeezes the iron table and looks at me. He says "Keri?" I say "It's hot as hell out here." David drinks his water down fast. I brush the sweat off my forehead and into my hair. David's eyes are clear. I say nothing. I want to "let Keri decide." I fuck her. David and I fuck her. No one fucks her. I remember to lean back in my chair. It's noon. I remember to cross my legs and I put on my sunglasses. I say to David, "Keri?"

The confession: "a ritual in which the expression alone, independently of its external consequences, produces intrinsic modifications in the person who articulates it"; a ritual of torture and pleasure, a ritual of narration.⁷

I take five rolls of black and white film from the Accademia delle Belle Arti, Florence, Italy. Images of Michelangelo's "David." Representations of representations of myself, Michelangelo, King David of the Israelites, slayer of Goliath, healer of Saul, murderer, adulterer. Multiple bits of historical refuse.

I write and I begin to watch myself write. I learn about watching.

Pauline Réage writes of O (or does she): "If only she could have closed her eyes. But she could not. Two gazes stalked her eyes, gazes from which she could not—and did not desire to—escape."[8] Why can O not divert her own gaze? Renéand Sir Stephen desire to "stalk" O. O could not escape. O does not desire to escape.

In the sou-*venir* shops, tourists jostle for position among books as black racks display postcards of Michelangelo's "David." I come to the "David" with millions of others.

The production of Truth is the production of "a certain representation of power" (i.e., "juridico-discursive") which "governs both the thematics of repression and the theory of the law as constitutive of desire."[9] Intervention in the "history of Truth" is possible only as a critique of representation. Can a representation of critique eviscerate Truth? A representation of a representation plays in metamorphosis.

When I photograph the "David," a representational reality seduces the male body, the male desire. I am before the lens: "I instantaneously make another body for myself, I transform myself in advance into an image."[10] The "David's" body and Michelangelo's body are mine.

Zarathustra's camel, "*wanting* to be well loaded," takes up what is *most* and speeds into the desert as if it could escape itself?[11]

Of course I am speaking of male homosexual desire?

Desire today has become "transferable" ("non-referential, un-referential") yet untransferred. Fed by the place left vacant (lack), desire is "captured in its own vertiginous image, desire of desire, as pure form, hyperreal. Deprived of symbolic substance, it doubles back upon itself, draws its energy from its own reflection and its disappointment with itself. This is literally today the "demand," and it is obvious that unlike the "classical" objective or transferable relations this one here is insoluble and interminable?"[12]

Photographing the "David," my organ is not the eye peeping through a plastic hole for "David" me-photographs. My finger presses lightly on the shutter release, metallic plates shift, I hear nothing. Instead of photographing I watch photography.

"When the unconscious itself, the discourse of the unconscious becomes un-findable," psychoanalysis becomes interminable. Jean Baudrillard holds that Jacques Lacan's categories of Real/Imaginary/Symbolic must be supplemented with "the hyperreal, which captures and obstructs the functioning of the three orders."[13] Rather, we experience an implosion of categories. When the "Real" drops away psychological symptoms oscillate between the Symbolic and the Imaginary. The hyperreal is superfluous.

It's 90°at Cape Cod. I pick up my empty water glass. I remove my sunglasses. I look at Keri and I shake my head. Small drops of sweat fell on my hand. I wait for Keri to come to our table. I wait for her to fill our glasses. As I eat my burger David talks to her in a non-stop stream. I see her laugh. She make small comments. Keri looks at David. I remember to fix my eyes on her eyes, my gaze waits. Keri's eyes move from David to me. It's July. I smile.

There is a seamless tonal curve from black (10) to white (0) through grey (5)?

My union with the "David" is fused by the technology of a single lens reflex which knits a camera body to my face, which becomes my eye, a frame that reconstructs vision. I see in photographs. The photographs are not of some "other thing." I covet this sight.

Has the phallus become liquid, exchanging hands at hyper-speed? For Lacan the phallus *circulates* within a theater of hetero-sexual masquerade, within the "comedy" of male and female interaction.[14]As the body disappears, however, the phallus, grounded in Symbolic history and Real experience, drops away. With the death of desire, the phallus (signifier of desire) dies: no one has or is the phallus because the phallus does not exist. As the gap between transmitter and receiver (need and desire) approaches zero, circulation becomes stasis, articulation, silence. This is "demand without content, without referent, unjustified, but for all that all the more severe—naked demand with no possible answer."[15]

Keri brings the sandwiches. I will remove my sunglasses. She wears a name tag. I remember to smile. David talks to her; asks her questions. He asks her opinion. I say "Hey, where is a good bar around here for this evening?" Keri says "I'll be at the Blue Angel. Why don't you go there?" I watch her yellow t-shirt curve around her tits. David says "O. K. Great. See you later." I say "What's its name?" I take a sip of beer. I want to think Keri has decided. Keri has decided.

A world of two dimensional representation concealed itself within the strategy of "perspective," a *masquerade* of reality. Photography innocently welcomed.

Is having the phallus a precondition for renouncing its presence?

"Because René was leaving her free, and because she loathed her freedom. Her freedom was worse than any chains. Her freedom was separating her from René."[16]

"We [men] should probably start by trying to grasp who *we are as men*, asking that from feminism rather than wondering what 'they' want from an assumed male us. We need to drop the academic masks, to pose at every moment the sexual determinations of the discourse we develop as we teach and write, to stop knowing as we do, as we want, as we impose."[17] These suggestions at first glance appear sensible and sensitive. But can I ever, as a male, ask "from feminism"? The eagerness of male feminists to thrust upon me what I "need" maintains and re-enforces a pedagogical positioning; indeed, men do "*pose* at every moment." A pretense to dis-empowerment grants full reign to another sadistic smile, to another passive/aggressive reaction.

Sex "itself" no longer exists.

"Photography creates my body or mortifies it, according to its caprice."[18]

"The specificity of [a body and of a] psychic economy can only be maintained as long as discursive practices are determined by the gender differences which they themselves project"?[19]

Having been re-made in the image of an owl (the specular centerpiece for a masquerade ball) O is absolutely divorced from her "lover" René. Sir Stephen and the Commander unfasten her chain, remove her mask and lie her on her back. They possess her one after the other.[20]

At the Blue Angel at Cape Cod I prod her. I ask about her sexual experiences. I said nothing. David is a doctor, so he says, "But don't you enjoy sex? Don't you orgasm?"

O's anatomy is matched up with clothing, instruments of torture, architectural spaces, metaphysical constructs.[21]

"The body is the inscribed surface of events, traced by language and dissolved by ideas, the locus of a dissociated self, adopting the illusion of a substantial unity—a volume in disintegration."[22]

Is the *Story of O* (narrated from the "third person omniscient") limited to *speculations* of male desire?

Representation is in relation to bodies: sexual identity as pornographic, the look of Calvin Klein, the Calvin Klein look, and desire's cathexis to narratives of "love" and "romance."

"He whom one awaits is, because he is expected, already present, already master."[23]

"The letter always arrives at its destination?"[24]

As the logic of masquerade teaches: to "drop" one mask is to pick up another (even if that mask is the "dropped mask"). A patronizing form of "male concern for feminist issues" is characteristic of the entire history of patriarchy as subterfuge. Unveiling the phallus implies veiling the phallus.

As I *analyze* the *Story of O* I am granted the ineluctable pleasure of extraction, the "unquestionable proof" of power.[25]

In an era of representational corporality, the subject, as principle of constancy, falls away. The Symbolic Order, the structure of exchange between the unconscious subject and the ego, is posited *a posteriori* . The Truth of psychoanalysis (conceived objectively or in terms of *aletheia*) is dumb.[26] Imaginary egos speak the Symbolic Order as representation. Situationally reconstituted, this ego shifts modes, "demands" interminably.

O's freedom is the condition for the possibility of renouncing that freedom. Roissy teaches that "you are totally dedicated to something outside yourself."[27] I am dedicated to nothing.

Desiring-production is that which crosses boundaries to "discover new lands and new streams," to open up "new worlds" and "new areas." Desire, moving in ever changing flows "does not 'want' revolution, it is revolutionary in its own right, as though involuntarily, by wanting what it wants." The "nature" of desire, however, to flow in an *undirected* manner, is intolerable to both fascism and multi-national capital. Patriarchy effectively channels heterogeneous desire through women as a "powerhouse" of male desire and as a "force of absorption"? Yet, the "new male ego could never have developed as a ruler-ego, one that was isolated from women and opposed to them, without the (admittedly enforced) cooperation of women themselves."[28]

Today, postmodern desire lives as "dead desire," as a digital paroxysm between polar oppositions within a network of "dead power." Patriarchal apologies are invalid when control and power are no longer at issue; yet men continue to simulate positions of control within socio-economic spheres. "This secret of power's lack of existence that the great politicians shared also belongs to the great bankers, who know that money is nothing, that money does not exist; and it also belonged to the great theologians and inquisitors who knew that God does not exist, that God is dead."[29] The mediascape constitutes the very male desire from which it comes.

Zarathustra's lion, *wanting* to "conquer his freedom and be master in his own desert," seeks out the dragon-lord who screams "Thou shalt" and says "I will" as if it could destroy itself.[30]

Stephen Heath writes that "pornography is a relation between men, nothing to do with a relation to women except by a process of phallic conversion that sets them as terms of male exchange." Men need to "examine the structure of the relations between men" to access "why men like porn (not piously, why this or that exceptional man does *not*)."[31] Yet as Heath (an exceptional man) admits, his writing is just more "pious words." More pious pleasures? Male desire functions here at its most insidious levels. Heath wants a God and he wants to fuck her. He states: "I *take* Irigaray and *use her* writing to end mine."[32] If "pornography" is "this society's running commentary on the sexual" then Heath's text is pornographic.[33]

I take photographs.

To "male feminists" Friedrich Nietzsche says: "Alas, where in the world has there been more folly than among the pitying? And what in the world has caused more suffering than the folly of the pitying?"[34]

"How peaceful and reassuring the hand of a master who lays you on a bed of rock, the love of a master who knows how to take what he loves ruthlessly, without pity."[35] O is repulsion. Why does her desire grip my mouth, dry my mouth, replace saliva with sweat and vomit?

A "recipe for male feminists" belies the entire project. (Men's relation to feminism is "an impossible one." Men can learn to write, talk and act in "response to feminism," and should try not to be "anti-feminist" or supportive of traditional "oppressive structures." Men understand their participation in the sexual domination of women on an abstract (rather than personal) level; a "move" to preserve male positioning within hierarchies of power. Since "equality" is a mask for the oppression of women, male feminists must recognize "difference."[36]The need to theorize, to insulate a position from critique, to cover one's ass, undercuts the ability to enact any radical "male feminism."

As the phallus signifies desire raised (*aufgehoben*) to the Symbolic level, latent desire from the Imaginary level (i.e., desire from the child directed to the mother) is concealed.[37]Phallic performance demands a veil.

The history of sexuality, for Michel Foucault, has not been one of continually increasing repression. The ability to take sex "into account," to analyze the object of our investigation "as a target of intervention," to employ strategic silences, has recreated the way our bodies act out sexuality. "Real" sexual activity has not been suppressed. The pleasure of power—the power of pleasure; mutually reinforcing each other, confirming, constituting an interpolar relation. Why does a science of sex lay out the "Truth" as an analytical visibility, a permanent transparency?[38]Discourse on sex and sexual pleasure have restructured our activities in manageable terms. An explosion of sex-speak has produced a new sex and a new flesh.

Science refuses to speak of "sex itself"; instead, it concerns itself "primarily with aberrations, perversions, exceptional oddities, pathological abatements, and morbid aggravations."[39] The desire of psychoanalysis always already conditions its discourse, conditions a relations of the subject to another subject.

Freikorps members, proto-fascists, "soldier males" who eventually formed the core of the S.S., provide us with an easy target. Male desire has always been critiqued (and venerated) in the guise of war and sport and science. Klaus Theweleit asks why the "fear of dissolution through union with a woman actually causes desire to flee from its object, then transform itself into a representation of violence?"[40] Does the cathexis of fear into "a representation of violence" imply that "representations of violence" are fear-productions? "On the basis of his clinical practice, Reich reports that soldier males often in fact suffered from sustained erections."[41]

Why is the pessimism offered by apocalyptic prophets not shared by a consumer public indulging in ultra-fashion and image purchasing?

Romantic desire for "union with the other" calls out in the name of holy transcendence and male orgasm. Theweleit presupposes an alienation (non-union) that can and should be overcome. Lacan's conception of the gaze forecloses this possibility. For Lacan, memory of dissolution implies the subject sustaining itself in a "function of desire," _not union_ . The gaze is _imagined_ by the subject in the field of the Other.[42] An experience of "dissolution" must be conceived as the revelation of a subject's condition as always already de-centered, a revelation which can only be enacted from a centered position (non-dissolved).

The continual valorization of positions considered traditionally "feminine" (decentering, liquidity, dissolution, fragmentation) is a popular ploy among "male feminists" who desire to act out personality traits historically assigned to women (passivity, sensitivity, naturalness, passion, etc.) and to reinforce conservative gender distinctions (women as hysteric, mother, virgin, whore,_"territory of becoming,"_ etc.).[43] "Oppression through exaltation."[44]

Photographs take me.

As images replace images with cinematic speed, romantics look around and blink. I've never had real sex and I don't want it. In the day and age of A.I.D.S., the sex/death link formulates a "sex without secretions."[45]The postmodern preference: media-sex. More bang for your fuck.

Zarathustra's child, *wanting* to will its "own will," *wanting* "a new beginning, a game, a self-propelled wheel, a first movement, a sacred 'Yes,'" forgets and embodies innocence as if it could create itself.[46]

Cinematic velocity forecloses pictorial comparison. The annihilation of the reflexive viewer inaugurates a war for ratings. Has cinema ever allowed us to question?

"The simulacrum is never that which conceals the truth—it is the truth which conceals that there is none. The simulacrum is true."[47]

The desire for fascism: As "constantly present and possible...*it can, and does, become our production*." At a certain point and under certain conditions the masses *wanted* it. The production of male-female relations is a crude example of it.[48] Heterogeneous and homogeneous elements present within individuals and societies are united in it.[49]

"Computers which employ digital languages (0/1) to store bits of information present distorted pictures of experience. Music, digitally encoded onto compact discs, is read as (0) or (1) by C. D. players and translated back into musical notes. While the digital systems increase clarity and distinctness (analogue recordings are less clear and distinct) they lose resonance (available on analogue recordings). This results from an inability to represent the infinite sound gradations between (0) and (1). The thrust for a more perfect simulation must continue." This analysis is obsolete. It manifests a nostalgia for a *real* which has always already been reconstructed. Within the mediascape the body is constituted along digital lines. Radios, amplifiers, TVs, sound systems, present only 0/1 sound to the human ear. Perhaps at first, a few musical aficionados object that something sounds "wrong." Soon the body adjusts; the ear adapts, "digital music sounds better." A self-fulfilling prophecy is enacted. The world has indeed become flat. The band plays "live Muzak."[50] I want my MTV.

In writing, perceived reality is "annihilated in order to preserve the life of an ideational representation," in a process which proceeds from compulsion and the reconstructs approximate models as "determinate paradigms."[51]

Today, in the postmodern era, sexuality is relegated to technology and the mediascape: authorized dealers of orgasmic pleasures, fantasy, and the body.

Psychoanalysis can no longer uphold a confessional mode. The "one who is supposed to know" seems confused. The analyst has become the analysand has become the analyst.

In postmodernity I am cinematic?

Philosophical inquiry, insisting on an apolitical, ahistorical, asexual perspective, effectuates precise images of human existence and experience.

Western literature moves from narrated presentations (myths and fables) to confessional representations of Truth (confessions).[52] The confession can no longer exist if concealment of transgression is not possible, if desire and activity are formulated within an obscene cinema. Today, however, surveillance (exterior/interior) and the policing of desire have become unnecessary in an era where the variation between models, between the screen of the movie theater and the screen of the body, have been eliminated. The desperate quest for an authority of reception and absolution, for a master to whip my inner thighs, has been abandoned. I cannot confess my sins because I don't have any.

As the arc of postmodern power circles back upon itself, transgression becomes recombinant (philosophers as capitalists, capitalists as artists, artists as preachers, preachers as movie stars, movie stars as presidents) or nostalgia (re-vamped styles as the avant-garde of fashion, neo-psychedelic as music's cutting edge).

Today the body's enunciation of a discourse on sex cannot be separated from the enunciated body's sexuality. Today the body's enunciation of a discourse on sex has replaced the enunciated body's sexuality. The noise of body moans.

As I speak I fuck?

"Man's desire is desire of the Other."[53] For Lacan, male desire functions (as it returns to the subject) as lack of a specific object of desire (*"objet petit a "*) and of the condition of being the desired of the Other. "Desiring-production" introduces an alternative which includes Lacan's conception as a limited case.[54] However, as models, both constitute reality; as reality, both are symptoms of their models.

Within postmodernity, re-representation emerges as quintessentially political. Re-representation makes "reality."

Literature is not based on experience. Approximate demos, support the continued search for more reality than the real. However, the complete codification of women (Demi Moore is Raquel Welch, Raquel Welch is Holly Hunter, Holly Hunter is Daryl Hannah, Daryl Hannah is Cher, Cher is Glen Close is...) presupposes then denounces the existence of "real women." Male desire drives the search for its object via lack. If this search is taken to its logical extreme then it self-destructs in ten seconds.

"Rarely have philosophers directed a steady gaze to these objects situated between disgust and ridicule, where one must avoid both hypocrisy and scandal."[55]

My anatomy is matched up with clothing, instruments of torture, architectural spaces, metaphysical constructs.

Excremental philosophy: the pressurized implosion of transcendental signifiers and bar room gab in a mutual hyperbolic spin, denuding political ramifications with the precision of napalm. We are left lip-syncing "just for the fun of it."[56]

Zarathustra does not cling to itself? A principle of intelligibility, a condition of constancy, the assurance of a transcendental signifier, the ground, drops away. A Zarathustra speaks of itself to itself and laughs angrily in self-condemnation.[57]

"On her way, she suddenly saw her reflection in one of the mirrors fastened to a door and which, together with another mirror covering part of the wall and a third on another door, formed a large three-faced mirror...she was no longer wearing either a collar or leather bracelets, and she was alone, her own sole spectator. And yet never had she felt herself more totally committed to a will which was not her own, more totally a slave, and more content to be so."[58]

Cinematic denial of our visual habits, "*seems* to introduce us into an *inverse* world, but a world of images and therefore without real malignity, one that can be put right again whenever we wish and that is thus literally *reversible.*"[50]

I want nihilism?

"Whoever sins by symbols will be punished by symbols."[60] My fate is now being enacted.

Sexuality, uncoupled from realism, no longer maintains the "functional requirements of a discourse that must produce its truth."[61]

The "obligation to conceal it was but another aspect of the duty to admit to it."[62] The desire to conceal my sex, insures a desire to reveal my sex.

"The agency of domination does not reside in the one who speaks (for it is [s/he] who is constrained), but in the one who listens and says nothing; not in the one who knows and answers, but in the one who questions and is not supposed to know. And this discourse of truth finally takes effect, not in the one who receives it, but in the one from whom it is wrested."[63] When the rituals of domination are perfected to the point of completion, domination ceases to exist?

"That which is thus alienated in needs constitutes an *Urverdrängung* (primal repression), an inability, it is supposed, to be articulated in demand, but it re-appears in something it gives rise to that presents itself in [humans] as desire (*das Begehren*)."[64] When the lacuna between the needs of a subject and what can be articulated in demand falls to zero—desire is cryogenized.

Pornography is condemned by "enlightened" individuals. Pornography is everywhere.

The phone begins to ring as I unlock the apartment door. It's 20°in Boston. The answering machine clicks on. After a few seconds I hear, "Hello. Hello. This is Keri. From the Cape? I know I haven't spoken to you for a while. But I..." I pick up the phone. I say, "Hello." She says she wants to meet for a drink at ten. I hung-up. I smile. My sister is not yet home from work. I turn on some lights and turn on the shower. Steam covers the mirror. As the hot water slaps my back I masturbate with efficiency. My eyes close and I reach up to touch my tits. I reach up to touch Keri's tits. I want my desire to remain unreadable. Balls of whitish come slip down the drain.

The twentieth century professes to loosen repressive mechanisms, proliferate tolerance, and diminish disqualification of "perverts."[65] In the completion of repression as tolerance have we all become perverts? Have we all become perversions?

When heterogeneity becomes transgression, when perversion is the Law, when the media has eclipsed the role of the family, when a computer is smarter than mommy and daddy, when a movie star is stronger than brother or sister, more beautiful, more handsome, more desirable than anyone on the street, when the fucking on screen forces the cock to become stiff and smooth.

I am the man who fucks women in films. I am the man who fucks women.

A representation of a representation fucks in metamorphosis. "I" am a shifter *sine qua non*. Tom Cruise, Tom Cruise is Anthony Perkins, Anthony Perkins is James Dean, James Dean is Mickey Rourke, Mickey Rourke is Marlon Brando, Marlon Brando is...

I watch carefully as Keri enters the bar. She gives the bouncer some proof and looks around. I smile at her. Keri is excited. She hugs me for a long time. She squeezes my face between her hands. She kisses my lips. I ask Keri what she's been doing. Keri asks me about my work. I spoke about Nietzsche. Keri asks me why I study philosophy. I say "To meet women." Keri takes my hand and laughs. I smile. I want her to say "You're brilliant. You're beautiful. I want to fuck you." I take a sip from my beer.

"No contemplation is possible. The images fragment perception into successive sequences, into stimuli toward which there can be only instantaneous response, yes or no—the limit of an abbreviated reaction. Film no longer allows you to question. It questions you, and directly."[66]

It was O, in the *Story of O*, "it was she who sometimes leaned back against a wall, pale and trembling, stubbornly impaled by her silence, bound there by her silence, so happy to remain silent. She was waiting for more than permission, since she already had permission. She was waiting for an order."[67] As I write of O I am pornographic.

When the project to delineate all possible positions is realized, those positions become obsolete. "If it is possible at last to talk with such definitive understanding about power, sexuality, the body, and discipline, even down to their most delicate metamorphoses, it is because at some point *all this is here and now over with* ."[68] To upset the opponent, can a Judo-pragmatic approach use an aggressor's own momentum?

After reading half of O I am bored. This paper and ink, this imagination; they are no match for a *cinéma verité*, a cinema from which there is no escape, where escape has been accounted for and even the guaranteed orgasms of "Jamaica" commercials leave one blasé.

Sex "itself" no longer exists?

"Precisely the sign of postmodern culture is to incorporate the arts into the network of symbols that are exchanged exactly in the same way as that of fashion."[69]

"Signs need flesh to make themselves manifest."[70] Always already invaded, the male body is perfectly colonized by re-representation in a postmodern society.

I watch Keri as I enter the bar. She is speaking on the phone. I see her jeans. Keri hangs up. I see her blond hair. She takes my hand. I see her leather jacket. She kisses me on the lips. It's 20°. I will smile. After two drinks I want to speak of sex. She says "I'm petrified of A.I.D.S. I think I have it. I definitely have it." I say "Are you sure? I mean, have you been tested?" She tells me about someone she fucked last year. I feel nervous so I tell her not to worry. I tell her I'm not worried. I want to say "I don't have it so you can fuck me." I remember to look at her eyes. The waitress approaches and I want Keri to order another round. She orders another round.

Technology's ability to represent experience within binary categories (nature/culture, wet/dry, dark/light, -/+, body/mind, evil/good, 0/1, passion/reason, feminine/masculine) reconstructs reality in accordance with its own formulation. Cinema as a hyper-perfect simulation of multi-dimensional space/time.

Postmodern nihilism petrifies my body. I am terrorized, I think. Affirming a digital reality is the "will to nihilism," a desire to "go under."

Identification: the principle of love. Why do I become erect and partici-pate (as Renédoes) "in whatever may be demanded of or inflicted on her?"[71]

Keri uncrosses her legs and leans forward. I watch her hair fall on the glass table. I moved the hair off my face. She says, "I'm petrified of A.I.D.S. I won't fuck anyone."

Digital simulation invades psychoanalysis: Lacan notes that the phallus "belongs to being, and man, whether male or female, must accept having it and not having it, on the basis of the discovery that [s/he] isn't it."[72] Insofar as all subjects participate in the masquerade, one either "seems to have the phallus" (male/1) or "seems not to have the phallus" (female/0). Lacan's *representation* is symptomatic of the individual's re-articulation by a binary reality. A restricted economy constrains the excesses once permitted within a general economy. Ambiguity has been exorcized. The phallus no longer circulates in liquid flows. A subject spoken by a digital Symbolic Order is now just "male (1)" or just "female (0)."

Filmic Truth: the principle of intelligibility at the *fin-de-millenium* .

Just past midnight I am drunk. I look at Keri's eyes. I smile. I say, "Ready?" She says, "Ready?" She will walk quickly toward the cars. I want Keri to say, "So would you like to come over for a drink instead of going straight home?" She says, "Why don't you come over for a drink instead of going straight home?"

At some point in history, sex derived its meaning and necessity from "medical interventions." Now, when fucking has become a simulation of cinematic positioning, from what can "sex" derive its "meaning and necessity"?

Details of O's body, of O's position are not sufficient. I fill in Réage's description. Male desire wants a clearer picture. I exchange O's face for those of old lovers. Now when I masturbate I can come.

A death in Nicaragua, in Burma, in the United States, is the visceral pleasure of representational murder. Bloodshed has been abstracted completely. I listen quietly to the T.V. evangelists and I Bible-scream: "We know of it only by report."[73] Edited mediation provides a visual world without emotion or reaction. We are forced to ask: "Does the newscaster lie?"

I unlock the door to my apartment. I am laughing. I breathe heavily. I put my finger to my lips. I don't turn on any lights. I open the Venetian blinds. The light from a street lamp will filter through the slats. I want to take Keri's photograph in this light. I want to fuck her photo. Keri throws her fur coat on the bed. I want to turn the stereo on loud. I can't hear anything. I get two glasses of cognac from the kitchen. I say, "Shut the door behind you."

In the face of postmodern subjectivity without desire, devoid of gender, class, race, politics, history: the imperatives of neo-biologism, retronaturalism, a modern rationalist messiah. An ultra-logical response.

Keri sits on the bed's edge. Her legs are crossed. I hand her a beer. I throw my leather jacket on the bed. She crosses her legs. I say, "Sorry the stereo's broken." I want to say, "Shut the door behind you." It's 20°outside. I won't know what to do. I say nothing. The beer is too cold. I look out the window. I look around my room: books and papers and knic-knacks.

"The cool universe of digitality has absorbed the world of metaphor and metonymy. The principle of simulation wins out over the reality principle just as over the principle of pleasure."[74]

I become conscious of Keri's presence only as she leaves. She says, "I'll see you this weekend O. K.?" Keri kisses me on the lips. She curls her arms around my body. I said, "O.K. O.K. Great. Great."

I am not blinded. I am irradiated. Rather I want insurance: the confident production of corresponding visual imagery for every sign, every lick by the Butthole Surfers, J. S. Bach or N.W.A., every bit of steak tartar or semen, every whiff of dog shit, the garbage pit, every porthole of my body. I want my MTV.

Keri takes her clothes off. I watch where she piles them on the floor. Keri watches me. I place my beer on a window sill. I remove my shirt. My cock is erect. I remove my pants. Keri's nipples are erect. My eye's fixed on her tits. I smile. I remember to look at her eyes.

Within the "play-world" of the mediascape, our every mode of social behavior is tested, popularized and forced into circulation: apolitical, ahistorical, and asexual processes insofar as they present the new image-politics, the new historical simulation and the new re-representational subject.

As I undress, Keri walks around on the bed. She smiles. I am embarrassed because my cock is already erect. I rub my tongue on Keri's nipples. I rub my tongue on Keri's tits. I rub my tongue on her cunt. I will take a rubber from my pants pocket. Keri says, "No. I won't fuck you." Keri dresses and leaves.

Representational spaces are cooled to binary oppositions: Is O passive or aggressive? Is Zarathustra passive or aggressive?

I am silent. I want Keri to shut up. My mouth will fuck her cunt. Her cunt fucks my mouth. My cock fucks her mouth. Her mouth fucks my cock. Keri says, "You can't come in my mouth." I come on my stomach.

"The body's external appearance is not immutable."[75]

When I enter the hospital to have my hernia repaired I am shaved. My penis appears skinny, flat. My body arches over to me-see. My penis is a raw chicken. My penis is thin.

I want to watch my cock go in and out of her cunt. I watch her cunt move near my cock. I watch her hair. Keri watches me. Keri said, "Do you have any rubbers?" I say, "No."

"The bright light of a May day turned the clandestine into something public: henceforth the reality of the night and the reality of day would be one and the same. Henceforth—and O was thinking: at last. This is doubtless the source of that strange sentiment of security, mingled with terror, to which she felt she was surrendering herself and of which, without understanding it, she had had a premonition."[76]

Keri says, "No. You won't fuck me." I will rub my cock on her cunt. I come on Keri's stomach.

The condom package says, "Each SHEIK is electronically tested for reliability. Sold in Drugstores. Made in U.S.A. Printed in U.S.A." Keri tears open the condom package. Keri holds my cock with her hand. She smiles. She pushes the condom over my cock with her hand. I want her to put my cock in her cunt. She puts my cock in her cunt. It's 20°. I watch Keri fuck my cock with her cunt. She rubs her tits. She rubs my tits. She watches me. I watch Keri begin to come. She began to moan. She watches me. I remember to move my cock so it presses harder on her cunt. I want to moan. I want her to shut up. I come. Keri shakes her head. I put my finger to my lips.

I am a series of images set in motion. My ego is the pleasure of suture. The "situation of suture" withholds a double lie: 1) that the situation cannot be described as suture and 2) that the situation corresponds to "reality." The pleasure of suture always already exists and, as a hermeneutics, never corresponds to "reality." Narrative cinema, by concealing its own situation, reveals the pleasure of ego existence to the viewer.

Keri slipped under my down quilt. I slip the rubber off my cock. I drop it on the floor. The rubber makes a loud noise as it hits.

Men, at one point in time, controlled the production of cinematic fantasy and engaged in the pleasures of spectatorship: sadistic/fetishistic scopophilia and identification via recognition/mis-recognition of an omnipotent ego ideal. Cinematic technology presented "an illusion cut to the measure of desire."[77] Now, desire is cut to the measure of an illusion. The continual production of new pleasures have been replaced with the reenactment of pleasure. The secret of great directors is to know that cinema does not exist.

"The chief criticism leveled by Deleuze and Guattari against Freud is that he invariably saw as the unconscious itself what were in fact representational forms of social repression, encountered in analysis on the level of displaced desire."[78] The "unconscious" only appears in "representational forms." An "unconscious itself," as some type of transcendental signifier, cannot present itself to consciousness in unmediated form. Psychoanalysis can only provide interpretations, "by means of which the conscious makes of the unconscious an image consistent with its wishes."[79]

I slip under my down quilt. Keri smiles. I laugh quietly. It's 20°. I drag my fingers over her thighs. I say, "You were thrashing around quite a bit." Keri says, "You like it. All the men I've been with really like it. When I first started fucking I didn't know what to do, how to act. I saw some porno flicks with women arching their backs and rubbing their tits and screaming. I started imitating the porn stars. Those guys liked it. The guys I was with liked it." I say, "But fucking me is different from what's on screen." Keri says, "I only know how to have sex like a porn star. Men like it." I say, "But having sex with men is different from what's on screen." Keri rolls over. She presses her ass against my cock. I press my cock against her ass. I will watch her ass move against my cock. Keri breaths heavily. "Get a rubber." She slips the rubber on my cock. "Fuck me."

"O felt herself being weighed and measured as the instrument she knew full well she was, and it was as though compelled by his gaze and, so to speak, in spite of herself that she withdrew her gloves."[80]

Invasion of the Body Snatchers discloses the secret of re-processed corporality: The pod-people have already been here.[81] They're us.

I hate Keri because she will fuck me. I hate Keri because she is a porno star. I am not a porno star. I think porn is misogynistic. I think porn causes rape. I think Keri is sick. I hate her because she will never fuck me. I took a sip from my beer. It is 20°outside.

Postmodern cinema performs a double-reverse jump cut as shards of glass from an exploding mediascape slice through flesh and leave the body in a bloody heap. An audience strip-tease to excite celluloid's transparent desire; the orgasms of masochistic pleasure, as the body becomes a screen. Out-takes of exhibitionism and melodrama are to be acted out in our seats. Entering a suture-stream of complete metamorphoses from persona to persona, from situation to situation. Simultaneously, the double negation of filmic pleasure and filmic desire which returns us to the theater without malice or cause. The come shot. No movement, no liquidity, only mirror imaginations, eternally reoccurring fractal deaths. Instead of fucking we watch movies.*

Notes

1. Klaus Theweleit, *Male Fantasies; Vol. 1: Women, Floods, Bodies, History*, trans. Stephen Conway (Minneapolis: University of Minnesota Press, 1987), p. 35.

2. Ibid., p. 302.

3. Arthur Kroker and David Cook, *The Postmodern Scene: Excremental Culture and Hyper-Aesthetics* (New York: St. Martin's Press, 1986), pp. 9-10.

4. Ibid., p. 21.

5. Friedrich Wihelm Nietzsche, "On the Three Metamorphoses," *Thus Spoke Zarathustra*, in *The Portable Nietzsche*, ed. and trans. Walter Kaufmann (New York: Viking Penguin Inc., 1954), pp. 137-40.

6. Theweleit, p. 261.

7. Michel Foucault, *The History of Sexuality, Vol. I: An Introduction*, trans. Robert Hurley (New York: Vintage Books, 1978), pp. 59, 62.

8. Pauline Réage, *Story of O*, trans. Sabine d'Estrée (New York: Ballantine Books, 1965), p.74.

9. Foucault, *The History of Sexuality*, p. 82.

10. Roland Barthes, *Camera Lucida: Reflections on Photography*, trans. Richard Howard (New York: Hill and Wang, 1981), p. 10.

11. Nietzsche, "On the Three Metamorphoses," pp. 137-40.

12. Jean Baudrillard, *Simulations,* trans. Paul Foss, Paul Patton, and Philip Beitchman (New York: Semiotext(e), 1983), p. 155.

13. Ibid., p. 157.

14. Jacques Lacan, *Écrits: A Selection*, "The Signification of the Phallus," trans. Alan Sheridan (New York: W. W. Norton & Company, 1977), p. 289.

15. Baudrillard, *Simulations,* p. 155.

16. Réage, p. 103.

17. Stephen Heath, "Men in Feminism: Men and Feminist Theory," *Men in Feminism*, eds. Alice Jardine and Paul Smith (New York: Methuen, 1987), pp. 45-46.

18. Barthes, p. 10.

19. Kaja Silverman, *"Histoire d'O* ; The Construction of a Female Subject," in *Pleasure and Danger: Exploring Female Sexuality*, ed. Carole S. Vance (Boston: Routledge & Kegan Paul, 1984), p. 325.

20. Réage, p. 203.

21. Silverman, p. 331.

22. Foucault, *Discipline and Punish*, quoted in Kroker and Cook, *The Postmodern Scene*, p. 244.

23. Réage, p. 111.

24. Jacques Lacan, "Seminar on 'The Purloined Letter,'" trans. Jeffrey Mehlman, in John P. Muller and William J. Richardson, *The Purloined Poe: Lacan, Derrida & Psychoanalytic Reading* (Baltimore: The Johns Hopkins University Press, 1987), p. 53.

25. Réage, p. 13.

26. Lacan, "Seminar on 'The Purloined Letter,'" *Purloined Poe*, p. 37.

27. Réage, p. 17.

28. Theweleit, pp. 270-72.

29. Baudrillard, *Forget Foucault,* trans. Nicole Dufresne (New York: Semiotext(e), 1987), p. 59.

30. Nietzsche, "On the Three Metamorphoses," pp. 137-40.

31. B. Ruby Rich, "Anti-Porn: Soft Issue, Hard World," *Feminist Review*, n. 13 (Spring 1983), p. 66, quoted in Heath, "Male Feminism," p. 2.

32. Heath, p. 30. (My italics). Furthermore, Heath serendipitously footnotes Adrienne Rich's text *Diving into the Wreck* (New York: Norton, 1973) as *Driving into the Wreck*.

33. Ibid., pp. 1-32.

34. Nietzsche, "On the Pitying," p. 202. See also Derrida's discussion of Nietzsche's writing on women in *Spurs: Nietzsche's Styles*, trans. Barbara Harlow (Chicago: The University of Chicago Press, 1978).

35. Réage, p. 187.

36. Heath, pp. 1-32.

37. Lacan, "The Signification of the Phallus," *Écrits*, p. 288.

38. Foucault, *The History of Sexuality*, pp. 1, 24, 26, 27, 45, 53.

39. Ibid., p. 53.

40. Theweleit, p. 44.

41. Ibid., p. 249.

42. Lacan, *The Four Fundamental Concepts of Psycho-Analysis*, trans. Alan Sheridan (New York: W. W. Norton & Company, 1977), pp. 84-5.

43. Theweleit, p. 125.

44. Ibid., p. 284. This critique of valorization emerged from an interminable dialogue with Teresa Podlesney. See her work on feminism and cinema, and her film *LaPhallus*, 1988.

45. Kroker and Cook, p. 23.

46. Nietzsche, "On the Three Metamorphoses," pp. 137-9.

47. "Ecclesiastes," quoted in Baudrillard, *Simulations*, p. 1.

48. Theweleit, pp. 221-5.

49. Georges Bataille, "The Psychological Structure of Fascism," *Visions of Excess: Selected Writings, 1927-1939*, trans. Allan Stoekl (Minneapolis: University of Minnesota, 1985), pp. 137-160.

50. Don Delillo, *White Noise* (New York: Penguin Books, 1984), p. 84.

51. Theweleit, p. 87.

52. Foucault, *The History of Sexuality*, p. 59.

53. Lacan, *Four Fundamental Concepts*, p. 235.

54. Gilles Deleuze and Félix Guattari, *Anti-Oedipus: Capitalism and Schizophrenia*, trans. Robert Hurley, Mark Seem, and Helen R. Lane (Minneapolis: University of Minnesota, 1983), pp. 1-50.

55. Foucault, *The History of Sexuality*, p. 24.

56. Kroker and Cook, pp. 10-14, p. 27.

57. Nietzsche, "The Sign", pp. 436-439.

58. Réage, p. 60.

59. Michel Tournier, *The Ogre*, trans. Barbara Bray (New York: Pantheon Books, 1972), p. 108. (My emphasis.)

60. Tournier, p. 302.

61. Foucault, *The History of Sexuality*, p. 68.

62. Ibid., p. 61.

63. Ibid., p. 62.

64. Lacan, "The Signification of the Phallus," p. 286.

65. Foucault, *The History of Sexuality*, p. 115.

66. Baudrillard, *Simulations*, p. 119.

67. Réage, p. 103.

68. Baudrillard, *Forget Foucault*, p. 11.

69. Kroker and Cook, p. 156

70. Tournier, p. 99.

71. Réage, p. 32.

72. Lacan, "The Signification of the Phallus," p. 277.

73. *The New English Bible*, Job 28.22 (New York: Oxford University Press, 1972), p. 591.

74. Baudrillard, *Simulations*, p. 152.

75. Theweleit, pp. 327 and 334.

76. Réage, p. 111.

77. Laura Mulvey, "Visual Pleasure and Narrative Cinema," in *Art After Modernism: Rethinking Representation*, ed. Brian Wallis (New York: The New Museum of Contemporary Art, 1984), pp. 361-373.

78. Theweleit, p. 214.

79. Ibid.

80. Réage, p. 69.

81. Don Siegel (director). Invasion of the Body Snatchers, 1956. Remade by Philip Kaufman (director), 1978.

---

* Editor's note: This is part of a longer work in progress which has been edited due to space limitations

IV

DADDY'S NO

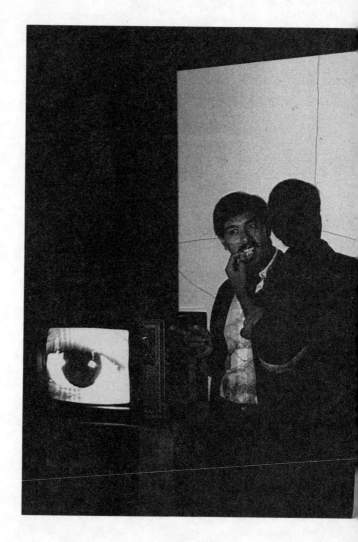

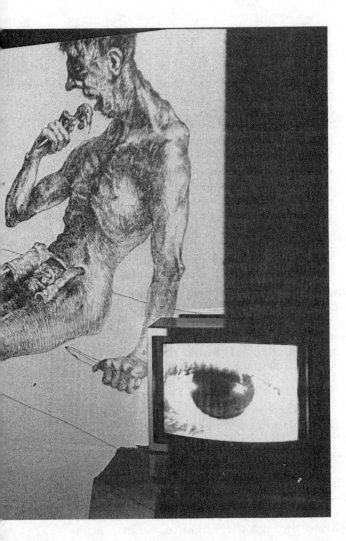

Photo: Critical Art Ensemble

14

THE PHALLIC MOTHER: PLATONIC META-PHYSICS OF LACAN'S IMAGINARY

Lorraine Gauthier

Just as in Plato? The "receptacle" receives the mark of everything, understands everything, except itself—without its relationship to the intelligible ever being established, in truth....And its function in relation to language, in relation to the signifier in general, would be inaccessible to it from the fact that it would have to be its support (sensible once again).[1]

Jacques Lacan has been a major force in the post-modernist attempt to dismantle the metaphysical foundation of Western thought. Working within the lineage of thinkers such as Nietzsche and Heidegger who have also attacked Platonic idealism, Lacan, like his contemporary, Jacques Derrida, locates the basis of metaphysical thought in the concept of presence articulated in Plato's definition of Being. In *Marges de la philosophie*, Derrida has shown how, according to Plato, Truth is capable of adequate reflection in the eternal presence of the Sun, the origin of knowledge expressed through the origin of vision. Yet, as Derrida goes on to demonstrate, the Sun, as a metaphoric expression, represses the truth about Truth, the fact that, as Nietzsche had understood, Truth is inexpressible, non-representable.[2] Lacan shares with Derrida this notion that it is metaphor itself which effects repression.

For both Lacan and Derrida, although metaphor represses Truth, Truth can nonetheless only be expressed through metaphors. Metaphors always miss the mark, they are but lies, errors, *méconnaissance*. It is this inherent structure of metaphor which guarantees that, as a trope constituted by an absent referent, it must necessarily fail to express Truth. Truth is, therefore, an absence of Truth. Truth, for them, is constructed as an absent signifier which they define, in linguistic terms, as a signifier of absence and which they articulate as *entre* or as lack. Rearticulating Heidegger's notion of a split being, Lacan specifically seeks to overthrow the concept of presence with that of an unbridgeable gap which makes Truth unattainable.

In "The Other and the One: Psychoanalysis, Reading and the Symposium" John Brenkman suggests that Lacan has indeed destroyed the foundation of the metaphysics of presence by successfully explaining the source of the gap in the desire for Truth, as articulated by Plato in *The Symposium*.[3] According to Brenkman, Lacan's work demonstrates how the refusal to accept the castration of the mother has led philosophers to seek the existence of one univocal, causal Truth. Such a recognition, Brenkman argues, is the goal of Lacanian psychoanalysis and the undoing of metaphysical idealism in that it seeks the reinsertion of the corporeal. The corporeal which is reintegrated, however, is that of a castrated maternal, a body lacking a signifier, unable to achieve human status except through the Phallus.

In her interpretation of Plato, Luce Irigaray, the French feminist philosopher and psychoanalyst, argues that the basis of metaphysics is less the concept of presence than the displacement of maternal corporeal presence onto the paternal ideal. For her, the metaphorical repression of Truth as absence exposed by Lacan and Derrida conceals yet another *méconnaissance*. In pursuing further the implications of Heidegger, Lacan, and Derrida's definition of metaphoricity as itself metaphysical, she discovers in the repressed referent of the metaphor not a metaphysics of presence, of Origin, as her contemporaries have done, but rather the suppression of a denial of corporeal maternal origin, repressed yet again in the signifier of absence, and thus maintained in the modern critique of metaphysics.[4]

Irigaray has not analyzed Lacan's work in the same detailed fashion with which she took on Freud's "Femininity" in her well known article "The Blind Spot of an Old Dream of Symmetry."[5] But Irigaray's reading of Plato's metaphysics and of its continued survival in Freudian psychoanalysis delineates the contours of an Irigarean reading of the "French Freud," the man who insists on returning to Freud to tell us what, in light of modern linguistics, Freud "really meant." Such a reading leads to a rather different conclusion than Brenkman's. It demonstrates that within his triadic division of human existence into the realms of the Real, the Imaginary, and the Symbolic, Lacan's conceptualization of the maternal has merely reiterated, in the language of modern linguistics, an age old devaluation and exclusion of the mother.

We find in Lacan some striking parallels to Plato—the emphasis on the visual and the characterization of birth as death, for example. Plato's

Truth passes through *mater*, the matter which Irigaray examines in her analysis of "The Allegory of the Cave," as a metaphorical expression/repression of maternal origin. Similarly, for Lacan, the truth of the subject in relation to the symbolic Other passes through the imaginary relationship of the ego to the other—and it is there, in the intermediary realm, as in Plato, that the mother resides.[6] Although Lacan recognized this matricidal basis, his work accepts it as necessary. It becomes in his thought the necessary precondition for a truly human symbolic existence. By claiming that "woman does not exist," that, as women, we enter the sexual relationship only "as a mother" (*quoad matrem*), that we are more closely linked to the realm of the real, the subhuman realm of chaos, Lacan rearticulates, in modern linguistic terms, the non-existence to which we have been relegated by the metaphysical concept of Being.

The close links between Lacan's work and Plato's matriphobia demonstrate the need to critically assess the works of post-modernist iconoclasts so that, as feminists, we may truly break metaphysicss' continuing matricide. In order to demonstrate how, from a feminist perspective, Lacan's work is less a deconstruction of metaphysical thought than a continuation of it, I will concentrate, in this paper, on Lacan's indebtedness to the Platonic and Hegelian idealism which he purports to destroy.

Truth as Non-Truth

In Plato's "Allegory of the Cave," Being is the Truth towards which we aspire. In Lacan's criticism of Platonic metaphysics, it is the definition of desire as lack, as articulated in Plato's *Symposium*, which best expresses his reconceptualization of Plato's concept of Being as *manque-à-être*, as non-truth. He argues that it is "in function of this lack in the experience of desire that [the human] being comes to a sense of [him/her] self in relation to Being." In his insistence that "within this lack of Being, he [*sic*] recognizes that he [*sic*] lacks Being and that Being is there in all those things which do not know themselves as being," Lacan is indebted to the Heideggerean concept of a radical split.[7] Inherent in Heidegger's *dasein* is a knowing and questioning Being whose interrogation posits the questioning self as subject in opposition to the questioned self as object. Against the Hegelian attempt to dialectically fuse self and other, Lacan and Heidegger attribute irreducibility and insurmountability to this constituting gap.[8]

This dichotomy between self and other closely resembles the opposition set up by Plato between Being and its representation, with this important exception, however. For Plato, the other is subsumed by the self. For Lacan, the self must submit to the authority and pre-eminence of the Other. In fact, whereas Plato's texts aimed at showing how the self as One constituted all others, Lacan's work aims at uncovering how first the real and then the symbolic Other is formative of the self. For Lacan, there is no totality, no One except for the gap which separates self and Other and by which Other constitutes self. Lacan thus opposes to the Platonic One, a concept of the Other which is defined as lack, an Other which in fact "does not exist."[9]

The Truth of the radical split expressed in the concept of desire as gap is not, however, a logical category of origin or of causation. Lacan argues that there is no original gap since the original experience of the subject has already been displaced onto objects or symbols to which the truth of his/her symptom and discourse refer. Truth, as displacement, is thus nothing but an erasure of traces which psychoanalysis, as a Heideggerian unveiling, attempts to expose. If there is an original repression, Lacan expresses it in a rather Nietzschean fashion as "the lack of Truth on truth."[10]

This lack of Truth is articulated by Lacan in his linguistic concept of truth as *cause*, as discourse. In the equivocity of the term *cause*, we find the Lacanian subject's trajectory, whose course conflates *telos* and origin much as the neophyte philosopher in search of Platonic Truth has done. As Irigaray has shown in her critique of Plato, *hysteron proteron*, as do the equivocal central terms in the "Allegory of the Cave," articulates the denial of corporeal origin through the conflation of origin and telos. Among these polysemic words, *hystera* is of particular importance. More commonly known as meaning uterus, *hystera* appears in the allegory in its second, more obtuse connotation of *hysteron*, things which lie behind. A variation of the word, *hysterein*, also means to be behind, but in temporal terms, suggesting that which comes later, which lags behind and therefore, what is yet to come, what lies ahead. Similarly, *proteron*, the antonym of *hysteron*, spatially means things in front, but temporally refers to what is prior, hence something past, what lies behind. These contradictory meanings are further complicated when the two terms are combined to produce the Greek locution, which is very important in the allegory: *hysteron proteron*, meaning opposites. In this definition, it is the spatial relationship, the behind of the *hysteron* and the in front of the *proteron* which are emphasized. The temporal future and past implicated in the definition of these words are discarded. This privileging of the spatial, both in the allegory and in the Greek language obscures, according to Irigaray, the fact that things which lie behind in the *hysteron* are reinscribed into those which come later, and that things that are prior in the *proteron* are projected onto what lies in front.[11]

The double connotation of *hystera* as uterus and as things which lie behind, of course, points to the unspoken relationship between womb and origin. This relationship is again suggested by the numerous terms Plato uses to define matter as that in which all things come to be, such as the word *mater*, which means mother, earth, and source.[12] Thus for Irigaray, it is no accident that the search for Truth, for origin, is articulated via an allegory of a cave, the womb of the earth. The prominent terms of Plato's allegory raise the central question of the relationship between woman and origin.

For Lacan also, *cause* is at once origin and *telos*. As the polysemic substantive derived from the French verb *causer* it means to cause, to talk, and also denotes a reason, a goal or an aim. It signifies, therefore, as in Plato's locution, *the* beginning of everything, that in which everything originates, that *through* which everything is articulated, and that *towards* which everything aims. For Plato this tripartite division of cause, means, and end is differentiated as the ideal, as matter, and as the phenomenal world of representation. Plato, of course, defines the real as the suprahuman realm of the ideal, whose corporealization passes through the intermediary realm of matter which must, theoretically at least, leave no trace of its role. In Lacan, the direction is reversed, the distortion of the passage is openly admitted and circumlocution is emphasized. Here, the prehuman realm of the Real must pass through the Imaginary to be articulated in the human realm of the Symbolic. In passing, it becomes distorted and hence constituted as non-truth.

In Lacan's formulation, *mater*, matter/mother, continues to occupy the intermediary position between the Real and the human. For Lacan, the primordial structuring gap which first appears in the realm of the Real excludes the mother from that realm much as she is excluded from Plato's realm of Ideal Truth. This original gap, as yet unexpressed and unrecognized, permeates the narcissistic sphere of the Imaginary, the equivalent of the Platonic *mater* where the mother resides. It finally expresses itself, even if only indirectly, in the human realm of the Symbolic where, once again, the maternal is exiled.[13] Just as the Platonic real, the ideal Intelligible Forms can find but approximate representation in the experiential world of human beings, just as the Sun is an inadequate metaphor for Truth, the Lacanian Real can only be approximately represented in the symbolic realm of human ex- istence.[14]

But since, as Lacan tells us, "something which is not expressed does not exist," the gap in the realm of the Real has no existence.[15] It is the truth of this structuring and as yet unarticulated gap in the realm of the Real which the Symbolic seeks to express. Truth, for Lacan, thus takes its guarantee from speech and not from reality. As he reminds us, "in the psychoanalytic anamnesis, it is not a question of reality but of truth" for "one accustoms oneself to reality, truth one represses." In his terms reality and truth are divorced in a way in which Plato could not have conceived.[16]

Plato's "Allegory of the Cave" is presented as an analogy of the search for Truth. It depicts the movement from reflection to reflection, from representation to representation until the Truth of Being that underlies all of these is revealed. The various stages of the allegory are but so many bridges built to span the gap between Being and becoming, between Truth and its representations.

For Lacan also, "truth is that which seeks the truth," much as Plato's *aletheia* is the negation of the original forgetfulness, the reclaiming of what was already there. In this search for and evasion of truth, akin to Nietzsche's fictive fixing of reality within a series of partial and perspectivist truths and to Heidegger's "errancy," truth, according to Lacan, instills itself within a realm of lies and errors, constituting itself as fiction. It is, however, no longer, as it was for Nietzsche, a question of desire imposing fiction as truth. Rather, desire is itself the fiction of truth, the truth of a "fictive" subject expressed in his/her discourse. For Lacan, what is indeed spoken in the *cause*, what is eternally displaced, is desire. In its Platonic definition as lack and in its Hegelian sense as recognition, this desire articulates truth as *méconnaissance*, as non-truth.[17] The truth of the subject's desire is its lack of truth, its continuous displacement.

This concept of truth, "instituted in the structure of fiction," is far removed from Plato's pedagogical concept of Truth as attainable knowledge. For Plato, as for Hegel, Truth and knowledge are one and the same. For Lacan "truth is nothing else but that which knowledge cannot understand." In fact, as he insists, "the division experienced by the subject, [is experienced] as the division between knowledge and Truth." Lacan's emphasis on the supremacy of language in his description of the speaking subject as a "spoken" subject reiterates the Heideggerean formula "language speaks." But if, for Lacan, language speaks, it speaks falsely. One needs to draw out the truth of the subject's speech as evidenced in his/her discourse, especially in the gaps, the slips, the metaphors, or the jokes where the insatiability of desire articulates itself, against the falsity or *méconnaissance* imposed on him/her by language.[18]

Within metaphysics, ignorance or contradiction is what delineates truth from error, from non-truth. For Lacan, *méconnaissance* is what articulates truth as non-truth and this *méconnaissance* cannot be grasped through the language of logic, but rather surfaces in the speech of the "subject," in his/her discourse, in which the "subject" of the *énonciation* and of the *énoncé* are different. Lacan underscores this when he remarks that "in the discourse which develops itself in the register of error, something happens through which truth can irrupt," and this truth is the "Truth of what his [*sic*] desire had been." From his perspective, it is in the field of psychoanalysis especially that the search for truth in the "discourse of the subject develops itself normally—in the order of lies, of *méconnaissance*, actually of *denial*," and denial, as Freud has taught us, is both expression and repression, or rather the expression of repression.[19]

Thus Lacan's critique of the metaphysics of truth replaces the concept of Truth with a concept of non-truth. But is this non-truth any less metaphysical for being the negative of metaphysical Truth? Is metaphysics adequately defined by Truth as presence, as original cause, or is this itself a metaphysical definition? Within Irigaray's definition of metaphysics as meta-physics, as that which lies outside the corporeal realm, the fundamental question would in fact be: has Lacan's critique of metaphysics gone beyond meta-physics? Has he succeeded, as Brenkman suggests, in reinserting the corporeal, i.e., the maternal body?

Some answers may appear, when, much as Irigaray has traced Plato's depiction of the neophyte philosopher's passage from the depth of the cave to the light of Truth, we explore Lacan's explanation of the subject's trajectory from the lack which constitutes his/her gap in the realm of the Real through to its symbolic expression. For the nature of what remains excluded from the Lacanian concept of the gap reveals, as does the nature of Plato's cave, the nature of the gap itself. And just as the truth of the analysand appears in his/her desire, so also, in the discourse through which Lacan traces the path of this disclosure, in his tracing of desire, the matricidal truth which underlies his conception of desire as lack irrupts.

As Lacan himself asserts, the concept of desire is ambiguous in its usage. On the one hand, it is "objectified," while on the other hand, it is "primordial in relation to all objectification."[20] In the eulogy to the god of love which the *Symposium* documents, Socrates defines the object of love and desire as "things or qualities which a man does not at present possess but which he lacks," thus defining lack in terms of the *manque-à-avoir* and the *manque-à-être* so crucial to Lacan's formulation.[21] The definition of desire as lack, constituted by an insatiability in which what is acquired constantly eludes it, was later taken up by Hegel. In *The Phenomenology*, the subject comes to knowledge only by way of a recurrent irreconcilability of itself with its object, a gap that is constituted and revealed by desire. Kojève, in his influential interpretation of Hegel states, "desire taken as desire, that is before its satisfaction, is in effect nothing but a revealed void, an unreal gap," and "being the revelation of a gap, being the presence of the absence of a reality, [it] is essentially other than the desired object."[22] It is in this lineage that we find Lacan.

Lacan's Hegelian definition of desire as desire for recognition locates it as its own "object" but because of the radical split between self and other, signified and signifier, desire as the desire for recognition retains the mark of the initial constituting gap. Expressed by the gap between the signifier and the signified this *manque-à-être* structures, for Lacan, the truth of desire. It is in the elaboration of these two seemingly paradoxical yet interrelated definitions of desire as lack and as recognition, that the concept of truth as lack appears, as does the gap which sustains its conceptualization.

For Lacan, truth seeks truth, as desire seeks desire. But desire, like truth does not exist until it is expressed. Yet paradoxically, both truth and desire are inexpressible. Metaphor articulates not only the means by which the search for adequate expression is conducted but most effectively represents the impossibility of definite expression which characterizes both truth and desire. This search for an appropriate signifier marks the path from pre-human infancy to human "subjectivity." Women occupy a specific position in each of the three stages of this search: the original gap in the realm of the Real; its necessary misrepresentation and eventual revelation as such in the realm of the Imaginary; and its more accurate though necessarily incomplete expression in the realm of the Symbolic. Just as Freud's mature woman must *be* the mother for lack of *having* her own mother, the maternal, in Lacan, will come to represent the *manque-à-être* through her *manque-à-avoir*, her lack of the Phallus.[23]

Desire as Gap:
The Original *Manque-à-être*

Although no gap is original, the gap is itself original. The gap is that by which life comes to be. The original and originating gap is produced at birth.[24] The gap as origin, as birth, occurs in the separation of the egg from the embryonic enclosure which sustains it. In each tearing "of the membranes of the egg from which the foetus exits in becoming a new born" Lacan asks us to imagine "a moment in which something escapes." And this something he humorously calls *l'homelette*, but more theoretically terms the *lamella*.[25] This *lamella*, Lacan tells us,

> this organ, which is characterized by non-existence but which is nonetheless an organ—is the libido. ...It is the libido, as pure instinct of life, that is to say of immortal life, of irrepressible life, of life which does not need any organ, of life simplified and indestructible.[26]

As initiation to life, therefore, this gap is marked by death, since, as Lacan insists,

> the real gap is that which the living being loses of his part of life through sexual reproduction. This gap is real because, it relates to something which is real, which is this, that the human being, from being subject to sex, has fallen under the exigency of individual death.[27]

It is this gap, "this part of himself that the individual loses at birth" which is represented by all the *objets a*. They serve to symbolize "the most profound lost object." And later, sexuality will install itself in this gap. In the realm of the Symbolic, this gap which constitutes sexuality revolves around the central "fact that the subject depends on the signifier and that the signifier is the site of the Other." But as Lacan tells us, this gap in the realm of the Symbolic "comes to take up once again another gap which is the real and anterior gap, to be located at the coming to be of the human being, that is, at the time of sexual reproduction."[28] Lying at the origin of life, therefore, the gap inaugurates the Real, a realm which he characterizes in its pure state as undifferentiated—unconstituted—chaotic, absolute and original—not yet symbolized—not yet the object of any definition.[29]

Birth, therefore, is the death of life. Within the separation of embryo and placenta, it is this death, this separation of self from self, which will be displaced endlessly and which gives the gap in the realm of the Real a position of some importance in relation to the future development of the human psyche. It structures desire as eternal displacement and constrains truth within the un-truth of errancy, of *méconnaissance*. It is this gap which the subject, in its search for an adequate signifier, must learn, not only to express and recognize symbolically, but also to accept, since it is, for Lacan, as for Heidegger, unbridgeable.

Lacan explores this unbridgeability through the myth of the *lamella* which he has invented to replace the myth of the original bisexual constitution of human beings articulated by Aristophanes in the *Symposium*.[30] This endless chasm differentiates Lacan's exploration from Plato's "Allegory of the Cave" which aims at bridging the gap created by birth by retrieving in Truth what was lost in birth. In the allegory, the prisoner attempts, in the final stage of his lengthy escape from the cave, to bridge the gap between the Sun and Truth, between the sensible and the intelligible, between life and death, or rather between the death inherent in sensible existence and the immortal life of the intelligible Ideal Forms. Like Lacan, Plato too, saw birth as a loss and a death as is evidenced not only in the allegory but in his reference to the myth of Er in Book X of the Republic:

> Now when all the souls had chosen their lives, they went in the order of their lots to Lachesis; and she gave each into the charge of the guardian genius he had chosen, to escort him through life and fulfill his choice. The genius led the soul first to Clotho, under her hand as it turned the whirling Spindle, thus ratifying the portion which the man had chosen when his lot was cast. And, after touching her, he led it next to the spinning of Atropos, thus making the thread of destiny irreversible. Thence, without looking back, he passed under the throne of Necessity. And when he and all the rest had passed beyond the throne, they journeyed together to the Plain of Lethe, through terrible stifling heat; for the plain is bare of trees and of all plants that grow on the earth. When evening came, they encamped beside the River of Unmindfulness, whose water no vessel can hold. All are required to drink a certain measure of this water, and some have not the wisdom to save them from drinking more. Every man, as he drinks forgets everything. When they had fallen asleep, at midnight, there was thunder and an earthquake and in a

moment they were carried up, this way and that, to their birth, like shooting stars. Er himself was not allowed to drink of the water. How and by what means he came back to the body he knew not; but suddenly he opened his eyes and found himself lying on the funeral pyre at dawn.[31]

When we note the similarity between Plato's definition of Being as immaterial, of the soul as non-corporeal and Lacan's definition of the *lamella*, Lacan's innovations appear even less unconventional. As in the rebirth of the Platonic eternal soul, Lacan's immortal life, although reduced to corporeal mortality is organless and bodiless.[32] The *lamella*, for Lacan, is

> something extra flat, which moves like an amoeba. Only it's a little more complicated. But it passes everywhere. And since it is something...which has a relationship to that which the sexed being has lost within sexuality, it is, like the amoeba in relation to sexed beings, immortal...since it survives this division, since it subsists beyond all fissipa-rous intervention.[33]

For Plato, it is *aletheia*, Truth as the negation of forgetfulness, as disclosure, that will lead the soul back to the omniscience and immortality which it enjoyed before its corporeal birth. As birth is achieved at the cost of the Truth the soul once possessed, the reclamation of that Truth, described in the "Allegory of the Cave," is achieved at the cost of one's corporeal life.[34] As Irigaray has shown us, the passageway which led from ignorance to Truth, from auto-reflection to self-contemplation stops at the door of death. It is the death of vision, of the pupil, of corporeality that allows us to see presence which has neither beginning nor material support.[35] The crossing of this threshold requires a jump, a leap which will never be accomplished in this life. It requires the transformation of the body into soul, which can then cross any division, any wall, any barrier. It is thus the corporeality of "man" which marks the divide between the sensible and the intelligible, between non-truth and Truth. Death introduces man to the life and time of the Father.

The morbidity that, in Irigaray's view, characterizes metaphysics is as central an aspect of Lacan's thinking as that of Plato's. The Truth of the Platonic philosopher is constituted by a desire for a knowledge that he lacks and which will be attained through the piercing of the pupil, the death of the body. Although, like Plato, the birth of human life, in Lacanian terms, is achieved at the cost of immortal life, for him, there is no reclaiming of the wholeness of the embryonic world. Nevertheless, the truth of the Lacanian subject is constituted by desire as gap in which death is also intricately woven. For Lacan, death inheres not only at the origin of corporeal life, in the realm of the Real to which Freud himself had linked the death instinct, but, more importantly for him, at the origin of the symbolic expression through which desire attempts to humanize itself and its subject. Death therefore, plays a central role in the Lacanian subject's second birth, his/her introduction into the Symbolic realm even though for this rebirth Lacan does not insist on the death of the body, as did Plato.

It is also no accident that those who lead the Platonic souls to the Plain of Lethe, to drink of the river of forgetfulness, are female, as are those who complete the cycle of sexual reproduction, the mark of death in life in Lacan's version. Woman robs life of its immortality. Her role as conduit to corporeal existence was clearly delineated by Plato as ambiguous and passive, as matter which lies between idea and representation. In Lacan, the articulation, as we will see, is somewhat different, but the message remains the same. For if Lacan's birth is more corporeal than Plato's, as the essential elements of the relationship within which self loses self, the embryo and the placenta repeat the exclusion of the maternal which Irigaray has disclosed as inherent in Plato's problematic of similitude, in the circularity of the self and its mirrored image, its other. This death within rebirth rearticulated by Lacan as the gap which structures desire maintains the exclusion of the maternal body from the site of truth. For what the infant loses at birth is neither its mother nor the uterus in which it evolved. The cutting of the umbilical cord, for Lacan, is the original split *within* the "subject" and not *between* "subjects," not between mother and child.[36]

Woman plays no role in the original gap which structures the human being, though passage through her is the cause of that structuring gap. She remains essential within the realms of the Real and the Imaginary, in the prelude to the child's attainment of full humanity. Just as Freud makes explicit, while retaining, the repression of the maternal, in Lacan's texts, the continued suppression of the maternal will make explicit the *hystera* which served as matrix for the developing philosopher in Plato's "Allegory of the Cave." Within the Lacanian realms of the Real and the Imaginary, the maternal, as in Plato's conception, will continue to serve an instrumental role, one which must be surpassed, as the site through which the child must travel on its way to human "subjectivity."[37]

The Maternal Other in the Realm of the Real

The pre-literate neonate has at its disposal no signifier except its cry. According to Lacan, this gives rise to a double error which structures the relationship between mother and child as pre-human. The cry signifies for the mother a need which she stifles by satisfying it thus preventing the child from entering into communication with her.[38] Conversely, the child, not knowing that it seeks more than its satisfaction, mistakes the mother for the site in which what it lacks can be found. In Lacanian terms, it erroneously constructs the mother as the site of the signifier, as the Other. The dependence of the prematurely born human infant which gives rise to the illusion that the mother is the site of the signifier produces thereby the fantasy of the omnipotence of the mother, defined by Lacan, as the "phallic" mother.

But these needs of the infant and its request for satisfaction are not what they seem to be.[39] They can represent what the infant has irrevocably lost through birth, that part of immortal life whose loss was represented by its separation from its placenta. The breast, as a response to a vital need is but another representative of this radical loss and, with all other such representatives, it assumes the form of what Lacan calls the *objet a*. But more importantly, Lacan, following Hegel, argues that in the prehuman infant, needs are from the very beginning more a demand for love than a request for satisfaction. Expressed as need, however, this demand for love remains unrequited, free to attach itself to yet another need, both need and demand becoming distorted in the process.

The movement from need to demand cannot be traced chronologically in the development of the infant since pure need never exists in the human. What this movement entails, theoretically, is a shift away from the desired object as that which satisfies a need, to a desiring subject who demands to be loved. This shift was originally articulated by Diotimus in her speech to Socrates where she pointed out to him the error inherent in concentrating on the desired object rather than on the desiring subject.[40] In Lacan's Hegelian conceptualization, demand for love is none other than the demand for recognition, the demand to be the object of desire of the mother. But here also, the narcissistic nature of Lacan's desiring subject can be traced back to its Platonic roots, to the text on which he has commented at some length. In the *Symposium*, Alcibiades accuses Socrates of misleading everybody by "pretending to be in love, when in fact, he is himself the beloved rather than the lover."[41] This is the narcissism of which Hegel speaks in his definition of desire as desire for recognition and it is this shift of register from object of desire to desiring subject which Lacan defines in the transition of needs to demand. He redefines the neonate's object of desire, its Other, that which satisfies a need, that from which a gap can be filled, in terms of the other, that from which it receives recognition. The mother, who played the original real Other, the source of the means by which the infant vainly seeks to express its desire through a request for the satisfaction of needs, is transformed into the imaginary other, object of the infant's desire for recognition.

In the pre-symbolic, pre-human realms, the infant's desire will be doubly determined by the mother, since desire arises in the gap between the request for the satisfaction of needs and the demand for love, both of which are represented by the mother. But according to Lacan, desire can be found in neither the desire for satisfaction nor the demand for love. It locates itself, rather, in "the difference which results when we subtract the first from the second."[42] In the gap, therefore, between the request for the satisfaction of a need and the demand for love we find desire and lose the mother. It is this structuring gap and the insatiability of desire which, for Lacan, locks both needs and demands into a continuous displacement in which satisfaction remains evasive.

In the illusive satisfaction of needs, the mother as real Other, offers to the child in the form of *objets a* the representation of the primordial gap by which s/he was constituted, of the loss initiated by the separation from his/her placenta. But representation is not signification, and according to Lacan, a signifier of desire the mother as Other is unable to offer. In the fusion of herself with the child, which her movement from the real Other to the imaginary other inaugurated, the mother will be unable to restore the gap.[43] And she will again fail to provide the infant with the signifier that would permit it to restore the gap and thus express its desire as desire for recognition. But her role is nonetheless crucial for the eventual symbolic resolution. As Lacan himself admits, "something is not extirpatable from the symbolic and this is the imaginary."[44] In setting up the interplay between self and other around the question of desire, the mother prepares the ground for the humanization of the child. Furthermore, her *manque-à-avoir,* the gap structured by her lack of a penis, will disarticulate her from the child, the other from the self. It will permit the symbolic to express the truth of the real gap, of the gap in the realm of the Real, as the constitution of the self by the Other. Thus the mother will serve once again as conduit.

Desire for Recognition:
The Maternal Realm of the Imaginary

It is in the redefinition of needs as demand for love that desire acquires its second definition as recognition without, however, relinquishing its first as lack. Through the concept of the imaginary, Lacan elaborates these redefinitions in which desire as recognition and desire as gap interact to produce a recognition of the gap and a gap within recognition. It is in the realm of the Imaginary, that the maternal flourishes. She becomes the medium through which the Symbolic sieves the Real to create the human in the recognition of desire as desire for recognition.

It is as other that the mother plays a significant role in the Imaginary. In very Hegelian terms, Lacan insists that "the desire of man [*sic*] finds its meaning in the desire of the other, not because the other holds the keys to the desired objects, but because its first object is to be recognized by the other."[45] Desire, therefore, like truth, narcissistically seeks itself since its object of desire is to be itself the object of the other's desire, that is, the ultimate object of its own desire. It is the child, as seen by the mother, that the child desires to be. In seeking recognition by the other, the child is seeking the signifier of its desire, is seeking to transform the other into the Other, the site of its recognition.

If this narcissism was the only element in the concept of desire as desire of the other there would be no reason why the mother herself could not break this narcissistic self-referentiality. But the equivocity of the French preposition *de*, with its objective and subjective connotations, establishes, for Lacan, the essentially closed circuit of the dyadic relationship between mother and child. *De* indicates that desire is not only a question of desiring the other but is also the desire to be the desire of the other, to be that which the other desires. The phallic mother, as the original real Other, must abdicate her position because she lacks the signifier of desire, the Phallus. Lacking it, she therefore desires it, since desire, in the Platonic terms which Lacan has appropriated, is the desire, amongst other things, to have what one lacks. Like the child, the mother searches for the signifier in the other, which in this mother/child relationship is the child itself. In order to be the object of the mother's desire, therefore, the child must become the Other, the Phallus, the site of all signifiers of desire. The subject, Lacan tells us, "is brought to really occupy the place of the Other, that is of the Mother."[46]

In this circumvolution, the child, lacking the requisite signifier, can neither express its desire nor represent itself to itself, as object of desire.[47] Something must therefore intervene between mother and child but its intervention must, like the presentation of Plato's Truth, be prepared. In Lacan, this intervention will be preceded by the insertion of a gap, in fact, of two different gaps in two very different and important stages, both demarcated by the visual, as in the intermediary stages in the "Allegory of the Cave."

Visual metaphors are crucial to the allegory as they are to metaphysics in general. Plato continuously uses the metaphor of the visible to clarify what is invisible. The relationship between the invisible and the non-visible, between Truth and the Sun, is the relationship between the absent signifier of the metaphor and the metonymic displacement of desire—a relationship which has been occluded by the metaphor itself. It is, therefore, a relationship between two absences. Platonic idealism, however, seeks the Truth in the present signifier of the metaphor, defining it as a mirror capable of adequately reflecting its absent counterpart.

Of all the visual metaphors which play a predominant role in "The Allegory of the Cave," mirrors, according to Irigaray's critique, are of exceptional importance because the reversions, inversions, and contradictions within the Platonic scope are most clearly exposed here. Mirrors not only epitomize the solidification of fluidity, but as reflective mechanisms they have their own blind spots. Mirrors have no memory, keep no trace of the imprint of that which presents itself to them and hence the irreducible inversion/reversion of all imprints cannot be detected. The fundamental metonymic displacement, the projection of depth onto surface, of containment onto reflection, of procreation onto imitation, all vague traces that are conjured away by mirrors. And of course mirrors reflect neither themselves nor the role which they play. They are self-effacing in the elucidation of Truth. Nothing is said of the fact that the positioning of the mirrors themselves, like that of the fire and reflective wall in the cave, determines what is reflected. As Nietzsche warned, mirrors only pick up the form and solidity which they presuppose.[48]

In Greek, mirror, as surface, as *topos*, also relates to matter.[49] In Platonic terms, the mirror, like matter, does not impose its own form on the image it reproduces. In fact, like matter and mother, like the absent signifier within metaphor, like Freud's cryptic writing pad, the mirror's sole purpose is to facilitate definition, representation, inscription while absenting itself from the production. Mirrors share with matter/mother the capacity to receive, reflect, and reproduce Being. As in all mirrors, the image is perverted, inverted and distorted through its reflection, through the deflection of the corporeal onto the ideal. In Irigaray's critique of Plato, it is this "ideologic," this reasoning through images, through reflections which has defined in its "terms and syntax" the metaphysical relationship to origin.[50]

Though mirroring as a tool of idealist perception was discarded by Hegel, Nietzsche, Heidegger, and their followers, it will present itself again in Lacan's famous "mirror stage" betraying a latent idealism in his theorization. Whereas for Plato, the mirror phase is used in the allegory to denigrate its reflective powers in favour of the Truth inherent in the One whose image it attempts to reproduce, in Lacan's mirror stage, the setting up of an alternate other and the articulation of the gap between self and other is at issue. In the maternal realm of the Imaginary, however, this gap remains as hidden as in the series of reflections found in Plato's uterine allegory. Like Plato's prisoner's journey out of the cave, Lacan's entire realm of the Imaginary as the prelude to the Symbolic, "is reduced, specialized, centred upon the specular image." His analysis of the intersubjective relationships experienced within that realm revolves around the gaze through which the subject becomes the object, the viewer becomes the viewed, and sees him/herself as such. Lacan insists on the importance of the three terms for, as he says, "there is never a simple duplicity of terms." It is not merely that I see the other. Rather, I see him/her seeing me, which implies a third term, to note that he/she knows that I see him/her. The circle is closed. There are always three terms in a structure, Lacan insists, even if these three terms are not explicitly present.[51]

This tripartite division reflects, of course, the tripartite division between Platonic Being as Existence, Being as Identity, and Being as Representation. The gap, between Being as Existence and its attributions as Identity is rearticulated through a variety of screens onto which Being is projected. The two most important of these, and in Platonic terms, the most appropriate, are the Sun and the soul. There is on the one hand, the presence of Being as Existence projecting itself onto the Sun. On the other hand, there is representation, the introjection of Being as Identity, as sameness, as similitude, as imitation, as reflection, within the soul. The eye marks the entrance to both, for it is in the blindness produced by the Sun, the forced opening of the pupil, the "consumption and extinction of sight," that the soul as the place/time of the reminiscence of Truth locates itself.[52] A *gap in vision* thus structures the articulation of the void inherent in Plato's concept of Being. In this gap, in the addition of Being as Identity, between Itself as Existence and its solar representation/ reproduction, not only is the univocity of Being's Existence undermined, but corporeality is negated.[53]

For Lacan, it is the *vision of the gap* which structures his concept of the subject. The recognition of one's corporeal self through its mirrored image distinguishes the human from the animal. Just as Plato's formulation exiled the body, in Lacan's conceptualization it is not the surface of the body itself but the surface reflected as form that allows the subject to appropriate the other, the speculative image, as self. For Lacan, the mirror stage inaugurates a "concept of self" through the "identification with the image as semblance."[54] Much as Plato's neophyte philosopher in the allegory would see his image as reflection, as self, before he saw his shadow as other, Lacan's subject must see his/her specular image as self before he/she recognizes this self as other. It is unquestionably the recognition of alterity which is at issue here, but an alterity which is constituted, much as Plato's, through sameness, through reflection.

In theorizing the child's relationship with its specular image as a narcissistic identification structured by the desire for recognition, Lacan emphasizes the gap between the seeing subject and the seen image. This split in the subject was of course there from birth but was occluded in the imaginary relationship to the mother as maternal object of desire. In the mirrored image, the child grasps itself as a whole at a time when it has not yet experienced this physically.[55] As Lacan insists "the mere sight of the total form of the human body gives the subject an imaginary mastery of his/her body, prematurely in relation to the real mastery."[56] What this image represents, of course, is the ego ideal and what it establishes is the gap between the subject and its ego.[57]

But despite this foray into a representation of the gap structuring the subject, the mirror phase cannot represent the lack inherent in desire no more than it could represent the Truth of Being for Plato. Lack is not representable. Referring to Parmenides, Lacan reminds us, What is missing in this reflection which gazes back from the mirror, in this *moi* in which the child conflates his/her self, is the truth of the desiring subject, the *je qui désire*. The gap that exists between the subject and its image, between the self and the ego, is the gap where desire resides, the gap which renders impossible the narcissistic search for self through reflection. A subject can no more be adequately reflected in an object, even its own reflection, than could Plato's Being find an adequate representation of itself in its attribute. Lacan bases his notion of subjective truth upon this very impossibility.

In Lacan's theory, the mirror stage rearticulates the realm of the Real, the site of the mother as the site as Other, as the impossibility of disarticulating self and other, of recognizing the gap that structures recognition. Just as for Plato the matter/mother could not offer any adequate reflection of Being, for Lacan, the mother cannot offer any adequate signifier of the gap. The desiring subject, failing to express its desire within the maternal realm of reflective imaginary, as it had also failed to do in the realm of the Real, takes up once again its search for the signifier of desire. The realization that the signifier of desire is not to be found on the mother's body brings on the castration complex, the next stage in the subject's journey towards the truth of his/her desire.

The castration complex, for Lacan, is not a question of the subject having or not having the Phallus. What is decisive is that the subject "learn[s] ... that the mother doesn't have it." In so doing, the subject seals "the conjunction of desire, in so far as the phallic signifier is its mark, with the threat or envy of the *manque-à-avoir*."[58] The recognition of the mother's *manque-à-avoir* will permit the subject to continue its search for the signifier to express its desire as *manque-à-"tre*. The mother is therefore characterized by the lack of the signifier rather than by the signifier of the lack.

Before desire learns to recognize itself as the desire for recognition, Lacan tells us, it "exists purely in the realm of the imaginary relationship, on the specular stage, projected, alienated into the other."[59] The recognition of itself as desire is also constituted by the visual, however. Castration, as Irigaray tells us, is really a matter of a *manque-à-voir*, rather than a *manque-à-avoir*. In Plato, the gap as pupil/hymen dialectically separated and united the depth of the cave and the shining light, un-truth and Truth, mother/matter and the ideal Father. In Lacan, the gap signified by the Phallus, lacking in the mother, represented by the father, differentiates and unites them. The conjunction of the visual and women's genitalia is notable in the philosophical premises of both authors.

For Lacan, the visual recognition of the absence within the mother allows the possibility of signification, of the symbolic expression of that which so far has eluded expression, even as it has articulated itself everywhere. The recognition of the Phallus as that which, as the privileged signifier of desire, supplants the absent penis, will pry apart the "self-enclosed circuit of desire" which structured the relationship of the child with the mother. As the demand for love held in check the destructiveness of the undifferentiated chaotic needs, so the Phallus as signifier must hold in check the incestuous absorption of self by the other, of the child by the mother.

But it can be argued that, in the Hegelian terms in which Lacan articulates his concept of desire as desire for recognition, the Phallus simply signifies its own desire and not the desired signifier of desire. One must remember Lacan's own play on words whereby the desire for (*de*) the other simultaneously represents the desire of (*de*) the other. Lacking the Phallus, the mother desires it as much as does the child who seeks the signifier of desire. In constructing the Phallus as the object of their desire, the mother and the child simply express the Phallus's own desire to be recognized as the object of desire of the other and hence narcissistically to be the object of its own desire. In wanting to be the desire of the other, the Phallus, like the desiring mother in the realm of the Imaginary, cannot be the Other, cannot offer the signifier that would recognize the other as a subject who seeks recognition through its desire. It does not recognize the other as a desiring subject unless this other desires it, unless this other makes the Phallus its object of desire and not the signifier of its own unattainable narcissistic desire. There is room for only one desire here, and only one desire recognizes the desire of the other as the desire for recognition. The supposed narcissistic bond between mother and child is theoretically reinserted between the Phallus and the subject who seeks the signifier of its desire. Just as through the attainment of Platonic Truth, through the death of the body, the Father is reabsorbed in the son, is inscribed within the soul of mortals thus achieving immortality; and bypassing the death of birth, Lacan's Phallus reinscribes itself into that by which it is represented. In the mother's and the child's desire to be "*le désir de l'autre*," the desire *of* the other must pass through, and in fact, must remain a desire *for* the Other. The Phallus as Other transforms their desire into its own reflection, mirroring, as it were, the narcissism of the signifier.

This narcissistic desire relegates the woman to the status of other and obliterates her desire unless it passes through his signifier. Is it any wonder that one of the unanswerable questions in this paradigm is "what do women want?" Rather than express desire as gap, the Phallus re-presses both sexes' desire for the original gap which it purports to represent. Reminiscent of Hegel's virile consciousnesses which, though sustained by life, are constituted by the threat of death, the Phallus, as symptom, as the signifier of repression, only serves to anchor this "virile" desire in the Platonic concept of sameness where Being as Existence reflects itself through metaphorical signification by passing through the concept of Being as Identity. In Lacan's work, this is camouflaged as the relationship between the symbolic Other as site, and the other as desire for recognition. The "subject," constituted by a desire qualified as male, seeks the phallic Other through the Platonic intermediary of the ego and the imaginary other. This backdrop of masculine self-reflexivity continues to be, of course, *mater*, matter/mother, the maternal Imaginary, the sphere of reflection through which she is excluded from *logos* connoted either as Platonic reason or as the Lacanian Symbolic.

Irigaray has shown how in Plato's exploration of Truth in the "Allegory of the Cave," the function fulfilled by matter/mother has been appropri-

ated by the Father and idealized. Matter/mother herself has been deni-
grated as a void or as a passive receptacle, outside of the scope of Being.
Brenkman has argued that in the *Symposium* Plato's metaphysical
definition of desire as gap was a denial of the mother's castrated body and
that this denial involved the appropriation of the maternal role by the
paternal function.[60] Lacan's concept of the Phallus, as the signifier of
signification, as the law of the signifier, also appropriates, in the realm of
the Symbolic, both of the mother's original roles in the realms of the Real
and of the Imaginary. It becomes both the source of desire, the other and
the origin of human symbolic existence, the Other.

This Other, Lacan argues, "is the locus from which the question of [the
subject's] existence may be presented to him [*sic*]." Psychoanalysis aims
at uncovering this Other, at laying bare the non-sense to which the
subject has been subjected. In the process the question itself must
change, however. The subject must take the Other's question, "What do
you want? and reappropriate it as "What does it want from me?"[61] But
does not psychoanalysis itself function as the Other that subjects? In
seeking the locus from which the question of the very existence of
psychoanalysis as a discourse may be presented, must psychoanalysis
itself not take its infamous question "What do women want?" and
transform it, in terms of the signifier of desire, into "What does it want of
them?"

Our Irigarean analysis suggests, quite simply, that the psychoanalytic
Phallus wants to maintain the mother as the intermediary, as the matter
through which its desire for itself can express itself. Whereas, in Plato,
presence was signified by a blinding light, the piercing of the pupil in
which the hymen, the mother, appeared, in Lacan, non-presence as
signified by the Phallus, the gap in vision, appears *on* the mother. The
matricidal articulation and repression of the Imaginary gives way, via the
phallic signifier, to the gynocidal exclusion of women, to the objectification and parcelling of our bodies, to the silencing of our voices. If, as
Brenkman tells us, Plato's journey began with the repression of the
maternal body, so has Lacan's.

As a psychoanalyst, Lacan is, of course, aware of this repression. It in
fact plays an explicit role in his articulation of the subject's "coming to
be." But in relocating the gap in such a way that the maternal is no longer
contained within it, that, instead, the gap is located on/in the maternal,
Lacan only succeeds in concealing, once again, and with yet another
phallic signifier, the gap created by the repression of our corporeal birth.
If Platonic Truth is the denial of the unrepresentability of origin, the
privileging of the phallic metaphor as the signifier of absence, is but a
distortion of this unrepresentability in which denial plays a crucial role.
And if Freud has taught us that to negate and to affirm is one and the same
thing, Lacan's articulation has shown us that to desire and to not want to
desire, to desire and to deny desire is also one and the same. In the
explicit suppression of the maternal Imaginary, in the displacement of

parturition onto a constituting gap created at birth *within* the subject, Lacan expresses, as yet a further footnote to Plato, the origin of his truth, of its representation as non-truth.

Notes

1. Luce Irigaray, *Ce sexe qui n'en est pas un*, (Paris: Les Éditions du Minuit, 1977), p. 98; *This Sex Which is Not One*, trans. by. Gillian C. Gill, (Ithaca, New York: Cornell University Press, 1985), pp. 89-90. From now on the page number within parentheses brackets refers to the English translation.

2. Jacques Derrida, *Marges de la philosophie*, (Paris: Les Éditions de Minuit, 1972), p. 320; *Margins of Philosophy*, trans. with notes by A. Bass (Chicago: The University of Chicago Press, 1982). For the role that matricide plays in Derrida's work see L. Gauthier "Truth as Eternal Metaphorical Displacements: Traces of the Mother in Derrida's Patricide," *Canadian Journal of Political and Social Theory*, 13, 1-2, (1989): 1-24.

3. John Brenkman, "The Other and the One: Psychoanalysis, Reading and the Symposium," *Yale French Studies* 55/56: 443.

4. Luce Irigaray, *Speculum de l'autre femme*, (Paris: Les Éditions de Minuit, 1974): p. 301; *Speculum of the Other Woman*, trans. by Gillian Gill, (Ithaca, New York: Cornell University Press, 1985), p.243.

5. Luce Irigaray, "La tâche aveugle d'un vieux rêve de symmétrie" *Speculum*, pp. 9-162; ("The Blind Spot of an Old Dream of Symmetry" in *Speculum of the Other Woman*, pp. 11-129). Other than "Cosi fan tutti," her critiques of Lacan are interspersed throughout several essays. "Cosi fan tutti," has been published as part of *Ce sexe*, (Paris: Les Éditions de Minuit, 1977, pp. 83- 101 (86-105). Among the essays in which she discusses Lacanian psychoanalysis the most notable are "La mécanique des fluides," *L'Arc* 56:49-55; "Le v(i)ol de la lettre"; "Le sexe fait comme signe," "Le practicable de la scène," and "Misère de la psychanalyse," in *Parler n'est jamais neutre* (Paris: Les Éditions de Minuit, 1985), pp. 169-88, 239-52, and 253-80.

6. For Irigaray's analysis of Plato's "Allegory of the Cave" see her essay "Plato's Hystera" in *Speculum*, pp. 242-364; "L' ύστέρα de Platon" in *Speculum*, pp.301-457.

7. Jacques Lacan, Le séminaire, livre II: Le moi dans la théorie de Freud et dans sa technique de la psychanalyse, (Paris: Les Éditions du Seuil, 1978), p. 262.

8. Lacan will go further than Heidegger in claiming a "radical heteronomy" which articulates the Real as discontinuity. See E. S. Casey and J. M. Woody, "Hegel, Heidegger, Lacan: The Dialectic of Desire," in Smith and Kerrigan, p. 98.

9. Lacan, *Écrits*, (Paris: Les Éditions du Seuil, 1966), p. 825.

10. Lacan, *Écrits*, pp. 522, 710-15, 805, 868.

11. Irigaray, *Speculum*, pp. 302-303 (244-45).

12. Luc Brisson, *Le même et l'autre dans la structure ontologique du Timée de Platon*, (Paris: Éditions Klinckslectk, 1974), p. 211.

13. The mother is excluded from the constitution of the gap in the realm of the Real, from the separation of the embryo from its placenta. In the realm of the Real, however, she will play the fictive role of the real Other, the source of all satisfaction, the bearer of the

signifier of signification, the phallic mother. The gap in the realm of the Real will be discussed below (pp. 18– 21).

14. Written this way, ex-istence represents the split which constitutes human subjectivity.

15. Lacan, *Le séminaire, livre II*, p. 354. This is a straight reversal of Parmenides' famous dictum that what does not exist cannot be expressed.

16. Lacan, *Écrits*, pp. 808, 256 and 521.

17. Lacan, *Le séminaire, livre XI: Les quatre concepts fondamentaux de la psychanalyse*, (Paris: Les Éditions du Seuil, 1973), pp. 172, 127; *Le séminaire, livre I: Les Écrits techniques de Freud*, (Paris: Les Éditions du Seuil, 1975), p. 290. Plato, Heidegger and Freud are the crucial references for Lacan's conception of desire as lack but it is Hegel's formulation of desire which informs his notion of desire as the desire of the other.

18. For an analysis of the relationship between truth, speech, and language in which Lacan compares the relationship of speech to language in the mad, the neurotic, and in the modern discourse of scientific objectivity, see Lacan *Écrits*, pp. 279-81. For a discussion of the relationship between Heidegger's and Lacan's notions of language see Casey and Woody in Smith and Kerrigan, pp. 75-112 and especially pp. 88-102.

19. Lacan, *Écrits*, pp. 808, 798, 856 and 518; *Le séminaire, livre I*, p. 290, 291.

20. Lacan, *Le séminaire, livre II*, p. 263.

21. Plato, *The Symposium*, trans. by Walter Hamilton, (Harsmondsworth, Middlesex, England: Penguin Books, Ltd., 1980), pp. 77, 82.

22. Alexandre Kojève, *Introduction à la lecture de Hegel*, (Paris: Gallimard, 1947), p. 12. For a clear exposition also see Jean Hyppolite, *Genèse et structure de la phénoménologie de l'esprit de Hegel*, (Paris; Aubier, Éditions Montaignes, 1946).

23. For Freud, the stake in the arduous task of becoming a mature sexual woman is to bear a penis substitute and to become a mother substitute. The revalidation of the woman as mother is not, however, a validation of her sex. As the rejected love object, the maternal becomes the internalized narcissistic role model for the little girl. This maternal identification is not even with her mother but with her mother-in-law as mother of a son and substitute mother for her husband. For Irigaray, therefore, Oedipus "legislates the impossibility of the daughter's return to the mother" except as imitation (Irigaray, *Parler n'est jamais neutre*, p. 293). Note: The change to pitch (12) and font (3) must be converted manually.

24. For Lacan, this birth is premature, since it not only produces a physically immature being but creates a being that is not yet human, a "subject to come," whose humanization requires a second birth.

25. Lacan, *Le séminaire, livre XI*, p. 179.

26. Ibid., p. 180.

27. Ibid., 186.

28. Ibid.

29. Lacan, *Le séminaire, livre I*, pp. 81 and 94.

30. Lacan, *Le séminaire, livre XI*, p. 187; Plato, *The Symposium*, pp. 59-65.

31. Plato, *The Republic*, trans. with intro. and notes by W. H. Cornford, (London: Oxford University Press, 1975), pp. 358-59.

32. Lacan, *Le séminaire*, livre XI, p. 187.

33. Ibid., pp. 179-80.

34. Nietzsche, following Plato, has also insisted that *Eros* and *Thanatos* were closely interconnected, and that the fluidity of truth had to be destroyed for even life to exist, and conversely, life was threatened in its very existence by Truth.

35. Irigaray, *Speculum*, p. 444 (354). It should be remembered that for Plato only the dead can see Truth.

36. If the placenta is indeed an "exclusively foetal tissue" this does not indicate that it has no relation to the mother. As Hélène Rouch suggests, the placenta is spatially closer to maternal tissues than to those of the foetus. It establishes a relationship between the two, a relationship whose fusional element is perhaps indicated by the fact that upon expulsion of the placenta, the mother also expulses the inner lining of her uterus. The insistence that the placenta belongs solely to the infant rather than being a passageway between mother and foetus is symptomatic of an ideology which dissects and isolates, a metaphoric hermeneutics which separates signifiers rather than emphasizing their contiguous relationship. See Hélène Rouch, "Le placenta: un parasite non égoiste," *Séminaires limites frontières*, (14 avril 1983): 8-10. For an analysis of the placenta as site see Julia Kristeva, "Noms de lieu," in *Polylogue*, (Paris: Les Éditions du Seuil, 1977).

37. The trajectory is complicated and so it is worth remembering the role she plays at both ends. As *objet a* she represents the gap inherent at birth. As castrated, she represents the gap inherent in "subjectivity" and hence opens the door to the Symbolic from which she nonetheless remains excluded, as she was from the original structuring gap. Although Lacan excludes the mother from any role in the coming to be of the structuring gap, he argues that she inaugurates the entire process by acting as the real Other for the neonate. It is because of this role that Lacan defines women "as much more entangled in the realm of the real than are men" (Lacan, *Le séminaire*, *livre I*, p. 187).

38. Lacan, *Écrits*, p. 691.

39. Needs, for Lacan, as for Hegel and Plato before him, are characteristic of the animal world. Lacan tells us, however, that while the infant is not yet human neither is it animal (Lacan, *Le séminaire*, *livre I*, pp. 242-43).

40. Plato, *The Symposium*, p. 83.

41. Ibid., p. 111.

42. Lacan, *Écrits*, p. 691.

43. According to Hegel, the satisfaction of needs results in the destruction of the other, its negation, its consumption, its absorption in the interest of the self. The satisfaction of a demand for love, on the other hand, validates the other at the expense of the self. Hegel resolved this vacillation between the absorption of and identification with the other through the dialectical fusing of self and other. But fusing is not what Lacan aims at. Like Heidegger, it is rather the irremediable separation of self and other which he emphasizes. But this separation consists of a tension rather than a severance, since the latter would obliterate the gap which constructs the separation within Lacan's theory. Destruction of the gap is as futile for Lacan as the destruction of the self or of the other was for Hegel and so, underlying the interaction of self and other in both their conceptions, is an assumption of the contrived existence of both self and other in which this destructiveness is constantly held in check.

44. Lacan, *Le séminaire*, *livre II*, p. 352.

45. Lacan, *Ecrits*, p. 268.

46. Ibid., p. 813.

47. Needless to say, the mutual recognition of mother and child, of their mutual desire as desire for mutual recognition is also impossible, again, given the lack of the necessary signifier.

48. Irigaray, *Speculum*, pp. 367-88, 414 (294-301, 331).

49. Brisson, p. 212.

50. Irigaray, *Speculum*, pp. 438-47, 400 (348-56, 320). Nietzsche's and Derrida's influence is apparent here. However, Irigaray imbues her criticism with an emphasis on the repressed maternal body which is lacking in theirs.

51. Lacan, *Le séminaire, livre XI*, pp. 310 and 244-45. The tripartite structure so prevalent in Plato's metaphysics and Hegel's idealism also structures Lacan's conceptualization in the three connotations of *cause*, the three realms of experience, and the insertion of the third term in the dyadic relationship of mother and child.

52   Plato, *The Republic*, p. 220; Irigaray, *Speculum*, p. 398 (318-19).

53   As well, Irigaray argues that Plato's unilateral and unequivocal conception of Truth is tautological. Being, he claims, can have but one Truth, that of its own Existence. It can abide no ambiguities, no obscurities, no phantoms. There is but Truth and non-truth. But, as Irigaray points out, while on the one hand the relationship between Truth and non-truth is defined by Being, on the other hand, the relationship between Being and non-being is defined by Truth.

54   Lacan, *Écrits*, p. 98.

55   It is of interest, as Irigaray points out, that the child, who is seeing him/herself in the mirror, is held by its mother. By what logic could the child differentiate his/her image from that of the mother's? Her inclusion, though seemingly fortuitous, cannot be purely accidental. See Irigaray, *Speculum*, p. 160.

56   Lacan, *Le séminaire, livre I*, p. 93.

57   The image also inaugurates "the possibility of the order of presence and absence, that is to say, the order of the Symbolic." Lacan, *Le séminaire, livre II*, p. 371.

58   Lacan, *Écrits*, pp. 693-94.

59   Lacan, *Le séminaire, livre I*, p. 193.

60   Brenkman, pp. 426, 448.

61   Lacan, *Le séminaire, livre XI*, pp. 226, 815.

15

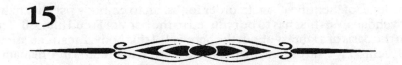

LACANIAN PSYCHOANALYSIS AND FEMINIST METATHEORY

Charles Levin

In epicene language, as distinct from language imagined as either neutral or androgynous, gender is variable at will, a mere metaphor.[1]

The letter as a signifier is thus not a thing or the absence of a thing, nor a word or the absence of a word, nor an organ or the absence of an organ, but a *knot* in a structure where words, things, and organs can neither be definably separated nor compatibly combined.

...the author of any critique is himself framed by his own frame of the other....[2]

Freud and Lacan: the Psychopolitics of Totemism[3]

In circles of social, cultural, literary, and film study—and among some feminists—Jacques Lacan has become something of an institution. He is commonly read in isolation from other psychoanalytic writers (Melanie Klein, Hanna Segal, Marion Milner, Edith Jacobson, Joyce McDougall, Janine Chasseguet-Smirgel, to name only a few apart from Freud himself, and his immediate circle). Even the best known of Lacan's contemporaries are rarely cited in the arts and social science literature, with the exception of Klein and D.W. Winnicott, who are mentioned very sparingly indeed. On the other hand, Lacan is taken seriously by nearly everyone doing up-to-date cultural or feminist research. And of course he is frequently cited on such matters as metaphor and metonymy, and on the relation of the tropes to the dreamwork. Nobody refers to Ella Sharpe, who developed this connection in the nineteen thirties.[4]

The reasons for this condensation of psychoanalytic thought into the lone figure of Lacan are no doubt obscure, but they may have to do with the logic of identification. In order for Lacan to embody psychoanalysis, psychoanalysis first has to be reduced to the body of Freud himself. Then, on the basis of a fantasy about the betrayal of this body, Lacan can attempt to reembody true psychoanalysis (the "return to Freud") in "the name of the father." Thus Lacan appears well situated both to share and to resolve the feelings of ambivalence which anyone approaching psychoanalysis is likely to feel.

Nearing psychoanalysis, especially in the atmosphere of a totemic fantasy such as this, it is easy to feel as if one is entering an already controlled space—specifically, the authoritarian father's space. Moreover, as Lacan was to point out, the dead father is rather difficult to dislodge from his privileged position in the carefully self-cancelling structure of an obsessional discourse. The deliberate patterns of displacement and deferral in Lacan's *Écrits* and seminars provide a seductive occasion for the deflection and management of (oedipal) ambivalence and conflict.

As Jane Gallop suggests in *The Daughter's Seduction*, Lacan's appeal to feminists may be related to the way in which he set himself up as "the cock of the walk," a kind of contemporary ally and lover who provides magical access to the feared and admired oppressor to be overthrown.[5] Lacan not only disposes of the master, but resurrects him as well: he is both a rebel and a redeemer, committing and then expiating the crime of desiring to partake in a fantasied omnipotence, such as that so commonly ascribed to Freud himself, and so universally resented in him. Lacan serves, in other words, as a conduit for projective identification onto the father.

The myth of Freud as primitive father is of course fundamental to psychoanalytic politics. If psychoanalysis is the dead body of Freud, then the rituals over his remains—the vigil against grave-robbers, the appropriation and resurrection of the corpus as the body of the analyst himself, sitting at the right hand of Freud—are as characteristic of Lacanian practice as they are of the International which so unceremoniously expelled him. Lacan, however, is neither father, nor son, nor brother, but a kind of trinitarian demiurge—like Thoth, a doyen of writing,

> [a] god of resurrection...interested... in death as a repetition of life and life as a rehearsal of death.... Thoth repeats

everything in the addition of the supplement: in adding to and doubling as the sun, he is other than the sun and the same as it; other than the good and same, etc. Always taking a place not his own, a place one could call that of the dead or the dummy, he has neither a proper place nor a proper name. His propriety or property is impropriety or inappropriateness, the floating indetermination that allows for substitution and play.[6]

Unfortunately, this resolution of the problem of Freud's space (his resting place) runs into its own complications, which emerge most clearly in neostructuralist developments of Lacan's thought. Deconstructionist symbolics are immersed in rivalry with the parents, obsessed with creation as a process of dismemberment and annihilation. The theory and practice of textuality have become a sort of allegory about what is stolen from the paradoxical father (the supplement, or name without referent or substance) and from the irretrievable mother (the virgin-hymen-origin, or substance and referent without name). This cosmogony is not exclusively Oedipal: it also draws upon the *Orestia*. In the Lacanian version of that less celebrated tragedy, however, revenge against the mother never seems to be followed by reconciliation with her law, and the taming of the Eumenides (primitive superego). The Lacanian father may be an oppressor, but he remains the only source of order, while the mother becomes, in a sense, much more dangerous: she is the betrayer, and this appears to be a feature of Lacan's thinking which persists, not only in the writings of Kristeva, but even in the anti-patriarchal discourse of Luce Irigaray, as Gallop suggests.[7]

Philippe Sollers is reported to have said that Lacan's political problems arose because he had "run afoul" of the psychoanalytic "matriarchy."[8] Princess Bonaparte (who ransomed Freud after the *Anschluss*) was not the only daughter (or imaginary wife) of Freud whose authority Lacan disputed. There were also Melanie Klein and Anna Freud herself, who between them presided over English-speaking psychoanalysis for nearly half a century. Implicit in Lacan's denunciation of "ego psychology," and his return to Freud, was the fantasy of a march against the domestication, the feminization of psychoanalytic theory. The publication of *Anti-Oedipus* during the heyday of Lacan's notoriety was a continuation of this hyper-masculine ethos, with its virile imagery of the social process, and its picture of Lacan himself as a family-oriented counter-insurgent who had emasculated desire by theorizing it as a lack.[9]

In general, the fact that Freud had a mother gets little play in the Lacanian imagination. But Freud actually seems to have had a privileged relationship with his mother. She had heard a prophecy that he would be a "great man," and told him about it. In some ways, Freud's feeling about his own creation, psychoanalysis, was like his mother's attitude toward him: he thought he had brought something significant into the world. A question—or a fantasy—arising out of this is the following: what if reading Freud were a gratification, rather than a mere competition for old space? What if Freud were not only the stern and prohibitive professor-super-ego, but also a kind of mother, or even what Melanie Klein called the "good breast?" And what if the "conquering hero" of which Jones speaks in his biography of Freud were really psychoanalysis itself (as an opening, as something to be pursued, an adventure), and not Freud the man, or any other man or woman? Perhaps, through his text, Freud was also able to say: "This is a new space I have found, which I want to share with you; but the world is still out there, and there is more to be discovered!" That is a symbolic relation to psychoanalysis very different from Lacan's, though it is not unlike the transference which Gallop managed to developed onto the work that Lacan left behind, in her *Reading Lacan*.

Some Lacanian Themes

An interesting example of Lacan's status in contemporary discourse on culture can be found in Jacqueline Rose's excellent introduction to the volume of essays on *Feminine Sexuality* by Lacan and his circle.[10] What is so typical of this essay is not the handling of theoretical issues (which Rose does very well), but the mythogenic rhetoric in which the exposition of Lacan's "re-opening of the debate on feminine sexuality" is couched. Rose rejects the arguments of those, like Jones, Horney, or Klein, who dissented, in one way or another, from Freud's various hypotheses on gender. Yet, in describing Lacan's insight into sexual politics, she only reiterates the original line of reasoning used against Freud's claim that the analysis of the "psychical consequences of the anatomical distinction between the sexes" leads to a kind of biological "bedrock."[11] Rose insists that it is to Lacan alone (and his discovery of the signifier) that we owe the possibility of a genuine critique of phallocentrism: according to her, Lacan revealed that the indexation of sexual difference on possession or absence of the phallus "covers over the complexity of the child's early sexual life with a crude opposition in which that very complexity is refused or repressed."[12] But nowhere in Lacan is there a discussion of this "complexity," or of early sexual life in general, apart from the child's relation to the phallus. One has to turn to non-Lacanian writers like Klein or Robert Stoller or Masud Khan if one wants to read about the subtleties of "pre-Oedipal" sexuality.

The essence of Rose's historical account of the sexuality/ gender debate within psychoanalysis lies in the claim that, with the exception of Lacan, psychoanalysts (and psychoanalytically inspired commentators) have "failed to see that the concept of the phallus in Freud's account of human sexuality was part of his awareness of the problematic, if not impossible, nature of sexual identity itself."[13] This is a very broad and misleading statement that seems to be based on two peculiarities in the self image of writers who identify with Lacan.

The first is a question of emphasis: it is probably true that the phallus plays a more fundamental and determinant role in Lacanian theory than in any other school of psychoanalysis. The second factor is that Lacan grants the phallus an objective status unusual in post-Freudian theory: it becomes a "symbolic" universal in the classical sense, acting independently of the body's history and of its associations.

Lacan's recognition of the problematic role of the phallus is perhaps not as unique as Rose makes out. In work that preceded his, Melanie Klein payed a great deal of attention to unconscious processes involving a kind of archetypal phallus like Lacan's. Indeed, one might say that the "thrust" of Klein's exploration of pregenital psychology was her insistence (contrary to Sigmund and Anna Freud) that the fantasy of the phallus (and its structural correlate, the superego) is not delayed until the onset of the classical Oedipal situation.[14]

In fact, there are striking parallels between Klein's early conception of infantile psychodynamics and Lacan's emphasis on the child's identification with the object of the mother's desire (again, the phallus). Lacan's view, however, is based on the assumption of a quasi-naturalistic symbiosis between the mother and the child—the classical conception of primary narcissism. The infant lives passively in an objectless state of psychic oblivion whose accomplice, for Lacan, is the mother's invidious desire. According to Lacan, this is a trap from which only the "symbolic" function of the father can save the child, by separating the phallus from the self (castration), and placing it in the objective external order of language, so that the child can be apprised of its own "lack."[15]

Whereas the Lacanian solution to the psychology of infantile dependency thus appears to be an intensification and objectification of the function of the phallus—a *raising* of its status within discourse—Klein's thinking moves in the opposite direction. Klein stresses the infant's *active* experience of its *own* desire in aggressive relation to the Other. If the phallus is a term, at the adultomorphic level of language and society, for one of the more primitive conceptions of power, then for Klein the infant does not *identify* with the 'phallus' in the simple classical sense, but actively appropriates it (as an elaboration of the breast and other experiences), in cycles of incorporation and projective identification. In brief, the problem for Klein's infant—or the "psychotic" child within us— is not how to *accept* the allegedly independent role of the phallus in the symbolic order, but how to *demystify* it. This involves coming to terms with unconscious fantasies of power (which may eventually have become displaced onto a gender sign system playing on presence/absence of the penis). The power fantasies (having to do mainly with omnipotence and retribution), inevitably conceal more profound feelings of envy and guilt that interfere with the infant's capacity to explore, elaborate, and internalize dimensions of pleasurable experience or trust in mutuality (the "good breast"). Of course, Klein's work is full of difficulties and I am by no means suggesting that she solves the socio-political problem of "phallogocentrism." But in contrast to Rose, I would argue that Lacan's work only compounds the problem, whereas Klein offers some useful new ideas. At least she is innocent of the absurd strategy (to be discussed below) of grounding the structure of significa-tion in the phallus, as if meaning derives only negatively from the body part the mother does not have (as opposed to the ones she does, which are of greater interest to the infant anyway).[16]

The justification of Rose's wholesale rejection of all but Lacanian developments of psychoanalysis lies in her contention that Lacan alone recognized that the unconscious "constantly undermines" the sexual subject. Stated in this general way, however, it is difficult to see how a Freudian grasp of the "link between sexuality and the unconscious" can be denied to everyone but Lacan. What *is* in fact specific to Lacan is a claim about the *structure* of the unconscious—namely, that it is seg-mented, like a written language, or any other system of inscription, and that it functions according to laws of association and contiguity. Lacan expanded this claim by suggesting that language and the unconscious—and by extension, sexuality—are homologously structured through their common link to an essential process of substitution, or what he often describes, in allusion to a number of competing and inconsistent linguis-tic models, as "metonymy." Substitutability is, of course, a basic property of any unit defined within a digitally constructed system of signification. If the unconscious could be defined as such a system, governed by mechanisms of displacement, then psychoanalysis would fulfill the Rationalist dream of a universal *mathesis*, whose object would be exhaustively describable in terms of linguistic "laws" or geometric and algorithmic graphs.[17] But whenever Lacan specifies the linguistic struc-tures of desire, he merely invokes a semiotic reformulation of the functions of the dreamwork and the structure of compromise formation in symptoms; or adumbrates a discourse model of some feature of superego conflict, like obsessional oscillations and manic flights.

Rose by no means accepts the positivistic interpretation of Lacan's work. But she does adopt its corollary, which is that subjective experi-ence (including the emotional experience of material object relations) is epiphenomenal, and not the proper object of psychoanalytic work. Neither Rose nor Lacan have much to say about unconscious feelings, perceptions, or processes. There are only unconscious contents: signifi-ers, bits of congealed signification, which are arranged in systems and patterns either controlling or undermining the illusion of subjectivity. The Lacanian Symbolic is an impersonal structural causality, which acts externally, like a social force.[18] The subject is only decentered in the sense that desire itself is thought to be something that cannot really be experienced, except in terms of its effects, which are always organized into (social) orders of signifiers. In this objectivistic conception of the substitution process, therefore, the basic psychoanalytic principle of the decentering of the subject is disconnected from the existential experience of indeterminacy and complexity inherent in subjectivity, and related instead to a quasi-sociological reduction: the subject is decentered for Lacan because it is determined—because, in other words, it will always be fixed in advance by society. The irony of this is consequently that whenever Lacanian thought attempts to demonstrate the "arbitrariness" of sexual identity, it in practice advances an argument for its necessity, by removing the sources of sexual structuration from the psyche to an ideal region outside the history of bodily experience as psychoanalysis has been able to understand it.

Theoretical Problems

The implications of Rose's sociolinguistic approach to the unconscious emerge clearly in her exclusion of alternative perspectives on the mirroring relationships of early infancy. In a passing dismissal of Winnicott's work, for example, Rose states: "The mother does not mirror the child to itself... she grants an image to the child, which her presence instantly deflects."[19] Rose's point is essentially an epistemological (or deconstructive) one, namely, that the subject has no originary identity, that the baby does not have an "itself" to be mirrored back to itself by the mother. But this sophisticated (essentially positivistic) vigilance against every hint of essentialism or misplaced concreteness conceals the inability of the Lacanian paradigm to grasp the problem of the infant subject's (relationship to its own) world of feelings and emotions, and the fulfillments and conflicts inherent in the infant's capacity for experience in relation to other bodily subjects. In other words, Rose emulates Lacan's tendency to replace the specificity of individual differences with the generality of a schematism.

Infants have very complicated feelings (ways of experiencing physical needs and sensations, as well as desires and emotions, some of which are observably violent). They also *elicit* an environment—they are not restricted to the pure reactivity of behavioural psychology and the theory of primary narcissism.[20] All of these qualities of the small child's subjectivity can be intuited, recognized, respected, and accepted by the child's human objects (the caretakers)—or at the other extreme, they can be ignored, denied, or utterly disqualified. Of course, the infant will always have to learn to take others into account more than he or she may wish to—Freud's reality principle, like Lacan's Symbolic Order, says essentially this. But when the infant's expressivity is systematically disqualified—or in other words, when the caretaker(s) can only "*grant* an image *to* the child" (as Rose would have it), while being unable to "mirror the child back to itself," the survival of the child will come to depend on an inordinate degree of self-repression and reactivity. The schizoid sense of the unreality of one's own being that develops out of this passive survival strategy of the ego is not due solely to the assumption of an illusory or Imaginary identity in a universal "mirror stage," as Rose, following Lacan, maintains; but also to a particular and local disregard for the infant's difference. Whether or not the "lack" to which Lacan refers is, in the last analysis, an ontological condition, it may also spring from a failure to acknowledge the child as an independent being in its relations with others. The desire for some kind of recognition of one's distinctness by another has nothing to do with the various red-herrings which Lacanians like to raise, such as the "ideology of the unitary subject": the infant's emergent sense of its own difference has nothing to do with the Western politico-juridical concept of individualism. So while Rose's views are certainly compelling, so are Winnicott's.

Rose's rejection of Winnicott implicitly assumes that the infant is a *tabula rasa*–a being that has to be "granted" an image. This is related to an important tenet of Lacanian theory: that the human neonate is in biological fragments, unable to use the senses, or to relate the senses to each other. This view is based on a misconception that can be traced back to Freud's earliest conjectures about infantile states.[21] The baby is pictured as a bundle of unrelated instinctual pressures, without objects, imperiously and impersonally seeking gratification. Lacan continued this tradition with his concept of the "*corps morcelé*." Of course, there is a great deal of truth in the model (which Rose emphasizes so much) of an originary fragmentation. But the truth of part drives and part objects is not biological in the sense of a primary epigenetic stage of development leading up to the mirror stage and the acquisition of language. Unintegration is a psychological phase in a rythm which persists throughout life.[22] Being in pieces is an aspect of life, we drift in and out of it, and it is probably no less or more "biological" or "cultural" than "femininity" and "masculinity."

Now, because Freud tended to think of "primary narcissism" as an originary, biologically-determined stage, his model of development placed a great deal of emphasis on the idea that "reality" is something that is gradually *imposed* from without, and that this is what makes us into social beings. In contrast to this view, Lacan argued that it is not reality, but "language," that is imposed from without; it is the "system" of lingual differences that turns us into social beings. Both of these points of view need to be taken into consideration, but it would be misleading to conclude that the psychological function of the "Other" is an objective structure (whether of language or reality), rather than the problematic emotional and aesthetic experience of another person.

At the metatheoretical level, there is not a lot of difference between Freud's stress on the reality principle and Lacan's emphasis on language. In either case, we are presented with what critics of Marxian economism call the base/superstructure model, and what critics of behaviourism call the "secondary drive" theory of human sociability. The infrastructure is always some version of the classical image of nature (e.g., the allegedly chaotic randomness of the body untutored by language or the reality ego); and the superstructure is always a conventional image of the arbitrariness of culture (in this case, socialization). The ways in which people actually relate to each other are viewed as wholly arbitrary orderings ("symbolic orders," to use Lacan's phrase) imposed upon the body by some reified external agency, usually called 'society' or 'economy' (or 'language').

The base/superstructure, secondary drive model works itself out in Rose's account of Lacan through a vision of human sexuality as a wholly ideological construction masking the "fragmented and aberrant nature of sexuality itself."[23] Sexuality as we know it, then—sexuality as constituted in language—is an arbitrary fusion of disparate bits and pieces of instinctual nature and unrelated psychic experiences into a false identity, a streamlined discourse inflicted on the hapless subject by the Symbolic Order. Of course, there is no doubt that the emotional meaning of bodily experience is extremely plastic, especially in early childhood, when something like polymorphous perversity is more prevalent. However, the Lacanian theory of infancy supplements this with an implicit myth of origins—that the state of nature is an originary chaos. If one is going to make a biological hypothesis out of sexual indeterminacy (a standard behaviourist assumption), then one also has to take into account the other psychobiological facts about neonates: their perceptual, emotional, and social capacities. For, as we have already seen, the newborn child is much more coordinated, aware, and sensitive to the external environment than most academicians were prepared to believe in Lacan's day.

The Text and the Anti-Text

The widespread belief that Lacan represents the only critical development within psychoanalysis since Freud has encouraged an overestimation of the arbitrariness of subjective psychosocial experience. Yet the apparent regularities of human sexuality (which tend to be either wildly exaggerated or grossly underestimated) cannot be explained entirely by the hypothesis of an endlessly displaced instinct or signifier. And so the doctrine of essential sexual randomness seeks compensation in an overly systematized, structural-linguistic (i.e., disembodied) conception of the symbolic process.

Lacan was perhaps the only psychoanalytic innovator of his generation not to take advantage of the fact that symbolization begins in the baby's body, rather than with the father's (Symbolic) intervention against the (Imaginary) "mother-child dual unity." His effective exclusion of the intimate role the mother plays in the child's symbolic and linguistic development in Western culture led him to pose the question of the psychic significance of the signifying gesture in an original way. Lacan's emphasis on the link between symbolization and the paternal order had the welcome effect of enriching philosophic criticism of the ideal types of linguistic "meaning" privileged in the rationalist tradition.[24]

But the deeper influence of Lacan's thought has been to reinforce the Cartesian ontological split on a new level.[25] Lacanian deconstruction depends, in practice, on a hypostatization of systems: in the Lacanian tradition, 'play' is derived theoretically from the manipulability of the formal elements that make up systems of signification, and not from the symbolizing body. The concrete and irreducible—what cannot be accounted for on the formal plane of rational codification—tends to be deduced from logical failures of the ideal type—the break-down of the formal system—as revealed through manipulation of the linguistic signifier. From this has developed the technique of deconstruction, which always interprets the informal as a by-product or effect of the formal. In consequence, post-Lacanian theory has found itself in the unenviable position of having to derive and to explain the tacit and arational dimension of experience (subjectivity, sexuality), while treating hypothetical 'systems,' such as language, as given.

According to Jacqueline Rose, language is always moving in two directions, or functioning in contradictory ways. At the superstructural level, language tends toward the *fixing* of meaning, the fusion of signifier and signified, which entails the "positioning" of the subject in the symbolic order and the imposition of an arbitrary sexual identity. At the infrastructural level, however, language engenders the *slippage* of meaning, which produces the displacement of the subject and what Rose describes as the "constant failure" of sexuality.

The problem with this account is not that it challenges the capacity of a substantive language to name sexuality—that point is well-taken; the problem is that it reduces sexuality to the insufficiencies and aporias of the signifying process itself. *Sexuality becomes the crisis of universal semiosis.* The point is not to deny the confluence of sexuality and language, but to show that the axis of Rose's linguistic perspective, in the traditional base-superstructure model, generates an abstract opposition between form (inevitably failing language) and material (a hypothetical deduction of sexuality as the excess or remainder of linguistic systems), which might be termed *the dialectic of the text and the anti-text*. The orientation of this epistemological framework is a double one. In the beginning, the world can be known only through the text, the order of writing, which is thus in a sense a kind of originary secondarity. Yet the knowledge gained by means of the text is always re-marked by an Other, the invisible and illusive anti-text, which exercises, *sui generis*, a powerfully disruptive influence.

In Rose's more sober terms, this means that sexuality (and by implication, all of our psychosomatic being, or 'body,' in the psychological sense) is a piece of social writing—a superimposition, or inscription. "For Lacan... there is no pre-discursive reality."[26] On the other hand, says Rose, there lies concealed beneath (and in a sense within) this observable but arbitrary order of signifiers, a kind of anti-text similar to a pure *potentia*, a formless plasticity subsisting in the blanks between the marks—in the margins, gaps and abysses which inhabit the order of discourse, with its visible plane of discrete elements arranged in systemic relations of opposition. The internal nothingness of this diacritical function, the *absentia* of *différance*, torments every structure imposed upon it, and therefore sexuality itself. Thus, Rose's astute definition of sexuality ("constituted as a division in language, a division which produces the feminine as its negative term"[27]) maps precisely onto the formalist opposition between inchoate 'force' (*différance*, desire, power, nature) and the superstructural plane of aleatory effects (the fictional order of human signs). At its Nietzchean best, this dialectic of presence and absence, mark and blank, phallus and castration, text and anti-text, gives Lacanian Rationalism a wonderfully Dionysian turn; at its worst, however, it deteriorates into the terroristic domination of the "simulacrum," the precession of the model, the combinatory, and the code, of which Jean Baudrillard speaks.[28]

Lacanian Anti-Lacanianism and the Problem of *Différence*

There has been an endless round of debates about all this. Lacanians, ex-Lacanians, and deconstructionists have argued interminably about whether the phallus is the penis, or is not the penis,[29] and about whether discourse may after all really be organized around something other than the phallus, some other principle, such as what Samuel Weber calls the "Thallus,"[30] or what Derrida variously termed supplement, hymen, and so on. At stake in all of these debates is the principle of difference—textual, sexual, and ontological.

One of Freud's greatest contributions was to draw our attention to the extraordinary emotional significance of the human body, and of parts of the body in particular, not least the penis. These parts (which of course include the mouth and anus, and constitute a zonal symbolic quite different from the binary genderal coding which so preoccupies Lacanians) are not only of narcissistic significance to children, but the sites of enormous struggles which sometimes last a lifetime.

As I have argued, when Lacan discusses the phallus, he is engaging the meanings of the body on a somewhat different plane.

...the phallus is not a phantasy, if by that we mean an imaginary effect. Nor is it as such an object (part-, internal, good, bad, etc.) in the sense that this term tends to accentuate the reality pertaining in a relation. It is even less the organ, penis or clitoris, that it symbolizes. And it is not without reason that Freud used the reference to the simulacrum that it represented for the Ancients.

For the phallus is a signifier whose function ...is...to designate as a whole the effects of the signified.[31]

As with the Symbolic, the phallus for Lacan is something abstract, hardly a part of the body, or even an experience; it is a metatheoretical function, a digital principle: in structural terms, the differential function of signification; in Gestalt terms (the terms of the mirror stage), the function of the 'figure' (standing out against a ground, but capable of oscillating with it); and in epistemological terms, the function of substitution as an originary condition (the simulacrum), the basic presupposition of philosophical deconstruction.

This discursive function of the phallus resembles a sort of rationalized version of children's common fantasy about the faeces. The wish of the phallic child is that the relations between human bodies be simplified into a kind of political economy. In a discursive variant of this, the exchange value would be the signifier, which embodies the condition of serial fungibility. In possession of the idealized (presumably anal) substitute for the parents' sexual maturity (their breasts and hair, the mysterious insides of the mother's body, the penis, and so on) the phallic child fantasizes a competition with the aggrandized parents, a satisfaction of their desires, a production of babies, even a self-production.

So the Lacanian phallus is essentially that which circulates in the form of *substitutability* (exchange value). Yet Lacan's enormous influence on all the various forms of contemporary discourse theory has always depended on his capacity to persuade us that the phallus is the conceptual embodiment of a kind of metalinguistic and metapsychological principle of *différence*. The contradiction here arises from the attempt to equate something very abstract and general (the principle of substitutability) with something very empirical and subjective (the perception that the world is not all made of the same thing). The conflation of fungibility and difference lies at the root of two ubiquitous contemporary phenomena: the philosophical school of deconstruction and the sociocultural problematic of simulation.

But difference is not a form, it does not circulate—in other words, difference has little to do with the psycho-linguistic ontology that post-Lacanian philosophy has transposed into a theory of textuality. If difference is both significant and originary, then it is unlikely that the phallus, either as a gender sign, or as the *Ursprung* of signification, can have anything *in general* to do with it. Difference is particular. It cannot therefore be systematized, or pinned up on a semiotic grid; which means that it cannot be reduced to the general, *formal* principle of the signifier, or to a coded diacritics, or to any of Lacan's "laws" and algorithms of the phallus and the father. But instead of simply abandoning the whole Lacanian paradigm, post-Lacanian thought has become inextricably mired in this problem of reserving difference by universalizing or formalizing it, and then having to rescue difference from the very attempt to save it.

Although difference cannot be thought in terms of the abstract and generalizing (or digital) differences of linguistic and cultural coding, the Lacanian phallus remains an important concept: not because it is the (dis)seminating 'knot' (*noeud*=penis) from which the textual unconscious is unravelled, but precisely because *the phallus is an idealization of desire*. It is a kind of 'defence': a *découpage* of unconscious process, a figural sublimation of desire. Schematically visible (but oscillating and self-consuming), it functions like the preconscious layer of a splitting process. Perhaps this is what Lacan meant when he said that the phallus "can play its role only when veiled."[32]

The Oedipal termination of infancy represents the linguistic crisis of the psyche: the marginalization of the dream state and of unconscious perception. The phallic defence is erected against the potential loss of the diacritical function itself, the threat of dissolution of formal or conscious difference in regression to unintegrated differences, differences without applied general structures to hold them in place for consciousness. In the transition from what Lacan pejoratively terms the Imaginary to what he misleadingly refers to as the Symbolic, the emotional intensity of the infantile body is subordinated to the phallic 'reality principle,' and superceded by the *functions* of differentiation and substitution.

The veiled phallus, the simulacrum, corresponds to the figure-ground problem of Rubin's double profile. The 'signifier' is like the 'right hand' side of a vertical split, the complement of which is the dreaded left hand of castration and death—the 'abyss.' Like the 'fort' and the 'da',[33] they are both available to consciousness, but mutually exclusive at any given moment. What is intolerable to phallic consciousness is neither the image of power nor the image of nothingness (both manageable idealizations), but the possibility of "dedifferentiation" (Ehrenzweig), the decodifying regression which leaves the psyche defenceless against itself. In the phallic defence against this possibility of undifferentiated difference (i.e., against the nondigital, alinguistic realm of unwilled order [Milner], meaning without theory, body without mind), the complementary sides of the idealizing Lacanian split, the 'phallus' and the 'hole,' dance brilliantly back and forth, generating endless folds of text, each reviving as the other fails, but never losing themselves in each other.

The Epicenity of the Text

The problem of idealization, and how it affects human sexuality (as an incorrigible part of it), is an important theme of Jane Gallop's masterly misreading of Lacan.[34] Gallop approaches the question in the most direct way possible—through the medium of her transference onto Lacan himself. She works through Lacan's texts in terms of her own impulse to rationalize and split, to idealize and devalue, to double each experience into manageably separate but interchangeable chains of affirmation and negation. A particularly impressive occasion for these reflections occurs in Gallop's encounter with Lacan's famous essay on the phallus.

After some twenty readings, Gallop had noticed that at the top of page 690 of the original French edition of *Écrits*, the word phallus itself was, inexplicably, not accompanied by the usual masculine article "*le*," as proper French requires, but by the feminine "*La*." The ramifications of such a lapsus for a close reader of Lacan are far from trivial. Like the phallus itself, the word "*La*" is, according to Lacan, a signifier without a signified. In the seminar "*Encore*," he frequently crossed out the feminine article when it appeared in conjunction with the word for 'woman,' declaring, "il n'y a pas *la* femme, la femme n'est pas toute."[35] One can imagine Gallop's readerly delight when she encountered the misprint "*La* phallus" at the very beginning of the page.

> A feeling of exhilaration accompanies my glide from "phallus" to "La." Loaded down with the seriousness of ideological meaning and sexual history, the phallus mires me in its confusion with the male organ. "La" seems to fly above all that in a disembodied ether of pure language, an epicene utopia where "gender is variable at will." But the "La at the top of page 690 is nearly impossible to read... although I am convinced of the arbitrary relation between signifier and signified, the masculinity of the phallic signifier serves well as an emblem of the confusion between phallus and male which inhere in language, in our Symbolic Order.[36]

In this passage, Gallop traces the two movements of language which Jacqueline Rose described. In the rising (or slipping) phase, the phallus, as signifier, is liberated from the penis, as signified, in order to become the figure of an asexual or perhaps bisexual freedom, the trace of an "epicene utopia." In the falling (or fixing) phase, however, signifier and signified are reconnected, to mark or "fix" the masculinity of the "symbolic order."

Jane Gallop's temptation was to soar. After twenty odd readings of the phallus, her discovery of the misplaced "*La*" makes her feel weightless—

she suddenly inhabits a utopia in which "gender is variable at will." And so it takes all the *avoirdupois* of the penis to bring her back down again. But Gallop is a brilliant allegorist. There is no question that the penis (or an alleged "symbolic *order*") returns Gallop to her body. Gallop just *is* her body, and never leaves it. She is never the inhabitant of an "epicene utopia," a "disembodied ether of pure language," where "gender is variable at will." What this clever Lacanian tale dramatizes is that there is no escape into language, that there is no such thing as the "liberation of the signifier," except as a fantasy of absconding from physical existence. The only alternative to embodiment is dismemberment or prosthetic hyper-evolution.

But since Lacanian theory presupposes and privileges the phallic significance of language, psyche, and culture, Lacanian feminism is left with the dismal prospect of endlessly displacing the gender significations of signification itself, and thus repeating the whole problematic of the Lacanian text. Such is the strategy evolved through deconstruction: to grant Lacan's ideal function (often performing under another name than the phallus) such a privileged autonomy as to permanently disjoin it from all play of meaning, all reference to the physical body; or to so generalize the linguistic function of the phallus as to make it mean (or "fail" to mean) virtually anything. But in either case, the phallic (or formalist) theory of difference only increases the power of the phallus to govern feminist discourse, while necessarily remaining linked to the genital organs through denial, or repeated denunciations of the confusion between the rarified "Symbolic" and its inevitable referent. If we take the foregoing as a more or less plausible rendition of what has been going on in radical academic discussion, then the question arises: why has Lacanianism become such a successful intellectual cottage industry? Why choose Lacan? Perhaps most compelling is the element of carnivalesque mockery which unconsciously drives the public celebration of ideals. The sheer grandiosity of the phallic function in Lacanian discourse is, in other words, virtually indistinguishable from Rabelaisian parody.

But there is another, duller explanation. The Lacanian phallus is, of course, implicated in a primary semantics, an originary loss of meaning, the *Urverdrangung*, which permanently splits the subject from himself, the signifier from the signified, in what Derrida has called "that seminal division."[37] This severance, this primordial absence and abyss, is accepted on the grounds that it is universal: woman no longer stands alone in suffrance of the alleged lack. But this invitation—the redistribution and equalization of castration—conceals a revolving door; for immemorial lack is precisely the ground, the metaphysical underpinning, of Lacan's hypostatization of the phallus as the principle of signification in the first place. And that is why the phallus haunts all deconstructive theories of language.

Lacan's ontology of the signifier never traces the movement of desire (as is sometimes claimed for it), but rather the vicissitudes of a defensive displacement of the whole question of the body and the unconscious in the cultural sciences. In this sense, Lacanian psychoanalysis is a salutary intensification of the rationalism of these sciences, a parody of the "linguistic turn," in which all the dead theoretical space of classical Reason, with its ontology of models and its epistemology of the discrete, is finally used up in a kind of self-conscious Hegelian involution.

Sexuality and the subject certainly "fail," as Rose argues, but in a Lacanian universe, they always fail in the same, structurally determinate way, and always in order to return in due time to the same "fix" in the "symbolic order." This kind of simulation of movement is only convincing in a purely textual frame of reference: it enacts an interplay of abstractions: the body reduced to the model of the text, and the rigidity of the text then escaped in the ethereal pseudo-naturality of the anti-text. We can see this in the way that the Lacanian reading of human sexuality never moves outside the circular paradigm of inscription—even as it slips in that momentary vision of an epicene utopia: for the "disembodied ether of pure language," the vacuum where the phallus can mean everything and nothing, and "gender is variable at will," is not the recovery of desire, or a reaffirmation of the uncoded (or decoded) body— but only the splitting and projection, the idealization of the text itself. "A configuration of veils, folds, and quills, writing prepares to receive the seminal spurt of a throw of the dice."[38] The endless structural play of abstract oppositions we have inherited (signifier vs. signified, mark vs. blank, phallus vs. castration, writing vs. abyss, presence vs. absence, father vs. mother, culture vs. nature)—none of this is ever disturbed in the slightest, no matter how it is manipulated, because the digital form of splitting is implicit in the code of inscription that Lacan laid down. The 'phallus' is the essence of textuality as an epistemology.

Notes

1.   Mary Jacobus, "The Question of Language: Men of Maxims and *The Mill on the Floss*," in *Writing and Sexual Difference*, ed. Elizabeth Abel (Chicago: University of Chicago Press, 1982), pp.37-52.

2.   Barbara Johnson, "The Frame of Reference: Poe, Lacan, Derrida," in *Psychoanalysis and the Question of the Text*, ed. Geoffrey Hartmann (Baltimore: Johns Hopkins University, 1978), pp. 167,165.

3.   This paper was first presented at Elspeth Probyn's Canadian Communications Association panel on "Feminist Perspectives in Communication," Winnipeg, June, 1986. An earlier version was published in *Borderlines* 7 (Summer, 1987).

4.   Ella Freeman Sharpe, *Dream Analysis* (New York: Brunner/ Mazel, 1978 [1937]), pp.9-10, 19-39.

5.   Jane Gallop, *The Daughter's Seduction: Feminism and Psychoanalysis* (Ithaca: Cornell University Press, 1982), pp.33-36.

6. Jacques Derrida, *Dissémination*, trans. Barbara Johnson (Chicago: Chicago University Press, 1981), p.93.

7. Julia Kristeva, "Within the Microcosm of the 'Talking Cure'" in Joseph H. Smith and William Kerrigan, eds., *Interpreting Lacan* (New Haven: Yale University Press, 1983), pp.42-4. Cf. Gallop, *The Daughter's Seduction*, pp.117-8; 113-5.

8. Stuart Schneiderman, *Jacques Lacan: The Death of an Intellectual Hero* (Cambridge: Harvard University Press, 1983), p.13.

9. Gilles Deleuze and Felix Guattari, *Anti-Oedipus: Capitalism and Schizophrenia*, trans. Robert Hurley, et al. (New York: Viking, 1972).

10. Juliet Mitchell & Jacqueline Rose, *Feminine Sexuality: Jacques Lacan and his ecole freudienne*, (New York: Norton, 1982).

11. Sigmund Freud (1937), "Analysis Terminable and Interminable," in *Standard Edition of the Complete Psychological Works of Sigmund Freud* (Vol. 23), trans. James Strachey (London: Hogarth, 1953-74), p.252.

12. Jacqueline Rose, "Introduction II" in Mitchell and Rose, p.42. This article has been reprinted as "Feminine Sexuality—Jacques Lacan and the ecole freudienne," in Jacqueline Rose, *Sexuality in the Field of Vision* (London: Verso, 1986), pp.49-81.

13. Rose, p.28.

14. Melanie Klein, *The Psycho-Analysis of Children*, trans. Alix Strachey (London: Hogarth, 1932; Virago Press, 1975), pp.135-6.

15. See for example, Anika Lemaire, *Jacques Lacan*, trans. David Macey (London: Routledge and Kegan Paul, 1977), p.92; also, Kristeva, op. cit.

16. One of the implications of Lacan's anchoring of the Symbolic in the paternal phallus is that desire itself is conceived in its most fundamental constitution as little more than a displacement of narcissistic envy, since Lacanian desire has its roots in the "desire of the Other," which for Lacan is originally the mother's projection of 'lack.' Deleuze's Nietzschean reading of Lacanian desire as *ressentiment* is thus entirely appropriate.

17. At a recent conference on "post-structuralism(e)" at the University of Ottawa (1983), the addresses of Ellie Ragland-Sullivan, Jacques Alain-Miller, and Stuart Schneidermann all traded on the medico-linguistic fantasy of Lacan's 'discovery' of the 'structures' of the unconscious.

18. For example, Louis Althusser, "Freud and Lacan," in *Lenin and Philosophy*, trans. Ben Brewster (New York: Monthly Review Press, 1971), p.216; Lacan (1964), *The Four Fundamental Concepts of Psycho-Analysis*, trans. Alan Sheridan (Harmondsworth, Middlesex: Pelican, 1977), pp.20-1.

19. Rose, p.30.

20. The outlook of experimental psychology has changed in the last ten years, largely as a result of more sophisticated infant research. For psychoanalytically oriented summaries and interpretations of neonatological research, see Daniel Stern, *The Interpersonal World of the Infant* (New York: Basic Books, 1985) and Victoria Hamilton, *Narcissus and Oedipus: the Children of Psychoanalysis* (London: RKP, 1982). The view of classical and Lacanian psychoanalysis is stated in Juliet Mitchell's review of Hamilton in "Psychoanalysis and Child Development," *New Left Review*, 140 (1983): 92-96.

21. Sigmund Freud, The Interpretation of Dreams, *Standard Edition* 5 (1900), p.588f.

22. For discussion of the idea that unintegration is part of a natural psychic rythm, see Anton Ehrenzweig, *The Hidden Order of Art* (Berkeley: University of California Press, 1967); Marion Milner, *On Not Being Able to Paint* (London: Heinemann, 1957); and D.W. Winnicott, *Playing and Reality* (Harmondsworth, Middlesex: Pelican, 1971).

23. Rose, p.28.

24. See Luce Irigaray, *This Sex Which is Not One*, trans. Catherine Porter (Ithaca: Cornell University Press, 1985); and *Speculum of the Other Woman*, trans. Gillian G. Gill (Ithaca: Cornell University Press, 1985). For further discussion of Irigaray, see also the article by Gauthier in this volume.

25. Cf. Jane Gallop, *Reading Lacan* (Ithaca, N. Y.: Cornell University Press), pp.59-60; p. 160.

26. Rose, p.55.

27. Rose, p.55.

28. Jean Baudrillard (1976).

29. For example, E. Ragland-Sullivan, "Jacques Lacan: Feminism and the Problem of Gender Identity," *SubStance* 36 (1982): 6-20.

30. Samuel Weber, *The Legend of Freud* (Minneapolis: University of Minnesota, 1982).

31. Jacques Lacan, *Écrits: A Selection*, trans. Alan Sheridan (New York: Norton, 1977), p.285.

32. Lacan, *Ecrits*, p. 288.

33. Jacques Lacan (1953), *The Language of the Self: The Function of Language in Psychoanalysis*, trans. Anthony Wilden (Baltimore: Johns Hopkins University Press, 1968), p.83.

34. Jane Gallop, *Reading Lacan*.

35. Jacques Lacan, *Le Séminaire: Livre XX: Encore* (Paris: Seuil, 1975), pp.13,68.

36. Gallop, *Reading Lacan*, p.140.

37. Jacques Derrida, *Dissémination*, p. 268.

38. Ibid., p. 285.

16

THIS IS NOT A PRESIDENT: BAUDRILLARD, BUSH AND ENCHANTED SIMULATION

Diane Rubenstein

Today the trompe l'oeil is no longer confined to painting.[1]

Jean Baudrillard

I mean, like hasn't everybody thought about becoming president for years?[2]

George Bush

The end of millenium American presidency reads as a perverse re-write of Baudrillard's sign theory: a gradual disobligation of the sign as we pass from the disenchanted and banal strategies of Ronald Reagan to the seductive enchanted simulation of Bush and his most 'fatal strategy', Dan Quayle, a man who "does not live in this century."[3] What has been lost in the non-visible transition from Reagan to Bush is precisely this move from hyperreality to seduction. The apparent continuity of Reagan-Bush and their cabinet cross-dressing (the same men in different suits) masks an epistemic discontinuity. For Bush is our first hysterical male president, the first *trompe l'oeil* president of Baudrillard's fourth order of simulation: fractal (1,000 points of light) and orbital (yes, we will go to Mars). With Bush we move from the hyperreal in-difference of Reagan to an objective irony, from a president as hologram to the *trompe l'oeil*. Reagan: the ectasy of the real in hyperreality. Bush: the ectasy of the fake in seduction.

Umberto Eco evokes what is at stake in this realm of the Absolute Fake in his depiction of Disneyland's reconstructed Oval Office: "Elsewhere, on the contrary, the frantic desire for the almost real arises only as a neurotic reaction to the vacuum of memories, the Absolute Fake is the offspring of the unhappy awareness of a present without depth."[4] We might as well insert the 'id'—a president without depth. The scandal that the *trompe l'oeil* poses for political and esthetic representation since the Renaissance is situated in its "unreal reversion" (p. 60). The aim of the reconstructed Oval office in both Disneyland and Washington is to supply a sign that will fool (*trompe*) the eye and abolish the distinction of reference. (Or, as in Bush's own words: "This isn't any signal. It's a direct statement. If it's a signal, fine."[5]) In the history of the late 20th century presidency, Bush marks a peculiar instance of the relation of reference to signification. While American presidents since Gerald Ford have been empty signifiers, rarely has there been such a Lacanian relation to language that Bush daily enacts. Bushspeak may be the closest approximation outremer of the Lacanian unconscious: ça parle. "It says what it knows while the subject does not know it."[6] With Bush, we have a presidential subject that cannot be understood as a signified (i.e., as objectively knowable). This is preparation for the final turn of the screw: Quayle as Baudrillard's fatal strategy, where "the metamorphosis, tactics and strategies of the object exceed the subject's understanding."[7] (Carter posed problems of a different psychoanalytic order. For he demonstrated the fissure between idea and affect. Carter always seemed to smile at the wrong time.)

The end of milennia presidency is a twin appeal to the "image repertoire" and the symbolic order. As image repertoire, it can be read as a litany of bad presidential performances: "LBJ abusing his dogs and exposing his belly; Nixon hunched and glistening like a concerned toad, Gerald Ford tripping over..." Reagan, as a hyperreal president could always satisfy our iconic interests: "Reagan was nice as Iago was honest because his image repertoire required it of him."[8] Moreover, Reagan was always tangible as symbol if not as image. In the difference between image repertoire and the symbolic order we can first glimpse the subtle passage from hyperreality to seduction. What sets Bush apart from Reagan is his intractable opacity. For Bush is a simulacra without perspective. He appears as a pure artefact (our "environmental" president, our "education" president) against a vertical backdrop. Bush replaces Reagan's tangibility with the "tactile vertigo of the afterimage." Richard Goldstein concurs: "now we're in the grip of something that no longer requires a spokesman."[9] This tactile vertigo recounts "the subject's insane desire to obliterate his own image and thereby vanish" (p.62). Life becomes a 'Jeff Koons tableau'. Koons the artist and Bush the seducer know how to let the signs hang. Bush/Koons, suspended in ether.

Bush not only follows the hyperrealism of neo-geo/Reagan but recalls the surrealism of Gerald Ford. Both share the same knack for the tautology: "Things are more like they are now than they ever have been."[10] (Ford) "It's no exaggeration to say the undecideds could go one way or another."[11] (Bush) They juxtapose physical against linguistic slapstick: Ford trips; Bush slips linguistically. If Gerald Ford recalls the Jerry Lewis of the Lewis-Martin movies in which a subjective irony might still be possible, Bush is most reminiscent of the movies Lewis produced after his split up with Martin.[12] An internally dissociated subject emerges in the linguistic parapraxis as Bush stages his own disappearance. Pronouns flee, then verbs in the vanishing act of his State of the Union address: "Ambitious Aims? Of course! Easy to do? Far from it."[13] We are left with nothing but the irony of the object which underscores the tie between Lacan's "linguisterie" and Bush speak: "what might be called a man, the male speaking being strictly disappears as an effect of discourse by being inscribed within it solely as castration."[14]

I   "Ghosts that haunt the emptiness of the stage"
Baudrillard (p. 60)

I'm going to be so much better a president for having been at the CIA that you are not going to believe it.[15]
Bush

What seduces us with Bush, as in the *trompe l'oeil* is its missing dimension. And if Ronald Reagan was a hologram, Bush is, in Baudrillard's words "a superficial abyss." Opposed to Reagan's televisual sarcasms ("How do I spell relief? V–E–T–O"), Bush is a visual non-sequitur. Bush affords the same perspectual pleasure as that of the *trompe l'oeil* (as well as its secret undermining of language) even as he takes us back to our earliest lessons of political representation. Since Machiavelli, power has always—already been a simulation model, only an effect of perspective. Baudrillard recounts that at the heart of the ducal palaces of Urbino and Gubbio were tiny *trompe l'oeil* sanctuaries, inverted microcosms whose space was actualized by simulation. These sanctuaries (studiolos) were blind spots in the palace and were placed at the heart of the prince's politico—architectural space. Through a subversive metonymy they invite an allegorical reading: that "the prince's power is only mastery of a simulated space. This is the prince's secret." (p. 65).

And we might wonder who is better than Bush, a former CIA spook, to preside over the seductive presidency and guard this secret. Seduction is, after all, the realm of the *secret*. Production, for Baudrillard, is "to materialize by force what belongs to another order, that of the secret; seduction removes from the order of the visible, while production constructs everything in full view, be it an object, a number or concept" (p. 34). Those people who doubt Bush's popularity at the polls, who castigate his caution (or prudence), are like those critics of Ronald Reagan who saw him either as a hypocrite or vacuous and thereby missed his remarkable sign function and theoretic challenge. The depthlessness and nonobligation of the sign is constitutive of the post-modern presidency. And if Reagan was conceptually tragic yet hilarious Bush profers a no less metaphysical hilarity: the acute metaphysical appeal of the *trompe l'oeil*.

It may appear bizarre to characterize Bush as seductive. After all, this is the man who *Newsweek* decreed had a wimp factor too strong a disability ever to become president. But we should not make the mistake of confounding the autonomous or disembodied signifier with charisma or its lack. Charisma, like vulgar notions of seduction, has everything to do with the body; seduction, on the other hand connotes a whole "strategy of appearances" interpreted in terms of "play, challenges, duels" (p. 7). Indeed, the Bush presidency when read against Baudrillard's *Seduction* seems less an instance of the wimp factor than a transvestite oversimulation of femininity. The same impersonator for Bush on *Saturday Night Live*, Dana Carvey, is also the punishing church lady. This oscillation between the two Bush persona uncannily evokes both of Carvey's characterizations, especially that of the phallic mother and her appeal for the male masochist. This recentering around the strong mother entails a concommitant displacement of male subjectivity. Political pundits such as Peter Hart and Texas senator Carl Parker have an idiomatic appreciation of Bush as feminine simulator. Hart calls Bush the "Don Knotts of American politics". Parker compares Bush's macho performance against that of Reagan: "Reagan can portray a real macho guy. Bush can't. He comes off looking like Liberace."[16] Both analogies are telling figures. Don Knotts was most known as Andy Griffith's inept deputy, Barney Fife, whose failed attempts to impose a law recall the hysterics of Al "I'm in charge" Haig. Knotts is the perfect second fiddle (as is Bush). His tremendous effort at and failure to control becomes a caricature of male potency. Knotts, like Bush, exemplifies the masochistic self victimization of one who is so visibly trying to please. Indeed, Knotts seems an ersatz made for television (pre-telethon) Jerry Lewis. While Liberace is a rhetorically charged topos, he too can be read like Knotts or Bush as an oversimulation of the feminine.

The transvestite is an apposite figure for Bush. Like the transvestite Bush parodies signs by oversignification. Bush, like Baudrillard, knows that "it is the transubstantiation of sex into signs that is the secret of all seduction." (p. 13) Moreover, what we witness with Bush as with male hysteria in general, is not the recoding of men as men but rather a process of uncoding.[17] As with Jerry Lewis, Bush's frenetic effort to "control the (political) spectacle finally yields to a male subject position which demolishes any prospect of a coherent masculine subjectivity."[18] Reagan's obtuse meaning was literally impertinent; Bush's persona is incoherent. Bush-wimp and the macho Bush; Bush with Barbara, Bush with Baker; the kinder gentile Bush of the new WASP cultural hegemony against the macho cowboy Texan who puts tobasco sauce on his tuna "yet always seems to look as if he has just escaped from a dude ranch."[19]

What fascinates us in Bush is precisely this unresolved and contradictory self-formation—the self-cancelling spiralling of signs that is also the fascination towards the neuter: one libido? or Barthesian nectarine which dampens oppositions? In *Sade Fourier Loyola*, Barthes discusses Fourier's classification scheme in which there is always a reserved portion (1/8). This reserved portion is liminal or *neuter*: "The neuter is what comes between the mark and the non-mark, this sort of buffer, damper, whose role is to muffle, to soften, to fluidify the semantic tick-tock, that metronome-like noise the paradigmatic alternative obsessively produces: yes/no, yes/no..." This portion is shocking as it is contradictory and disturbing. It is necessarily ambiguous and it undermines meaning. The neuter is a 'qualitative, structural relation' which subverts the very idea of norm and normality. "To enjoy the neuter is perforce to be disgusted by the average".[20] And despite his many protestations, Bush is no average guy.

Yet Bush is a transvestite-feminine dissimulator in a parodic sense: "The seduction is itself coupled with a parody in which an implacable hostility to the feminine shows through and which might be interpreted as a male appropriation of the panoply of female allurements" (p. 14). This repudiation of the feminine is most evident in a contest situation, such as the Bush-Ferraro debate in which Bush "kicked a little ass" (a good ole Texas phrase) or in his televisual dual with Dan Rather "that guy makes Leslie Stahl look like a pussy".[21] His repudiation of the feminine is twinned with an overcompensation of masculine behavior that can only look to Jerry Lewis' Nutty Professor for an equally apt hysterical enactment. The Bush wimp is like the Lewis-Kelp character cured of what ails (Ailes) him via a substitute ego of simulated virility. Bush as wimp is transformed to macho-Bush only by an excess of masochistic self-victimization. Dana Carvey's brilliant parody of Bush's campaign self-management is to the point: "Voice low. Voice getting lower. Doctors tell me it can go lower still."[22] The exhibition of Bush—suffering throughout the entire 1988 campaign is enacted via the body: His voice is lowered, his mannerisms contained. Moreover, the oscillation between a passive and a hypermale (often misread as the opposition between Peggy Noonan and Roger Ailes) underlines the lack of a stable balance within a single male subjectivity, thus joining Bush to the ranks of other late 80's male hysterics: Pete Rose, General Noriega and Bob Saget.

Like the transvestite, there is nothing latent about Bush. It is only latent discourse that tries to hide the secret of appearances. Seduction is a manifest discourse offering us the lure (*leurre*) of the secret of appearances. What Bush offers is nothing less than the faker than the false—Oprah Winfrey's head on Ann-Margret's body on the cover of TV Guide. Bush becomes in this reading a blank empty sign that bespeaks the anti-ceremonial of anti-(political) representation. I repeat: Bush is a manifest character. Maureen Dowd and Thomas Friedman describe him: "When you sit across from the president, it is like holding an X-ray plate up to the light. You can see if he feels defensive or annoyed or amused. He is often distracted, toying with something on his desk."[23] Dowd's depiction of a distracted Bush makes him no less seductive in Baudrillard's sense: for the absence of a focused look, like the absence of a face, highlights the attraction of the void that lies at the base of all seduction: "The mind is irresistibly attracted to a place devoid of meaning" (p. 74). As our *trompe l'oeil* president, Bush 'bewitches' us with his missing dimension. And if Reagan simulated his constituency, Bush quite literally mirrors it. Like the seducer, Bush says "I'll be your mirror." But this is not in some American interest group liberalism sense of "I'll represent you or reflect you." Rather Bush offers to be our deception. "I'll be your deception", the mirror ensnares us with its come-on of "Let's Pretend".[24] Bush is as transparent and false as the plastic bag holding the crack 'purchased' in Lafayette Park—a wholly fake enactment with malfunctioning video equipment and a pusher who couldn't find the White House.[25] Rarely do we have a president with such camp potential. Yet the question still lingers which male hysteric: Pee-Wee Herman or Jerry Lewis; male hysteria with or without anxiety?

> II   I do not like broccoli. And I haven't liked it since I was a little kid and my mother made me eat it. And I'm president of the United States and I'm not going to eat any more broccoli[26]
>
> George Bush

> I'm legally and emotionally entitled to be what I want to be. That's what I want to be and that's what I am.[27]
>
> George Bush

It is this void, this missing dimension that ties Bush the *trompe l'oeil* president to Bush the hysterical male presidency. For it is the inner absence that terrifies the hysteric. Bush is described by Steven V. Roberts as a man in his middle sixties who "still didn't know who he was or where he wanted to go."[28] This panic is sometimes evinced in a self-reflective comment: "I'm looking introvertedly and I don't like what I see". This uncertainty and terror over his fragile concept of identity is underscored by his manic 1988 campaign insistence that "I'm one of you." This rhetorical tick (like the hysteresis of Koch's "How'm I doing?") was repeated eight times in his New Hampshire speech and in numerous states: Massachusetts "Born there. I'm one of them, too." Texas: "I'm one of them, too." (or in dialect: "Ah am one of y'al.") Connecticut: "I think it might be kind of nice to have a Connecticut kid in the White House."[29]

So much insistence on Being (The Dasein in all its naked stupidity). Barthes notes that the hysteric asks "Am I?" Bush's profound lack of a sense of self is momentarily assuaged by the appeal to voter registration: "I'm legally and emotionally entitled to be what I want to be." Bush displaces the question of identity to one of a posited self signified by documentation ("my Texas hunting license, my Texas driver's license and my voter's registration card")[30] as it also gives him the freedom to play roles and refuse any one fixed identity. The *trompe l'oeil* underscores the lack in male subjectivity.

Indeed there is a certain pathos in Bush's frenetic attemps to establish an identity (if not a residence—the unheimlich/homelessness of a suite in a Houston hotel serves as his primary address). Bush reminds us that hysteria is "the effect and testimony of a failed interpellation." Moreover, Bush's self questioning recalls Lacan's reformulation "Why am I what you're telling me that I am?" Zizek situates the hysterical question in the failure of the subject to assume symbolic identification. "The hysterical question opens the gap of what is in the subject more than the subject of the *object in subject* which resists interpellation."[31]. The Bush-lack is tied to the Lacanian (m)-other as Bush answers charges that he is a carpetbagger: "When I ran for office in Texas they said this guy's from New England. I said, wait a minute, I couldn't help that, *I wanted to be near my mother at the time.*"[32]

Baudrillard compares the hysteric and the seducer in their deployment of signs. The fear of being seduced leads hysterics to setting up "booby trapped" signs. Indeed, the entire 1988 campaign can be read as one long booby trapped sign as if Bush entirely lacked the capacity for secondary revision. With Bush there is a dizzying array of parapraxes, elisions and repetitions. Bush is aware of the problem: "I have a tendency to avoid on and on and on, elegant pleas. I don't talk much, but I believe, maybe not articulate much, but I feel."[33] Bush is self-conscious, defensive and non-ironic about his linguisterie. He fondly replays his Pearl Harbor Day lapsus when he gets flustered in the debate with Dukakis: "It's Christmas. Wouldn't it be nice to be perfect? Wouldn't it be nice to be the iceman so you never make mistakes?"[34] The Bush parapraxes can include foreign words: "muchissimo grazie" and thinking of "comme ci comme ça" as a popular hispanic phrase.[35] But it is in electoral campaigns and contest situations that his unique rhetorical talent merges most fully.

The primal scene of the 1988 campaign was the May 1988 rally in Twin Falls, Idaho, when Bush admits to having sex with Reagan: "For seven and a half years, I have worked alongside him and I am proud to be his partner. We have had triumphs, we have made mistakes, we have had sex." Correcting this lapsus ("we have had setbacks"), Bush commits an even greater blunder comparing himself to a "javelin thrower who won the coin toss and elected to receive."[36] Nor is this the first time the electoral parapraxes have concerned masculinity. In 1984 Bush offered to "lay his record on manhood against Mondale's anytime."[37] Or, commenting on the Anderson challenge in 1980 "If we win in Michigan, it would be like a jockey or a marathon man with lead weights in both pockets."[38] (The 1984 convention provoked considerable anxiety as Bush suffered from convention envy forcing the phallic comparison: "It doesn't have the drama of San Francisco. But our halo blowers are as good as theirs. Our flag wavers are taller, stronger and better.")[39]

As stated earlier, the Bush parapraxes range from elision (forgetting about Reagan's governorship while praising Deukmejian at a 1988 rally as the best governor of the state on record) to the just plain silly: "Tell me, general, how dead is the Dead Sea?" to Jordanian Army Chief of Staff.[40] The explicit goal of Bush's administration is to "make sure that everybody who has a job wants a job" [41](a much more ambitious aim than mere full employment). It is against this question of desire that Bushspeak should be read: not as over-exuberance leading to "misspeaking" but as an excess of decoration (a linguistic surplus value) over meaning which may be one reason he is so difficult to translate. Bush baffles his translators with his use of colloquialisms derived from popular culture (especially baseball) and Texas slang. Bush tells the Japanese to "stay tuned", the Soviets to "lighten up". He uses baseball references in a discussion of Panamanian stragy: "American will stay at the plate". Yet it is Bush's rhetorical appeal to Yogi Berra, master of the tautology ("You can observe a lot just by watching" "déjà vu all over again") and oxymoron ("No one goes to that restaurant anymore, it's too crowded") that most frustrates the French translator.[42] Yogi Berra's rhetorical duplication recalls that of Magritte's calligram[43] and once again underlines the figure of *trompe l'oeil* in Bush's presidency. Bush also enacts (with considerable hilarity) the difference between the logic of the unconscious and that of the ego. As mentioned earlier, Bush's slips exemplify Lacanian "linguisterie": that side of language that language has left unformalized."[44] These are most obvious in verbal slips, jokes, interruptions and dreams.

There is a manic insistence and disjointed character to Bush's discourse.* Even more than President Reagan's anecdote about his drive down Highway One, Bush exemplifies the Lacanian *dérive* (or drift): "being dragged by currents and not knowing where it is going."[45] An emblematic Bush drift is the following quite literal *dérive* as Bush floats around the Pacific Ocean after his fighter plane is shot down near Japan:

> I was shot down and I was floating around in a little yellow raft setting a record for paddling. I thought of my family, my mom and dad and the strength I got from them. I thought of my faith, the separation of church and state."[46]

Or we can consider Bush on his goals for the summit with Gorbachev:

---

* (Mary McGrory notes that the non-sequitur is the one grammatical form Bush has mastered.)

> We had last night, last night we had a couple of our grandchildren with us in Kansas City—six-year-old twins, one of them went as a package of Juicy Fruit, arms sticking out of the pack, the other was Dracula. A big rally there. And Dracula's wig fell off in the middle of my speech and I got to thinking, watching those kids, and I said if I could look back and I had been president for four years: what would you like to do? Those young kids there. And I'd love to be able to say that working with our allies, working with the Soviets, I'd found a way to ban chemical and biological weapons from the face of the earth."[47]

Bushspeak as such typifies the split between savoir and connaissance: it is a savoir without connaissance inscribed within Lacan's discourse of the messenger slave: "the subject who carries under his hair the codicil that condemns him to death (who) knows neither the meaning nor the text nor in what language it is written, nor even that it had been tatooed on his shaved scalp as he slept."[48]

In other words, Bush's 'linguisterie' shares with Barthesian "betise" the eruption of an unconscious truth in an unacceptable manner: incoherent, fragmentary, non-grammatical. At times Bush exemplifies something resembling a classic nineteenth century hysteric such as Anna O. It seems as if English is not Bush's native language. While many of Bush's slips appear merely stupid or of trivial significance, it is at precisely such moments when meaning is fractured that we glimpse a "missing letter"[49]—a break in the cohesion of the ego. When asked if the economic decline is over, Bush states emphatically: "The slide show is over." Also, the possibility of no further contra-aid "pulls the plug out from under the President of the United States."[50] Both slips reinscribe the after-image cyborg quality of his presidency. For Bush's digressions, non-sequiturs, lapses, repetitions recall those of an analysand rather than the narrative closure of an authorial subject (i.e., the President of the United States).

One of Bush's most interesting and parodied linguistic tropes is his use of the word 'thing': "Did you go through that withdrawal thing?" (to a recovering drug addict); or its numerous guises: the "feminist thing", the "hostage thing", the "vision thing", the "gender thing", the "ethnic thing"[51]... Bush's thing-thing is like Lacan's "petit objet a", a surplus object, a left-over of the Real which eludes symbolization. And like Lacan's "object a" it "partially represents the function which produces it."[52] This 'thing-thing' allows a hysterical Bush to identify with the Other's lack as well as his own. There is always something which escapes this presidential subject and this lacking object releases his desire.

For Baudrillard, the seducer and the hysteric differ in their manipulation of signs. If seduction mocks the truth of signs, the hysteric plays with signs without sharing them. (p. 120) Bush does both: seduction as challenge, hysteria as blackmail—an effective double game strategy.

Bush, like an hysteric, turns his body into a mirror. He is what he does and does not eat (pork rinds, broccoli).[53] But this is a mirror that has been turned against the wall by effacing the potential seductiveness of his body (after all, he is relatively good looking and fit) by de-sexualizing it. This de-sexualization can be read against the classic scenario in which strong female subjects (Marilyn Quayle, Barbara Bush) are obligated to assume male lack. (To the extent that Bush is also a male-masochist, this is his fantasy as well). The gaze of the sexual (m)other of the Bush presidency is quite different from Nancy's fawning. Barbara Bush answers the call to look upon and accept male lack. The denegation of her Wellesley commencement address acknowledges and embraces male castration (even and especially as it rewrites the First Lady as a man). Marilyn Quayle insisted during the campaign that she was not getting paid to be Dan's advisor even if she was doing what an advisor would normally get paid for. We witness a reorientation: a recentering of the Strong Mother and a combination of female magnaminity and male masochism.[54] Barbara Bush is so popular because she is so reassuring. But her reassurance is not that she allows herself to visibly grow old, but rather that she encourages us to be passive without guilt.

If Barbara follows the Lacanian route of the acceptance of male lack, Bush in his desexualization offers us an ultimatum: "You will not seduce me. I dare you to try." Yet as Baudrillard notes, seduction shows through in negation. The dare is one of its fundamental forms. A challenge is met with a response. This is the real sense of "read my lips" and not, as Peggy Noonan would have it, an attempt to establish unequivocal meaning.[55] Bush closes down the game by dramatizing his refusal to be seduced (i.e., cash in on his popularity) yet at the same time dramatizing a need for seduction.

Bush, seductive and oblique, is the perfect end of millenium president. If Ronald Reagan showed the signifier in a 'permanent state of depletion' (the Barthesian third or obtuse meaning), then Bush proffers another sign strategy: the obliquity of the seducer who knows how to let the signs hang. Who needs a White House astrologer when you have a seducer who knows when signs are favorable and has the requisite male masochism to enjoy suspense? We recall Baudrillard's words with a poignancy for the events of last fall. Bush is the luckiest man in the world, some say. I disagree. Bush only appears lucky because of the uncanny deployment of a seduction strategy:

> Signs are favorable only when left suspended and will move of themselves to their appointed destiny. The seducer doesn't use signs up all at once but waits for the moment when they will all respond, one after the other, creating a unique conjuncture and collapse. (p. 109)

Notes

1. Jean Baudrillard, *Seduction*, trans. Brian Singer (translation modified), (NY: St. Martin's Press 1990) p. 64. All references to *Seduction* appear in the body of the text and refer to the Singer translation.

2. *Spy* magazine, August 1988, p. 98. See also *The Wit and Wisdom of George Bush*, Ken Brady and Jeremy Solomon, ed., (NY: St. Martin's Press, 1989), p. 27.

3. *Spy* magazine, November 1988, p. 128. The full quote runs as follows: "The holocaust was an obscene period in our nation's history. I mean this century's history. But we all lived in this century. I didn't live in this century."

4. Umberto Eco, *Travels in Hyperreality*, (NY: Harcourt, Brace, Jovanovich, 1983), pp. 6–7.

5. *New York Times*, March 10, 1980, p. B10.

6. Bice Benvenuto and Roger Kennedy, *The Works of Jacques Lacan*, (NY: St. Martin's Press, 1986), p. 166.

7. Mark Poster, *Jean Baudrillard: Selected Writings*, (Stanford: Stanford UP, 1988), p. 188.

8. Mark Crispin Miller, *Boxed In: The Culture of TV*, (Evanston, IL: Northwestern UP, 1988), p. 80.

9. Richard Goldstein, "The New Wasp Hegemony in the Wake of Bush", *Enclitic*, Vol. 11, No. 2, Issue 22, pp. 8–14.

10. Mark Green and Gail MacColl, *Ronald Reagan's Reign of Error*, (NY: Pantheon, 1987), 9.

11. *NY Times*, November 4, 1988, p. 14.

12. I am indebted to Scott Bukatman's brilliant reading of Jerry Lewis: "Paralysis in Motion, Jerry Lewis's Life as a Man", *Camera Obscura*, 17 May 1988, pp. 194–205.

13. *NY Times*, March 9, 1990, B1, Maureen Dowd, "Bush–Speak. Not Pretty. Catching On".

14. Kaja Silverman, "Historical Trauma and Male Subjectivity" in E. Ann Kaplan, ed. *Psychoanalysis and Cinema*, (NY: Routledge 1990), p. 111. (The reference is to Jacques Lacan, *Seminaire XVIII*, p. 4.)

15. *Spy*, August 1988, p. 98.

16. Brady and Solomon, pp. 13–14.

17. Lynne Kirby, "Male Hysteria and Early Cinema", *Camera Obscura* 17, May 1988, p. 126.

18. Bukatman, "Paralysis in Motion", p. 195.

19. NY Times, May 6, 1990, Maureen Dowd and Thomas Friedman, "Those Fabulous Bush and Baker Boys", p. 58.

20. Roland Barthes, *Sade, Fourier, Loyola*, (NY: Hill and Wang, 1976), p. 107–109.

21. Brady and Solomon, *Wit and Wisdom*, p. 44.

22. *NY Times*, March 9, 1990, B1, Dowd, "Bushspeak".

23. Dowd and Friedman, "Those Fabulous Bush and Baker Boys", p. 62.

24. On this topic of 'Let's Pretend' (as well as the way Poppy Bush continually pops up), Bush recalls Pee-Wee Herman. See the article by Constance Penley, "The Cabinet of Dr. Pee-Wee: Consumerism and Sexual Terror", *Camera Obscura* 17, May 1988, for implicit comparisons between Bush and Pee-Wee on playing house, "I know you are but what am I?" and especially: "No! None of that stuff! Game's over", pp. 133–135. Penley's article is also excellent for a treatment of the *unheimlich* in both Pee-Wee's and Bush's playhouses.

25. NY Times, December 16, 1989 p. 10, Richard L. Berke, "Bush's Drug Deal: The D.E.A. Meets the Keystone Cops." See also Richard Baker "Let's Pretend", *NYT*, September 27, 1989, p. 37.

26. NY Times, March 23, 1990 p. B1, Maureen Dowd, "Presidential Decree: No More Broccoli."

27. Brady and Solomon, p. 26. (*Washington Post*, Nov. 3, 1984, p. A6).

28. Steven V. Roberts, review of *The Quest for the Presidency* 1988, *NY Times Book Review*, Dec. 10, 1989, p. 38.

29. Brady and Solomon, "Turning Inward", pp. 25–26.

30. Brady and Solomon, p. 26.

31. Slavoj Zizek, *The Sublime Object of Ideology*, (London: Verso, 1989), p. 113.

32. Brady and Solomon, p. 38.

33. Brady and Solomon, p. 36, (see also p. 38 for a similar formulation).

34. *NY Times*, Sept. 26, 1988, A17.

35. Brady and Solomon, p. 19.

36. *International Herald Tribune*, May 13, 1988, p. 3; *NY Times*, May 12, 1988, A32.

37. *Ms* magazine, May 1988, p. 24.

38. NY Times, May 19, 1980, p. B13.

39. Brady and Solomon, pp. 37–38.

40. Brady and Solomon, p. 24.

41. *Wall Street Journal*, Sept. 18, 1988, p. 1.

42. *Wall Street Journal*, June 18, 1989, p. 1. Gerald F. Seib, "Paradonnez–Moi, Mr. Bush: In French You Make No Sense".

43. Michel Foucault, *This is Not a Pipe*, (Berkeley: UC Press, 1982), pp. 22–25.

44. Bice and Benvenuto, p. 167.

45. Bice and Benvenuto, p. 173.

46. Brady and Solomon, p. 35 (citing Mary McGrory, *Washington Post*, September 29, 1988, p. A2).

47. Brady and Solomon, pp. 36–37.

48. Bice and Benvenuto, p. 173.

49. Bice and Benvenuto, p. 169.

50. Brady and Solomon, pp. 20, 23.

51. For more examples see Brady and Solomon, chapter seven "That 'thing' thing", pp. 73–77.

52. Bice and Benvenuto, pp. 177–181.

53. *NY Times*, May 1, 1990, p. B1. Maureen Dowd, "The President's Tastes, Down Home to Less So".

54. See Kaja Silverman's reading of "The Best Years of Our Lives" in E. Ann Kaplan supra.

55. Peggy Noonan, *What I Saw at the Revolution*, (NY: Random House, 1990), p. 307.

Meprobamate, Neura-
mate, Sedabamate,
Equanil, Diazepam, Ox-
azepam, Chlordiazepox-
ide HCl, Librium,
Reposans-10, Valium,
Tranxene, Atarax, Hy-
droxyzine HCl, Sine-
quan, Doxepin HCl,
Adapin, Elavil, Chlor-
mezanone, Trazodone,
Trialodine, SK-Amitripy-
line, Tofranil, Maproti-
line, Amitril, Emitrip, SK-
Pramine, Amoxipine,
Desipramine HCl, Phen-
elzine, Tranylcypromine.

Photo: Marc de Guerre

Contributors

Mark Lewis is a writer and artist and a member of the collective Public Access in Toronto. His current project involves *Lenin in Ruins*, a photographic essay on contemporary politics in Eastern and Central Europe.

Attila Richard Lucas is a Canadian artist living in Berlin. He is best known for his mythological paintings on sacrificial power, from Berlin skinheads to American military cadets.

Elke Town writes on Canadian art and culture.

David Hlynsky, a photographer living in Toronto, is currently completing a documentary (street photography) project on Eastern Europe.

Jennifer Bloomer, Associate Professor of Architecture at the University of Florida, teaches design and theory, and is a Fellow of the Chicago Institute for Architecture and Urbanism. She is currently massaging her dissertation into a book, *Desiring Architecture: The Scrypt of Joyce and Piranesi,* forthcoming from Yale University Press; and, as the work of her fellowship, is, with Nina Hofer, building constructions and writing a book which together "twist the separatrix" of the structure/ornament dichotomy. She is also plotting *The Domesticity Project* with Catherine Ingraham.

Marc de Guerre is a Toronto artist and writer.

Art in Ruins and Art. The name is a program. The English team of artists Hannah Vowles and Glyn Banks call themselves Art in Ruins and the name has a double meaing. Art in late-capitalist society has lost its mythic autonomous character. On first sight it serves as a satisfaction for cultural needs, and is bound to the capitalist system of exploitation, which is more orientated to commercial aspects than to the human. Art becomes a spectacle, which is running on empty. The spectacle fulfills its function, if it can mask the contradictions of the system. The artist within it is the sole subject on which the objects (as no longer existing subjects) can elevate themselves. Art in Ruins, art finds itself only as a ruin, in a state of dissolution.

Avery Gordon teaches in the graduate sociology program at the University of California, Santa Barbara. She writes on feminist theory and postmodern thought.

Charles Noble divides his time between Banff and Nobleford, Alberta where he farms with his brother. He has published four books of poetry. The latest is *Let's Hear It For Them* (Thistledown Press, 1990). "A Suite of Single Symmetries" has been selected into a new sequence (with some title changes) from *Haywire Rainbow* (Press Procépic, 1978).

Critical Art Ensemble (CAE) was founded in Tallahassee, Florida, in the summer of 1987. It is a collective of five artists who believe not only that cooperative work within a group allows for the realization of art that could not be produced by an individual working alone, but also that this work should be guided by a contemporary critical spirit.

Carole Spitzack is Associate Professor of Communication at Tulane University. Her research interests center on relations between the body as cultural construct, subjectivity, power, and ideology. She is author of *Confessing Excess: Women and the Politics of Body Reduction* and co-editor of *Doing Research on Women's Communication: Perspectives on Theory and Method.*

Teresa Podlesney is a graduate student in New York University's Department of Cinema Studies. Her writing on the construction of whiteness and womanhood maps the connections between neo-manifest-destinarianism, revisionist histories of the Western US, Cinemascope and hair colour technologies.

Geoffrey Bendz is a freelance photographer living in Montréal.

Angela Miles teaches at the Ontario Institute for Studies in Education. She is the author of the monograph *Feminist Radicalism in the 1980s.*

Peggy Phelan teaches at the Tisch School of Performing Arts. She has written numerous articles in the area of film theory.

Chris Tysh, originally from Paris, France, lives in Detroit where she teaches and writes. Lecturer at Wayne State University, she is the editor of *Everyday Life* and In Camera Publications. Her books of poetry include *Secrets of Elegance* and *Porne.*

Shannon Bell is a pornographic woman. She is contributing to taking the seed out of dissemination in cultural, political and academic contexts. Popular culture publications on female ejaculation include: "What shoots and sprays and shoots and sprays? A woman," *Rites* For Lesbian and Gay Liberation, vol.5, No.9, 1989; "Kvinner spurter de ogsa!," *Cupido*, Nr. 4/1990; "Nice Girls Don't Do It," (a docuporn film) made by K. Daymond. Current non-ejaculatory publications include: "The Political-Libidinal Economy of the Socialist Female Body: Flesh and Blood, Work and Ideas", Dialectical Anthropology, Vol.15, (1990), No. 1.

Berkeley Kaite teaches in the Graduate Program in Communication at McGill University in Montréal. Her book *Semio-sex: The Pornographic Moment of Transgression and Desire* is forthcoming from Indiana University Press (1991).

Stephen Pfohl teaches sociology at Boston College and is the President Elect of *The Society for the Study of Social Problems*. He is the author of the forthcoming book, *Death at the Parasite Café*.

Teri Weidner is an artist living in Boston.

Andrew Haase lives in New York City and is working in the logics of the political. He is a graduate student in philosophy at SUNY Stony Brook.

Lorraine Gauthier teaches in the Women's Studies Department at York University. She has written numerous articles on French feminist theory including, "Truth as Eternal Metaphorical Displacements: Traces of the Mother in Derrida's Patricide," for the *Canadian Journal of Political and Social Theory*.

Charles Levin is a practicing psychoanalyst in Montreal. His work, "An Essay on the Symbolic Process," won the 1990 Prix d'Excellence de l'Academie de Grands Montrealais. He is the translator of Jean Baudrillard's *For a Critique of the Political Economy of the Sign*, and has published many papers on psychoanalysis, social theory, and aesthetics, including "La Greffe du Zele: Derrida and the Cupidity of the Text," "Art and the Sociological Ego," and "Carnal Knowlegde of Aesthetics States."

Diane Rubenstein is Associate Professor of Political Science at Purdue University. She is the author of a book on French fascist intellectuals, *What's Left?: The* École Normal Supérieure *and the Right* (1990) and many articles on poststructuralist rhetoric. She is currently at work on a book on Baudrillard and American politics.

ACKNOWLEDGEMENTS

Cover Art
Mark Lewis, *They Sucked a Filthy Tongue No Mother Could Ever Love*

Page vi
Attila Richard Lukacs, *True North*, 1 of 4 panels, 1987
Diane Farris Gallery, Vancouver

Page x
Photograph by Marc de Guerre, *untitled*

Page xii
Photograph by Marc de Guerre, *untitled*

Pages 5, 7, 9, 11
Photographs by David Hlynsky

Page 12
Art in Ruins, Hannah Vowles and Glyn Banks, 'Oversite', 1987, installation detail, Edinburgh, Scotland

Page 56
Photograph by Critical Art Ensemble

Page 71
Photograph by Geoffrey Bendz

Page 91
Photograph by Mark Lewis
He Licked His Lip Until it Bled, 1987

Page 92
Cover: © Harlequin Presents
Love's Sweet Harvest by
Sally Heywood

Page 148
Attila Richard Lukacs
Still, 50" x 80"
Diane Farris Gallery

Page 166
Photograph of Shannon Bell
by Ruthann Tucker

Page 170
Photograph taken from *Paris Passion* Magazine, Paris, France
Summer edition, 1989

Page 186
Illustration by Teri Weidner

Pages 210 and 211
Photograph by the Critical Art Ensemble

Pages 266 and 267
Photograph by Marc de Guerre